# What Does Love
# Have to Do with It?

# What Does Love Have to Do with It?

## Excruciating Lessons on My Path to Enlightenment

Do what you came to do.

Mary

**Mary DeYon**

iUniverse, Inc.
Bloomington

**What Does Love Have to Do with It?**
Excruciating Lessons on My Path to Enlightenment

iUniverse books may be ordered through booksellers or by contacting:

iUniverse
1663 Liberty Drive
Bloomington, IN 47403
www.iuniverse.com
1-800-Authors (1-800-288-4677)

ISBN: 978-1-4620-7086-2 (sc)
ISBN: 978-1-4620-7088-6 (hc)
ISBN: 978-1-4620-7087-9 (ebk)

Printed in the United States of America

iUniverse rev. date: 12/13/2011

*For Heath, Melinda, Kyrstin, Addyson,*

*DeLaynie and McKynlee*

# CONTENTS

# FORWARD

The Universe rewards the action step! In her new book, Mary DeYon has expertly demonstrated this principle to its fullest expression and manifestation. Her vignettes paint a wonderful and profound example of how to deal with the struggles and adversities that each of us face on this path we call life.

In my 16 years of private practice, it has become my personal and professional observation that each of us in life have two basic choices when faced with adversity:

1. We have the choice to allow ourselves to be defeated by the particular struggle in front of us.
2. We have the choice to become empowered and strengthened by the particular struggle in front of us.

Mary has chosen to become empowered and face her obstacles positively.

When written in Chinese, the word "crisis" is composed of two characters. One represents **danger**, and the other represents **opportunity**.

The choice is yours and yours alone! You have an incredible opportunity in each struggle that crosses your path to grow and become stronger because of them.

What action steps will you take as you go through life? The rewards are great and many. You will see this as you follow Mary on her journey to enlightenment!

Many blessings on your journey,

Allen Knecht, DC
Certified N.E.T. practitioner
Emphasis on Functional, Mind-body, Integrative Medicine

# MY TRIBUTE TO
# SONGWRITERS

Music has connected me to my soul in a way that makes life worth living. From the postwar bebop of the 50's to the social change of the 60's through the fun of the 70's and onward, I have enjoyed and grown from the power of the words of songwriters.

Their melodies have lifted my spirit like wine or chocolate—only without the calories. Without them, my life would lack luster.

The chapter titles of this book suggest songs that have inspired me to laugh and cry throughout my journey, the soundtrack of my life. Thank you, singers and songwriters!

A Note for my Readers

I always dreamed of writing a book. Over the past 40 years, I unintentionally wrote 58 books in the form of diaries, notebooks and journals—all on the subject of me. These were not daily rundowns of events but rather dumping grounds of frustration where here or there, an insight would shine through, bringing transformation. In this way, I evolved from being a depressed, hopeless victim to a person fully alive, capable of ecstatic happiness.

When I sat down on my fiftieth birthday and read through my dramas I found tragedies and comedies intertwined to weave the story of my life. From there I was led to a writing class and then to the teacher who became my coach. She lovingly coaxed stories out of me that I didn't want to tell—even to myself.

And then I couldn't stop. My dream of writing a book became a desire so deep it kept me going for several years as I struggled with writing the tough parts—coughing up hairballs, I called it.

I again felt the powerlessness of living with an alcoholic father and the strictness of Catholic School. I replaced that victimhood by fighting back and trying to control every aspect of my life. I unconsciously married the very kind of man I was running from—twice. From Al-Anon and Adult Children of Alcoholics meetings I realized the overwhelming task of controlling was not only futile but exhausting. I began letting go and asking God to take over.

Slowly I learned what was mine to control and what wasn't. Then I began really living.

Through writing this book, counseling, group therapy, Feng Shui, Reiki, N.E.T. and other energy work along with Al-Anon, I was able to conquer my fear of telling the family secrets or being burned at the stake for believing in a spirituality different than I was taught in Catholic School. I learned to love myself enough to stop the abuse from me and others. I now live in a magical place of grace where I feel divinely guided every day.

These stories are my perception of my life. Some of the names have been changed to protect the guilty. I've capitalized some Moms and Dads out of reverence for them.

As Freud said, we are only as mentally healthy as the secrets we keep. I must be sane now because I have no secrets left . . . here they are.

# CHAPTER 1

## *Cherished*

The first time I fell in love was in seventh grade. All of my previous teachers since first grade were nuns. Then came Mr. Stevens, my history teacher. He was so ruggedly male, giving off an enticing mix of Old Spice and cherry tobacco whenever he passed my desk handing out test papers. His brown tweed jacket with patches on the sleeves made him look even smarter than I already knew he was. He mesmerized me as he moved across the blackboard writing about the three branches of government. "Whenever you hear people getting angry about rising taxes," he said, "think of everything the government does for us. It protects us in war, keeps our food and water safe, and builds roads. And just think, if every time you mailed a letter you had to hire a plane, it would cost a lot more than three cents." *Such wisdom,* I sighed.

At home, Dad griped about never getting ahead because of taxes. Mr. Stevens really knew how the world worked.

I fantasized about being married to him—different than my other fantasies when I pretended to be married to Pat Boone. With Mr. Stevens it was different. It was real love.

One Sunday morning Mom and I filed into our usual pew at church with my sisters and brothers. Dad was in the balcony with the organist, planning the songs he'd sing for Mass, and at the same time keeping an eye on us—just like the nuns at school, always right behind, watching. If we didn't behave we got the paddle when we got home. Dad had handcrafted it out of wood and drilled holes in it for added stinging. But most often we were good, anticipating our reward right after church—doughnuts from Williams Bakery. My favorites were cream sticks—maple bars filled with whipped cream. Just thinking of biting into one made me smile as I sat there in my pew.

I snapped back from my reverie when I spotted Mr. Stevens in front of me. He held his wife's arm as she genuflected. Then he placed his hand on the small of her back and guided her into the pew.

So. He had a **wife**. She was petite without an ounce of fat. Her pale blue suit and matching pill·box hat made her look like a blond Jackie Kennedy. She was perfect. And I was not.

As Mr. Stevens sat back in his seat I could smell the cherry tobacco and Old Spice. He wore a navy blue blazer with gold buttons. The collar of his white shirt peeked out of his jacket. His perfectly trimmed hair revealed his strong neck.

Ah, here was one more thing to fall in love with: Mr. Steven's hairline.

From the balcony Dad sang *Ave Maria*. Mr. Stevens took Mrs. Steven's hand in his and smiled down at her. I could see from the look in his eyes that he cherished her. I was heartbroken. That night I cried myself to sleep.

In the morning I grabbed my diary and wrote: "*When I grow up I'll find a man just like Mr. Stevens who will cherish me. I will create the perfect home for him, cook his favorite meals and raise our children with love. Every night he will come home and share the outside world with me.*"

But things don't always turn out like you plan.

# CHAPTER 2

## *The Dark Side of the Sun*

The summer before my senior year of high school Dad announced we were moving from Ohio to Phoenix. I was filled with a confusing mix of dread at leaving friends, school, and home, while at the same time sensing the thrill of the adventure. We packed the red Chevy station wagon for the big trip west. Mom and I hauled the cooler of milk, beer and lunch meat to the car, "I'm so glad you're here to help," she said. "Since Linda is staying behind to finish nursing school."

As if my older sister Linda was ever any help. She always had her nose in a book. I wondered if she was really reading or just hiding so she wouldn't have to do anything.

"Say goodbye to the trees and take your last breath of fresh air," Dad said. "You won't get any of that once we get to Arizona."

I had seen pictures of the desert, but it always looked fake like the scenes on *Bonanza*. I felt a glimmer of excitement over getting to see the real thing. Maybe it would be even better than *Bonanza*.

Then again, maybe not.

We hugged relatives and neighbors goodbye and were on our way. Day after day on the road we slept in cheap motels and sucked down cereal each morning with Dad yelling, "Toots Sweet, move it! Has everyone gone to the bathroom? There'll be no stopping until lunch."

We sped along with my brothers whining, "Are we there yet?" as Dad downed Pabst after Pabst to calm his nerves.

Traveling across the panhandle of Texas I had never felt so isolated and alone. Where were we going? When we stopped for lunch the hot wind blew sand in my mouth as I got out of the car. "Yuck," I spit. "It's miserable here."

"You think this is bad, wait'll we get to Phoenix," Dad said. "You can fry eggs on the sidewalk."

"Yeah, right," I rolled my eyes as I carried the water jug to the picnic table.

Mom was slapping baloney on Wonder Bread. A gust of wind lifted that baloney like a Frisbee and sailed it across the road. Dad whipped around, picked up a baloney slice, and flung one himself. "Stop it, Jack," Mom said, handing him another Pabst. "You're worse than the kids."

At the next stop, Dad bought cowboy hats for my brothers: John 13, Chris 11 and Joe 6. He gave them each a can of Budweiser and sat them on a white fence for a picture. It was supposed to be funny.

Back on the road the landscape changed into a flat desert that seemed to go on forever. I wondered where Dad was taking us. This is what pre-Columbus people must have seen when they thought the world was flat. I'd known a lot of disappointment in my life. Mr. Stevens was married. Doughnuts were only for after church. My sister Linda got all the good grades. But I steeled myself for even more disappointment in this lonely desert landscape. I prayed Lawrence of Arabia would come over the next sand dune and save me.

In Phoenix, row after row of houses lined row after row of streets with an occasional palm tree for an accent. It was all I saw for miles.

"Camelback Mountain," Dad said, pointing to a pile of reddish brown rocks. "See how it looks like a camel laying down."

*Dad's had way too many Pabsts or he got into his Jack Daniels a little early today,* I thought as we pulled up to Aunt Lorna's house. It looked just like the one next to it and the one across the street.

In fact it looked like every house on the street, except that her door was blue.

As we began unloading the car, I dropped my brother's crayons in the driveway. When I went out for the next load, everyone was standing around watching the rainbow of red, green, blue, orange and yellow melting down the concrete to the street.

"See, Mary Pat!" Dad shouted. He was always yelling. What was it this time? "See," he said with a twinkle in his eye, "I told you, you could fry an egg on the sidewalk! Here, let me show you."

Dad disappeared into the house, came out with an egg, cracked it on the bumper of the car and spread it on the pavement. The white of the egg immediately bubbled up and turned brown at the edges. This wasn't Ohio, for sure.

"Jack, stop wasting eggs and carry this suitcase for me," Mom sighed, shaking her head.

As we settled into our new house, Mom and Dad said I could go to Camelback, the public high school, or Gerard, the Catholic School. I chose the Catholic school since it would be smaller. Besides, I was used to Catholic schools.

I loved the blue skies and sunshine every day in Phoenix, and yet I was as lonely as I'd feared. All the cliques had been formed by senior year. I missed cheerleading. I thought about the last basketball game I cheered in Ohio. Our team was always in the state championships and last year was no different. We were favored to win this game, so I thought we had more games to play, but the other team made a shot at the buzzer and beat us. We were out of the tournament. I stood there stunned while the other team's cheerleaders ran onto the court. Under the bleachers I sat down and cried into my red and black pom-poms. I wasn't ready for cheerleading to be over. Then I began thinking that everything as I knew it would soon be over.

Mom tried to keep my spirits up every morning in Phoenix with, "Good morning, Mary Pat, it's a beautiful day in Central Arizona this morning."

But it didn't help. Night after night, home alone, I read and reread the psychedelic cloth-covered autograph book my friend Mary put together for me.

"Don't worry," Janie had written. "You'll make lots of friends in your new school, just like here."

"Write to me when you have time out from all your dates," Dianne said. *Yeah right.*

Most ironic of all, my old classmates had made me a burlap banner with rose colored writing that said, "Don't Let the Sun Catch You Crying." I hung it over my bed and sobbed into my pillow until spring.

Finally I did get a date. He showed up right on time. I was in my room when I heard the doorbell. As I started down the hall I heard Dad say, "Mary Pat won't be able to go out with you. She's sick."

"Okay, thanks," Manuel said. "I'll call her tomorrow."

"No, don't bother," Dad said, shutting the door. "She'll still be sick then too."

I stood in the hallway, hearing the door click shut. "Dad," I yelled. "What are you doing?"

"I told him you were sick," Dad said with his hands on his hips. "You are not going out with a wetback!"

"A wetback? He's Mexican?"

"With a name like Manuel Lopez?" Dad looked at me like I was stupid.

"But Dad," I cried, "he's the Skateboard Champion of Arizona!"

"I don't care. You are not going out with a Mexican."

I ran down the hall to my room, flipped over my soggy pillow and cried the night away. I knew I wasn't allowed to go out with colored guys, but I'd never guessed that Mexicans were colored, too.

My hopes for this new place were a collage of melted dreams, like the crayons running down the driveway. I tried to make the best of things. Kathy, a classmate, invited me to a Catholic Youth Organization meeting. Finally I had somewhere to go.

As the meeting started, Sara, from my Latin class with her perfectly bobbed hair, stood up. "No offense, Mary Pat," she said with a glance at Sister Anthony, "but I thought we weren't allowing any new members."

What was this about? Then I remembered. Earlier that day Sara's boyfriend had spoken to me after class. "Hey, you're new here," he'd said. "Where are you from?" He smiled and winked. Sara watched from across the room. Now she was getting her payback.

I sat frozen in my seat as the meeting continued for what seemed like hours. Kathy smiled but I could tell she felt bad for bringing me. I just wanted to get home and retreat into a bag of M&M's.

And so it went. The entire year would have been a disaster, except our neighbor hired me for the Classified Advertising Department at the *Republic and Gazette* Newspaper. It thrilled me to be earning my own money. I could buy lots of clothes—every Catholic girl's dream after navy blue jumpers, plaid skirts and white blouses. And, I was meeting all kinds of different people.

I liked sitting in my cubicle with a headset, taking ads over the phone. "How many puppies did you say you had for sale?"

With my next customer I kept repeating, "Excuse me, did you say you had a CAR to sell or you made PAR golfing today?"

Mona, the supervisor, heard my struggle and came over to help.

"Thanks, Mona," I told her. "He sounded like he was drunk or a hair lip. I couldn't tell which."

Mona giggled and her plastered Sassoon haircut jiggled a little. For once, my sense of humor was appreciated. For too long I had been berated by nuns yelling, "Mary Pat, do I have to call your mother again?"

I loved working at the newspaper. This was a place I could shine. My coworkers were like me: misfits in their respective high schools and colleges. Kathy, my one friend from Gerard, came to work there too. She was tall with an athletic build and a back to nature glow. Her laugh made me feel at home. She always knew what she wanted in life. She was going to be a nurse and was light years ahead of me in maturity.

Kathy saved me from being totally alone at my new school. One night we were reluctantly going to a school dance. As we drove into the parking lot and saw all our classmates hanging around, it looked like a costume party. There were girls in mini skirts and fishnets with blouses cut down to the navel. Their makeup was enough to shame Alice Cooper. The guys wore T Shirts and frayed jeans. After seeing these kids in uniforms every day, it was quite a shock. Did wearing uniforms make you lose all sense of fashion?

"Are we really going in there with those yahoos?" Kathy asked. "Look at them. Let's cruise Central."

That night I had my first taste of Boones Farm Apple Wine with some guys from public school. How racy! Booze and public school boys! I was beginning to feel a freedom I hadn't felt before and it was exciting. In my diary I wrote: "*Life in Phoenix is getting better.*"

# CHAPTER 3

## *Believe in Magic*

In my first year of college, I began seeking a spirituality that was an alternative to the fire and brimstone I'd heard from the pulpit every Sunday growing up.

I read about Buddhism in *Autobiography of a Yogi* and was spellbound by this new way of looking at life. The book ended with the day the Yogi's spirit left his body. It was actually the day I was born. This really stunned me and I became intrigued by the Buddhist idea of reincarnation. Rather than ascending to heaven, wearing robes and singing like angels or descending to burn in hell for eternity, the Buddhists believed you could come back and try again.

All the Christian religions had the Bible as their basis. And yet I'd never really read it. In Catholic school our Bible lessons were sanitized for us into little blue catechism books. Now, at last I started reading the Big Book and was shocked as I began to see Jesus as a down to earth guy with a great sense of humor. I decided anyone who changed water into wine was alright by me.

Back in grade school I had felt powerless. Nothing I was taught ever seemed right. This was in contrast to when I was very young, and Mom talked about God in a way that connected me to Him. I felt I was a part of something much bigger than me and my family. I felt I could rely on that power to guide me and I always had a guardian angel to protect me.

But as the years passed in Catholic school, I learned I wasn't good enough to pray directly to God. I could pray to a saint, or the Blessed Mother, or Jesus, who would go to God on my behalf. In fact, my best bet at getting prayers answered was to go to the saint I was named after. This was tricky. I knew I wasn't good enough to go to Mary, the Mother of God, so I had to find an alternative. I came upon a solution choosing St. Patrick because of my middle name. St. Patrick was cool—he had driven the snakes out of Ireland. So for my 9th birthday, I received a statue of him in his Kelly green robes with snakes winding and twisting all around his feet. I kept him on my bedside table and prayed to him every night for forgiveness of my sins.

I was working at the *Republic and Gazette* when I met another spiritual seeker, Candy. She was tall and willowy, with long, wavy, strawberry blond hair. She had a peaceful, gentle aura. Her IQ was off the charts. FORTRAN, DOS and Organic Chemistry were part of her class schedule. She wore flowing peasant blouses with tattered jeans and long halter dresses in tie-dye or flowery prints, the perfect image of an Earth Mother.

Candy had grown up Southern Baptist. Like me, she wanted to find a philosophy of life that made sense.

A couple of guys at the *Republic and Gazette* told Candy and me about *The Power of Positive Thinking* by Norman Vincent Peale and *Think and Grow Rich* by Napoleon Hill. As we read, we learned we could have whatever we wanted in life if we could visualize it. We started by driving up Camelback Mountain and touring a sprawling adobe mansion that was for sale.

The all-white rooms were bright with high arched ceilings. The living room was what Candy always wanted, big enough for a grand piano. While she was at it, Candy figured she'd visualize stables and acreage so she could ride all the horses she would buy.

As for me, I wanted a whole room lined with mahogany bookcases from floor to ceiling on three walls filled with my favorite books, *Wuthering Heights, Gone with the Wind,* and *Letters from the Earth.* The other wall would consist of tall windows that looked out at the beautiful view. I could see myself curled up in my cordovan leather wing back chair reading after dinner, while the twinkling lights of Phoenix appeared as the sun set in a turquoise and coral sky. Once we had visualized our ideal homes, we started reading all kinds of spiritual books. We'd discuss what we'd read at Coco's Restaurant between studying and drinking mega doses of coffee. We took a Transcendental Meditation class and received personal mantras similar to the "Ohm" chant. It was a great way to "drop out" of my racing mind and get away from thoughts like, "You know you were born in original sin and you'll never be good enough."

I liked going to that "happy place" of not thinking. It really came in handy, I found, at places such as the dentist's office. At last I could turn off life and the sound of the drill. But even better, meditation was cool—even the Beatles were meditating now.

At the same time, I often felt blasphemous. Catholic school had taught that anything like this was from the devil. And yet I was so electrified by what I was learning I was compelled to go even deeper. One weekend Candy and I were enjoying the coolness of the fall weather with the top down in my bronze Mustang convertible, our long hair flowing in the breeze. Gordon Lightfoot had just finished singing, "Sundown ya better take care," when we heard a KDKB advertisement for *The Silva Mind Control Method.* This weekend seminar could teach us how to program our minds like a billion dollar computer. We had to do it. We scraped together the money and were giddy with the anticipation of what we'd learn in this class.

The weekend arrived and soon we were learning the importance of controlling our thoughts: how thoughts influence what we draw to ourselves. In one exercise we imagined smelling orange blossoms. This was easy to do since the valley was filled with them every spring. Within seconds Candy started sneezing and sniffling as her eyes watered up. Highly allergic to orange blossoms, she had made the experience real in her own mind, and her body was reacting physically.

We were blown away.

That weekend seminar taught us several things I use to this day. For instance, we learned how to increase our memory. I could visualize my grocery list by arranging the items on the hood of my car, the goofier the better. I imagined toilet paper held on by my Mustang hood ornament with the end of it trailing in the breeze. Toothpaste oozed out of the tube running into the toilet paper. And to finish it off, eggs were frying on the hot metal of the hood with the edges turning brown and curling up, just like Dad's demonstration on the driveway.

Class went on for three days. To graduate, we had to pass the ultimate Mind Control Test. Each of us brought information about sick people we knew. On index cards we wrote the person's name, age, and where they lived. To conduct the test we were to choose partners we didn't know. I had noticed Dave the first day, looking like Van Morrison with his bushy hair and soulful eyes. I sprinted across the room to team up with him. As he sat down across from me he held his index card to his forehead reminding me of Johnny Carson doing his Carnac routine and said, "My person's name is Dottie. She's my aunt. She's forty-nine and lives in Sedona."

I settled into position to conduct the test. I closed my eyes and took a long, relaxing breath. I then imagined going to the laboratory they had told us to create in our minds. Dottie immediately flashed on the screen.

"Dottie has red hair," I said, "and she's wearing a brown and white polka dot dress."

"Yes!" Dave jumped up, "Aunt Dottie always wears polka dots. And how did you know she had red hair?"

Dave was as excited as I was about being able to "read" this person. We sat stunned for a moment, and then I prepared for the next part. I was to scan her body for her ailment. Within seconds, I saw a huge black lump attached to Dottie's neck.

"Does she have cancer?" I asked. "Somewhere around her throat?"

"She does!" Dave exclaimed. "A tumor on her thyroid!"

I let out a shaky breath and continued. We were instructed to fix whatever we found, leaving the person better than before. I visualized grabbing scissors, cutting out the tumor and throwing it away. In those moments I felt a tremendous surge of power.

I never did learn the results of that visualization of Dottie, but to this day I remember that experience, and the sense of healing I felt for the woman I'd never met.

That night Candy and I were flying high with all we'd experienced that weekend. Since we couldn't sleep we decided to make cookies. We infused them mentally with all the energy of this newfound way of thinking. Our "Alpha Cookies" were a hit brightening everyone's mood who tasted them.

Right before I finally could sleep I wrote in my diary: "*This isn't Catholic School for sure!*"

# CHAPTER 4

## *The Times are Changing*

Ali worked at the *Republic and Gazette* with Kathy, Candy and me. Almost 6 feet tall, she had a razor sharp wit and a sultry giggle. She had a wardrobe of shoes that would make Imelda Marcos proud. In spite of her height, Ali wore fabulous wooden high heels and walked like a runway model.

Like me, Ali grew up a staunch democrat in an Irish Catholic family. We discovered our commonalities and spoke with pride about John F. Kennedy's election. As we continued sharing, I relished hearing Ali's political views. She was always up on the latest shenanigans of Nixon and how many more soldiers were killed in Vietnam that week.

With my new friends, I'd found a whole new world, and now I was discovering a mindset to match. My only angst was what to wear with my Army Surplus jeans to the next party on Saturday night. Life was fun. We were coming of age at an amazing time and wanted to make a difference in the world.

The Civil Rights Movement had opened our eyes to see that all of us were created equal, even women. Despite this, I felt the pressure of finding a career in a stereotypically women's field. Ali and I were going to be teachers and Kathy, a nurse. Candy was the only one to break from the herd to become a brain surgeon. I admired her courage. Even so, we couldn't defy the way we'd been taught to view ourselves as women. Looking back, this came out in many of our conversations.

"Can you believe Debbie is going into business?" Candy asked as we were applying makeup before a party.

I shook my head as she turned back to the mirror. "She's just looking for her Mrs. Degree taking those all male classes," I said, separating my eyelashes with a safety pin.

I can laugh about it now, but it would take a lot more life experience before I would begin to feel free as a woman in our society.

In the meantime, the question remained: what would my major be? What would I like to teach? As I thought about it, I realized I'd always liked writing. I decided to major in English. My writings hadn't been well received by the nuns in high school, but maybe in college others would finally understand what I was trying to say.

As the weeks wore on, I felt like a misfit in my creative writing class. I didn't like wasting time describing silver, glistening trees lining a frozen lake. I wanted to write about people, experiences, and all the new ways I was beginning to view the world. So I changed my major to Journalism where I could write about real life. As the class continued, I learned the emphasis on facts. "Just the facts, ma'am" was no answer to my yearning to write about and understand people. After careful thought I decided to forget about writing altogether. I should work with people. I figured I could make an impact with handicapped people like my sister Ann.

Annie was born a year after me and needed a lot of care. She was deaf and legally blind, with a cleft palate and an unformed bone in her nose. My memories of Annie forever impacted my growing up, and my way of seeing the world.

One distinct memory is of an afternoon before Annie had the surgery to close the roof of her mouth. Mom was feeding her in the high chair while a service man crouched in the corner, repairing the refrigerator. As Mom slipped a spoonful of beets into Annie's mouth, she sneezed. The beets flew out of her nose all over the repairman's blue striped shirt.

The repairman stood up slowly. With horror he looked down at the red splotches covering his shirt, and saw Annie covered with the same spots. "My God," he gasped. "Is she all right?"

"She's fine," Mom laughed. "It's just beets." The repairman laughed too as Mom handed him a towel to clean up.

Annie had many operations over the years, mostly on her face and eyes. One surgery removed the iris of her eye and replaced it with a lightweight plastic to fit over her eyeball. It had been hand painted to match her other blue eye.

The night Annie came home from the hospital we were gathered around the TV watching Ed Sullivan. She was rubbing her new eye when suddenly it popped out and fell on the floor. Her eyeball rolled across the braided oval area rug and stopped on the hardwood floor, staring up at all of us. The room was silent. No one moved. Then Annie burst out laughing and pointed to her eyeball. We all burst into laughter and soon we were rolling around on the hardwood floor with Annie and her new blue eyeball.

Sometimes my Mom would insist I take Annie when I played at the neighbor kid's houses. My friend Julie's older brother would mock her nasal, barking voice. They would call her retarded and make fun of her deformed face. I would cry after I brought her home. I was mad at those boys, but also embarrassed about having a sister like Annie. These interactions continued, on into my teens. And as time went on, I continued to feel angry, ashamed, and embarrassed because of Annie. And then the guilt would set in.

Now was my chance to make up for all that. When I was in high school I had enjoyed volunteering for Annie's groups where there were all kinds of handicapped kids. Some deaf, some blind, some with Down Syndrome. They were all so loving and got so much joy from baking cookies or laughing at a cat matted from the rain. They were fun to be around. I thought I'd like helping the handicapped: I could go into speech therapy.

And so I began my courses at Arizona State University with great optimism. This was it! My place in the world and my chance to make a difference.

My first client was a man who had just had a heart attack. His speech center was affected and the only thing he could say was: "Furbish." Ted would hold the sides of his head shaking it back and forth sputtering, "Furbish, Furbish."

He was only forty-five and had five kids and a wife to support. It was a tragic case, but now I was here on the scene to change all that. Like Aunt Dottie's cancer, I felt Ted's speech impediment was something I could correct with my *Silva Mind Control* skills.

Approaching the situation, I knew he could take in information. Without fail, he understood what we said to him. He always read the newspaper in the waiting room before our appointments and followed every bit of instruction I gave him. But I could feel his frustration build whenever he tried to speak.

I worked with Ted all semester and finally had him responding to what were called psychological sets. I'd say "salt and," then he would say "pepper." When I said, "black and . . . . . .," he'd say, "white." After three times a week for four months this was all the progress we had made. Once again, my expectations were not matching my reality. I became as discouraged as he was.

I tried again with a new client. A stuttering mother of six children, Sally was thirty five years old and drove for hours to get to our sessions at the college. She had a great sense of humor and laughed that none of her children stuttered even though she was the one who taught them to talk. She told me terrible stories of abuse from her childhood by a father who beat her repeatedly when she stuttered. I was saddened by this woman's story, but admired her strength.

When I first assessed Sally's condition my entire Diagnostics Class watched behind a two way mirror. I had sat there many times myself behind the glass watching other students go through the battery of questions for their patient's particular speech problem. In order to have the patients relax, we didn't tell them they were being watched. This was light years before the Medical Privacy Act.

It was only the second time I had met Sally. She burst through the door with a big smile and a breathy, "Hi, Mary P-Pat." She wore bright red shorts that matched her lipstick. Several strands of pearls fell to her waist making her look like an old time flapper.

As she sat down on a metal chair she jumped up and cried, "M-my, m-my, they d-don't spare any exp-pense on the air conditioning, d-do they?"

I laughed pulling up a chair across from her. "No, sorry, it's always freezing in here. Are you okay? Are you ready for this?"

"You b-bet," Sally said balling up her right fist and pounding the table.

I began with my usual questions, "Have you always stuttered? Did anyone else in your family stutter? Have you received other counseling or therapy for your stuttering?"

Finally, when I asked, "Is there any word you never stutter on?" without pause she said, "Shit. I can say shit anytime I want and never stutter!"

Laughter erupted behind the mirror and Sally covered her mouth with both hands, embarrassed.

Good! I giggled and then explained about the class viewing us. To my surprise, and the delight of all of us, she laughed too. She shook her head, and without a hint of a stutter she good—naturedly turned to the mirror and said, "I'm sorry."

I understood the stress of people like Sally. I had a lot of stress at home. Dad was always yelling at me at the dinner table for being gone too much. Added to that was the intensity of working with these speech therapy clients, and the result was stomach problems. When I talked to Mom she said, "You need to see Dr. Haggard."

The doctor ran some tests and when I went back for the results he sat me down. "Young lady, you are only 18 years old and you have an ulcer! What in heaven's name are you doing?"

"Uh, trying to work and go to school, I guess." I explained, feeling sheepish. *You sound just like my Dad,* I thought. *He's always yelling at me.*

He must have read my mind since he said, "I know from your Mom that Jack is hard on you kids," he sighed leaning back while pushing his glasses higher on his nose. "But you have got to get a hold of yourself. At this rate, you'll be dead by the time you're

30." I sat back in stunned silence. I was working hard to fulfill my dream of making the world a better place. How could I possibly do it differently?

In my diary that night I wrote: *"Maybe it's time to move out of the house."*

# CHAPTER 5

## *Nothing Left to Lose*

The more I thought about it, the more I couldn't wait to get out, away from Dad's tirades. Kathy had begun talking about moving as well, together with Nancy, another friend from work. "Hey!" I said. "Why don't I join you two?" Not long afterward, we found a one bedroom apartment we could afford. Two of us could sleep in the double bed and one on the fold-down green couch in the living room. The couch matched the avocado hump-and-bump carpet. But hey, it had a pool and with a little fine decorating, like a purple tie dyed sheet to hang on the wall, it would be cool.

One Sunday morning Nancy went to her Mom's to do laundry. Kathy and I got up early to clean before church. It took all of 20 minutes to vacuum, dust and mop. As we were deciding whether to go to Sunday Mass or not, Kathy sat back on the funky green couch and lit a cigarette.

I leaned across our wobbly coffee table inhaling the smoke. That cigarette smelled really good. It seemed like a perfect reward for finishing our chores.

"Can I have one of those?"

Kathy smiled and handed over the pack. She looked at me. I looked at Kathy, and the minutes ticked by on the clock: 9:45, time to leave for mass.

Since Kathy and I had both gone to Catholic School, we knew it was a mortal sin if we didn't go to church on Sunday. But lately the church had been changing its rules. We were even allowed to go to Mass on Saturday night and it counted for Sunday. Some Masses weren't even in Latin anymore and we could eat meat on Fridays now.

Maybe we could just sit here smoking our cigarettes, and maybe after all, we wouldn't go to hell.

And maybe the rules would keep changing and by the time they figured it out we'd be home free.

The rules were tricky to begin with. For instance, I always wondered what happened to all those Catholics who went to hell years ago, for eating meat on Friday. When the Pope changed the rule, did God send St. Peter down to hell saying, "Okay, all of you in here for eating meat on Friday, you're free. The rules have changed. Come with me, you can go to heaven now."

When they got to heaven, I wondered if their charred bodies and raggedy loin cloths stood out among all the others in flowing, pristine, white robes. Or were they issued new robes and really absolved of their sins?

As I was wondering, I came back to our dilemma: to go to Mass or commit a mortal sin. We decided not to go. Kathy flipped on the TV and I moved to the couch smoking cigarette after cigarette waiting for the heavens to break open with Charlton Heston roaring, "You will be forced to live in eternal damnation!"

But nothing happened. Except I liked the high I got from cigarettes. It was different than the food high which calmed me, and cigarettes didn't put on weight. In fact they took away my appetite. I lost 12 pounds with Merit cigarettes, and knew I had a friend for life.

As the weeks passed, we decided to have a party celebrating our new apartment. The guests were a gathering of work colleagues and college friends. My goal for the evening was to drink a whole six pack by myself. Now that was sure to make my parents proud.

Stan, one of the guys we worked with, brought a friend to the party. Greg was such a fireball of energy he seemed much bigger than his 5 foot 9 inch frame. He had shoulder length thick dark hair and intense brown eyes that twinkled with life. I was usually drawn to the strong silent type, like Heath on Big Valley. But there was an attraction to this guy I couldn't explain.

Greg had life figured out. He was just about as smart as . . . well, Mr. Stevens of course, the smartest guy I'd ever known.

Greg was graduating with a degree in Chemical Engineering. We got to talking and before long we were seeing each other every weekend.

Greg graduated and began looking for work. He went to a barber and returned with a short trimmed haircut that I had seen before. I studied him in amazement as he turned around to show me. Here it was, the hairline I loved, just like Mr. Stevens. That's all it took. This was the man for me.

After a brief courtship, Greg surprised me with an engagement ring with diamond flower petals and sapphire leaves attached to a gold wedding band. The plan of my life was coming together. We talked about how I would continue school until I graduated the next year, working as a speech therapist until we had kids. Everything was picture perfect.

I chose a wedding dress that made me feel like a princess. It had a fitted lace bodice with a sweetheart neckline. The skirt dripped with layers of lace that made my waist look as small as Scarlet O'Hara's. I had never worn anything like it.

The bridesmaid's dresses were chiffon in pale pink, sky blue, mint green and daffodil yellow. Each girl was to pick her favorite color. My mother was enjoying the wedding planning since Linda had eloped. Mom was especially happy because Greg was Catholic.

Embossed invitations with flowery lettering invited our guests to join us on the evening of October 23rd. The caterer had suggested Chicken Kiev, Potatoes Au Gratin and a Seasonal Fruit Salad. The cake would be decorated with flowers in the same pastels of the bridesmaid's dresses.

Two months before our big day, Greg showed up at the door with a guilty look and a bouquet of daisies. "I want to go back to school," he said. "to get my Masters. Can the wedding happen later?"

"But-but-but, my dress!" I stammered. "The invitations! The caterer! Aunt Donita is coming from Ohio! What am I going to tell my Mom?"

Greg shrugged and shook his head. "Just . . . give me some time," he said.

My day as a fairy princess wasn't to be. As the summer passed, Greg spent most of his free time with friends playing racquetball and going to the gym. After all, he had put a ring on my finger. I wasn't going anywhere. Surely I'd be there when he decided to get married.

I felt like a fishing boat bought and put in storage until spring. After a couple of months of feeling sorry for myself, I finally called him up and told him it was over. I threw myself into my work. Who needed a man?

I dedicated myself to helping Ted and Sally with their speech problems. I stayed up nights researching the latest medical treatments for heart attack victims. Whenever I had a free moment I would pore over extensive studies about the effects of abuse on stutterers. I mentally went over any mind trick I had learned from my Silva class. I stopped going out with friends. All I did was go to work and school, study and eat.

My only break came on Saturday nights. All my roommates were out with their boyfriends, so I'd bake brownies while listening to the Allman Brothers album, *Eat a Peach*. I'd dance to *Blue Skies* until *Mary Tyler Moore* came on. Then I'd sink into my Lazy Boy eating brownies and know "I could make it after all."

By the end of that semester I was worn out. I went to my counselor at school, Mrs. Curtis. "I can't believe how slow progress has been with Ted and Sally," I said, looking down at my hands, the fingernails chewed away. "I've been working with them for three months."

"Dear," said Mrs. Curtis, leaning forward, her long silver necklace clunking on the desk. She reminded me of Lady Bird Johnson, with one big sweep of hair to the side of her head. "I hate to tell you this." She paused as if about to share a dark secret. "I think you are just too sensitive to be a speech therapist," she finally sighed.

"What?" I couldn't believe what I was hearing.

"I've been watching you. You take on your clients' problems as your own. You just care too much." She sighed again and shook her head. "I'm sorry, Mary Pat, I'm afraid you need to find a new major."

I slumped back in my chair, crushed. Maybe what everyone had told me since I was a kid was true. I was overly sensitive—always getting my feelings hurt. When would I ever learn? I remember Mom saying, "Quit being so sensitive!"

Then Dad would warn, "The world is going to eat you alive if you don't toughen up."

And now, caring too much had gotten me nowhere. Would I ever make a difference in the world, dream a dream that came true, or find someone like Mr. Stevens? My universe seemed utterly hopeless.

I decided to get as far away as I could from any profession that caused me emotional pain. I felt relieved, but also lost. I left college to give myself time to think. Now my pathway to save the world one person at a time was gone, as well as my fiancé. In my diary I wrote: "*I haven't felt this alone since the nun broke my arm in fifth grade.*"

# CHAPTER 6

## Lies, Lies Everywhere There's Lies

It was one of those rare spring nights in Ohio when the air was warm enough to play outside without a jacket. The street was filled with neighborhood kids, some catching lightning bugs in jars, some playing kickball, some riding their bikes down the steep Munson Avenue hill screaming, "Look, Ma, no hands!" Our moms were gathered together on the porches talking.

My friends and I were turning cartwheels through a jump rope. Julie was the best at this. Her timing was perfect, and she always landed like a gymnast doing an Olympic vault. My timing was getting better, but I was still shaky on my dismount. On my next turn, I miscalculated and became tangled in the rope. When I landed it felt like a sword cutting through my wrist and I screamed in pain. My friends helped me up, and, holding my wrist, I ran up the steps of my house to find Mom.

"Sit down, honey." she said. "Okay. Can you move your fingers?"

I did. "Oh good," she said, "its not broken, just a sprain. You'll be fine, thank God, since your Dad is gone and I don't have a car to take you to the hospital!"

At school the next day, my wrist was still swollen. In penmanship class, Sister Mary Theresa barked her usual command to all the fifth graders: "Sit up straight, pen in right hand, left hand flat on the desk!"

Sister paraded up and down the aisles with her ruler, correcting postures as she went with a whack on the back or a rap on the hand. When she got to me she stopped at my desk. She looked down her glasses and studied me as I pulled my hand along my paper. My wrist was stiff and not cooperating. "Mary Pat," she said sternly. "Lay your left arm flat."

"I can't," I said.

Her face reddened. She gritted her teeth. "Do it!" she screamed.

"It's swollen," I said. "It won't lay flat."

With her face scrunched up like a prune, she dropped her ruler as she marched to the back of the room. She bent her knees and with a grunt, hoisted with both arms the 1932 Webster's unabridged dictionary from its pedestal. She heaved it along with her, step by step, until she reached my desk. Then in one swift motion she raised the dictionary over her head and slammed it down on my wrist.

I passed out.

When I woke up I was in my great uncle Bud's office. He was the pastor of our parish and the principal of our school. I looked over and saw him on the phone, no doubt with my mother. "Why did you send Mary Pat to school with a broken arm?" he asked.

I could imagine my mother's embarrassment, being accused like that. She was probably answering him softly, saying, "I'm sorry," and "I didn't know." Probably she was mentioning the fact she didn't have the car today. "Don't worry," he said. "I'll take Mary Pat to the doctor."

Once at the doctor's office, I lay freezing on the examining table while my arm throbbed. The bright lights overhead gave me a headache. It seemed like I'd been there forever, with no one but Uncle Bud in the room. "Where's the doctor?" I finally asked.

"Looking at the X-rays," said Uncle Bud.

I kept wondering why they made me take off my white uniform blouse. It was only an arm—did they really need me half naked? I still had my slip on, but nobody ever saw me in my slip except my mother or a doctor. And with the cold air, I could feel my nipples standing up beneath the silky material, betraying me. Sure enough, in the chair at my side, Uncle Bud was peering over his horn-rimmed, pop bottle glasses to stare at my chest.

I wanted to hide. It was bad enough lately, constantly embarrassed by the tell-tale swelling. I'd begged and begged Mom for a bra. "You don't need one yet," she said. "Your sister is two years older and she hasn't even got one."

Linda was not developing like I was. She didn't have to face the threats that I did. I was terrified the boys in my class would turn their attention from Bonnie, who was newly endowed with developing breasts, to me, their next victim.

Nurses came in and strapped down my injured arm. Uncle Bud took my free hand until the doctor finally came in.

"Your wrist is shattered," he said. "You have several broken bones. I'm going to try to set it, but you're probably going to need surgery later."

"Okay," I said. "So, can I go?"

"After I set your arm," he said carefully lifting my wrist. He spoke gently like Ben Cartwright teaching Little Joe a lesson. "This is really going to hurt," he said, giving me a concerned look. "Now, take a deep breath and count backwards from ten."

I squeezed my eyes shut and began, "Ten . . . nine . . . aaaaggghhh!" A pain like I had never felt reverberated through my body. I couldn't breathe.

As they wrapped my arm in gauze and slathered it with cold plaster, I hoped Uncle Bud would stop leering at my breasts. I felt such shame, such betrayal. These nuns and priests were supposed to be the next best thing to God! How could they hurt me like this?

As Uncle Bud drove me home, I couldn't look him in the eye. When we reached my front door, Mom rushed out and grabbed me "Are you all right?" she asked, breathless. "Thanks, Father Bud, I am so sorry to have sent her to school like that. I don't know what I was thinking."

When he left, Mom spun around on her heel to face me. She gave me a solemn stare. "Mary Pat," she scolded, "Why on earth didn't you tell me your arm was broken last night?"

"It wasn't broken last night," I said. "My teacher broke it today."

Mom blinked at me, incredulous. A long moment passed. "What," she finally asked, "are you talking about? It was broken when you got to school. Father Bud said so."

"No, Mom."

She shook her head.

"It wasn't broken until this morning, in class," I repeated. "Sister Mary Theresa broke it."

Her mouth dropped open, and then she clamped it shut. "He is a priest and wouldn't lie," she said carefully. "Now go to your room until you can tell the truth."

In my room, I lay on my bed with my face against my good arm. I was crying because my arm hurt, but even more because Mom didn't believe what that nun had done to me. And, I couldn't even imagine trying to explain to her the shame I felt about Uncle Bud's leering gaze.

I felt so lost and alone. This nun and this priest, who were also my teacher and my uncle, had hurt and betrayed me. How could God's representatives on earth be so thoughtless and cruel?

It could only mean one thing: I deserved it. I wasn't good enough.

The pain pills kicked in and I found a place of great euphoria, drifting off to sleep.

When I awoke, my arm was throbbing. I went downstairs to find Mom. I found her in the kitchen biting into a strand of spaghetti and with a huff she said, "I never know when this stuff is done!"

I asked for a pain pill and without meeting my eyes she quickly handed me one. I went back up to my room, crawled under the covers and hoped I could hide there for the rest of my life.

As time went on, my arm healed but my shame didn't. The only good thing I'd taken away from the experience was the euphoric feeling of those pain pills. I missed that hazy happiness.

If only I could find that bliss again.

I started looking in the kitchen.

Night after night, I began sneaking into the kitchen when everyone was asleep hoping there was cake or pie left over from dinner. If not I'd graze on leftover chicken or potatoes or whatever the fridge had to offer. If the family had devoured everything at dinner, I'd smear peanut butter on Wonder Bread and eat until I got that high. It wasn't as good as the pills, but I could reach the same semi-comatose state. And, it never betrayed me. It was always the same high, there for me whenever I needed it.

Later that summer I began babysitting twin boys. I loved all the cool food they had at the Brickman's house. At home, we baked all our breads, pies, cakes and cookies, but at the Brickman's there were store-bought Twinkies, Hostess cupcakes and Reese's Peanut Butter Cups. They even had mashed potatoes in a box.

I was enamored with the idea of taking that box down from the shelf, boiling some water, adding those papery little snowflakes to a bowl with some milk and butter and reaching my food high in five minutes or less. It was an unconscious place: safe, where no one could hurt me. I was insulated from the rest of the world.

Then one night Mom caught me standing at the refrigerator, gulping down cold green beans swimming in clumps of bacon grease. "My goodness!" she gasped. "No wonder you've been putting on weight!"

The next thing I knew, she was restricting my eating. But I had ways of outsmarting her.

On Saturday mornings, Mom had a system: my sister and I could choose to clean the living room and dining room, or the kitchen. If you chose the kitchen, you had to bake all the desserts for the week's school lunches and suppers. With all that baking, the kitchen detail took many hours longer than cleaning the main rooms, so Linda never wanted it. With a sigh, I pretended to be making a great sacrifice as I took on kitchen duty. All morning I would eat cookie dough, cake batter and pie filling, getting the food high I sought. Mom never caught on or I would have been banished to cleaning the toilet and vacuuming.

The rest of the week, though, I had to be on the lookout. Linda loved to catch me in the kitchen between meals. "Mom, Mary Pat's eating again!" Then she'd start chanting, "Mary Pat is VERY FAT." Years later, my family wondered why I dropped the "Pat" from my name.

It was typical for Linda to take me down a notch. From the time she was born, she had been treated like a princess. The first baby in our family had died, so when Linda was born Mom and Dad were ecstatic. In the pages of pictures of her first birthday, she was surrounded by dolls, stuffed animals, and a rocking horse Dad had made himself. Even on my best Christmas, I never scored that big.

There were pictures of Linda sucking her thumb, Linda drinking her bottle, Linda playing on the floor, Linda crawling, Mom holding Linda, Dad holding Linda, Grandma holding Linda and every relative who ever visited us holding Linda.

There were only three baby pictures of me in the family album. One, naked in a bathtub, one naked on my stomach, and one with chocolate smeared all over my face. All the ways I'd really rather not be remembered.

When I was born, Linda wasn't happy to share the spotlight. And then came even more sisters and brothers, and, as in most families, we each coped in our own ways.

It was easier to handle when everyone had their own role. Linda, for example, was the smart one. I knew this because when I was nine I heard Mom talking on the phone to her best friend, "Linda never has to study to get all A's," she said. "But Mary Pat really works hard to get B's and sometimes A's."

And so it was.

In the same week as Mom's phone conversation Dad brought home pictures we had taken at a photographer's studio. "Everyone says she is a real beauty," Dad said pointing to my picture.

I felt good. Maybe if I wasn't smart, at least I could be pretty.

And so, we each played out our roles. Linda always had her nose in a book and remained aloof. I tried to always be perfect. Annie was handicapped, so we all looked out for her. John tried to please Dad, like me. Chris was the only one who really stood up to Dad.

And then came Joe. Joe was the baby, my baby. I was eleven when he was born and I played with him instead of my dolls. He was so cute with bright blue eyes, porcelain skin, and the sweetest blond curls. Mom let his hair grow long and everyone thought he was a girl. We dressed him up in a red velvet dress and took pictures. He's never forgiven us.

Looking back, it's funny how each of us had a different perception. You would think we had been born into different families. For instance, when Dad would line us up to do calisthenics shouting, "Hut, 2, 3, 4!" like he was still a drill sergeant. Linda thought we were playing army. I thought it was a grueling form of torture.

To me, home was chaotic. I found any reason to be gone. But it wasn't that easy getting out. If you were making money it was okay to leave the house, and this motivated me to do more and more babysitting. I liked making money. With my earnings I would sneak to the corner store to buy my favorite—Reese's Peanut Butter Cups.

One day, after dreaming about that perfect blend of salt and sweetness on my tongue, I bought three.

The first, I wolfed down because I wanted the sugar rush. The next I broke in half moons, fitting one in my mouth and letting it melt into my soul. In this way, performing my ritual, I reached heaven with the other half.

Only one left. I broke it into pieces. I chewed the first piece. I savored the second piece—and then, from the corner of my eye I saw Linda coming down the street. Why was she always there, like a nun over my shoulder, watching my every move? I gulped the last piece. As she passed she said, "Mom's looking for you."

I sighed with relief. She hadn't seen me eating! I didn't have to endure her taunts. But my joy was over. I hadn't gotten a chance to enjoy that last morsel. And then, a while later, I put my hand in the pocket of my grey parka and realized there was still one piece left. Oh my God! That last piece of peanut butter cup on my tongue was the most delicious thing I'd ever experienced.

My only other pursuit at that time in my life was working on perfecting the backbend. On our front steps I descended lower and lower, holding onto the railing until I finally reached the ground. When I could do it on my own, I ran to show my accomplishment to Bill, our next door neighbor.

Bill wore crisp white shirts that said, "Acme Distributing" on the back and "Bill" on the front. He drove a big white van with the same "Acme Distributing" logo on the side. A medium sized man with a brown, balding comb-over, Bill had a nice smile and the demeanor of a Maytag repairman—kind of lost, but there to help. His son was grown and gone and he loved to watch all of us kids playing in the side yard between our houses.

With Bill watching, I was able to repeat my performance without a hitch. With both of my hands I reached up over my head to the ground and formed the perfect back bend. Then I collapsed on the ground.

Bill clapped yelling, "That's great, Mary Pat!" Then he laughed and said, "But if you can get all the way down there, you can certainly get up the same way without falling to the ground."

Struck with this idea, I went through my back bend a few more times, and tried straightening up. Finally I did it! I couldn't help but grin proudly. Bill smiled back and said, "Follow me."

Step by step, he led me around the hedge and through the gate, into his backyard. It was a forbidden place since his wife, Florence, didn't like us kids playing there. Bill turned with his finger to his lips and whispered, "Shhhhh. This will be our little secret."

Bill guided me around the massive oak tree, through Florence's prized rose bushes, past the grapevines hiding the fence to the alley that ran behind our houses. His eyes darted left then right.

What was I in for?

Bill unlocked one side of his garage door. He flipped on the light and I almost fainted. The entire garage was filled with boxes of candy! There were endless shelves of brightly colored boxes. Even more brown boxes were piled high with Acme Distributing stamped on the side. Rows and rows of mouth-watering M&M's, Mars Bars, Pez dispensers, and my all time favorite-peanut butter cups. Why hadn't I known this was here?

This was a far cry from Dad's garage with its table saws and drill presses.

"Pick out three," Bill said standing guard at the door. "Go ahead, anything you want."

I took my time walking up and down the aisles. There were Paydays in bright blue and white wrappers, licorice in both black and red and Gumballs in every color of the rainbow. I bit my lip with indecision. *I only get three?* I thought to myself.

At last I decided to venture into the unknown. I reached up to a big, brown and white wrapped candy bar with red writing. It read, "Luscious Coconut Covered in Chocolate with Almonds." That would surely not disappoint me in my hour of need.

And then, a safe choice would always be my cherished favorite, peanut butter cups.

Now I only had one choice left. It was a moment requiring extreme concentration. Bill smiled patiently as I slowly strolled the aisles, scanning every item. It would have been devastating to miss one, and make a wrong choice. Then I saw the bright green box of Doublemint chewing gum. It would last me a while—even the name said so. I chose a pack, completing my choices.

"Don't tell the other kids what's in here," Bill said.

"I won't, for sure!" I hid the candy under my shirt and yelled over my shoulder as he closed the garage door, "Thanks, Bill!" Then I ran to hide out in my room.

I loved that man. He always had a twinkle in his eye when he saw me. I'd smile back, as together we shared our great secret. I worked on mastering more gymnastic feats to earn another trip to Candyland. Sadly, I was never granted another visit. But even so, my love affair with food continued.

I gained even more weight. It was a great way to hide from the world, but Mom didn't like it. She took me to the doctor. "I'm embarrassed to be seen with such an overweight child," Mom said exasperated. "Can't you do something?"

I sat there more hurt than I'd ever been.

The doctor wrote out a prescription: diet pills.

Wow, these were really great. I was never hungry and could stay up and study all night. It felt almost like those euphoria-producing pain pills. But with this medication, I didn't need a broken arm. In just a couple of months I lost thirty pounds.

In my diary I wrote: *"Hopefully Mom won't be embarrassed to be seen with me anymore."*

# CHAPTER 7

## *Cheated and Mistreated*

Now that my fiancé and my profession in Speech Therapy were gone, I tried to figure out what to do with my life. I began working full time at the *Republic and Gazette* and heard about an opening in Display Advertising. This was my break! I could just see myself visiting car dealerships and real estate offices helping advertisers create their ads each week.

As I entered the Advertising Manager's office he sat up with a big smile. Herb had always been friendly when I'd see him around the building. I thought of him as kind of a father type, but right now he wasn't looking at me like I was a daughter. He seemed to focus on my bright yellow miniskirt as I sat down trying to keep from squirming in my seat and asked about the job.

"You must be kidding," Herb said, looking up to answer my question. "We don't hire women for these positions."

I sat up straight. "Why not?"

"Well, these jobs pay a lot and we can't waste that income on a woman," Herb said. "A man needs the money to raise a family."

I scratched my head as I left Herb's office. This was the same company that wouldn't allow us to wear pants because pants were immodest. Yet we could sit at desks all day with all but an inch of our thighs showing in our micro mini skirts. That was modest? I went back to work really confused.

Later that year my friends and I decided to celebrate the fact that I had NOT been married for a year. We went to our usual place, the Blue Goat Pub on Hayden in the river bottom. We liked the Blue Grass bands that played there on weekends. The cool desert breeze was the finishing touch to the perfect fall evening as we sat outside around a wooden spool table.

We were playing Cardinal Puff, a drinking game, and got sillier as we drained our pitcher of Miller Lite. Several guys walked up. "Can we get you a refill?" one asked.

"Sure," we said in unison as they sat down and joined in the drinking game.

Next to me sat a tall slender guy with medium brown hair and a Fu Man Chu mustache. "Hi, I'm Dan. Did they call you Mary Pat?"

"Yea," I said toasting with my beer.

"Are you Catholic?" he asked moving closer.

"What gave it away?" I asked. "My guilt ridden face or my name?"

"Your name mostly," Dan said. He settled into the seat beside me with a grin. "What are you guilty about?"

"Everything," I sighed.

"Well maybe I can help you with that," he smiled.

I was intrigued by his answer and liked this kind of banter. His sense of humor was quirky and cute, attracting me along with his quiet charisma. On the same night I met Dan, I met his roommate, Jim. He was a little older than us and I could see why he was the voice of reason in the group.

There was a party every weekend in those days. We'd meet at friends' houses with our backgammon boards and drink, smoke dope or do whatever drugs were available, playing games until the early hours of morning. Jim and I talked as Dan sat in the corner bobbing and weaving from the Quaaludes downed with Coors. I drank but I didn't really like pot. It seemed so antisocial, smoking it then laughing in the corner by yourself since no one else got the joke.

Some, like Dan took the pills. I had surely liked the pain pills when I broke my arm and then later the diet pills, but these pills weren't prescribed by a doctor and they scared me. But this is the way it was in those days. And here was Dan, another party lover just like Dad.

Dad was always a hit at parties. Mom rolled her eyes and hid when he started his latest one man show of irreverent jokes. But at home he spared us the racy stuff and baited us kids with questions like, "How long is a piece of string?" or "Where does the light go when it goes out?"

Dan's style was quieter, but he had Dad's charisma. He came from a similar background, growing up in the Midwest. He wasn't Catholic, but the Protestant's closest offering, Episcopalian. Not only did our backgrounds match but our neuroses seemed to match also. He was a budding addict, though I didn't know enough to have called him that. There was just this quality I couldn't name that made it seem natural to be with him. I could hardly believe how fast it all happened. Soon we were married.

---

I tried to adjust to my new role as wife. At the grocery store counter I looked down at the check in my hands, having just signed my married name. I stopped and thought, *who is that?* Here I was with my husband's name on me, just like his Cutlass or an embossed shirt. Was I my husband's possession now? Everything seemed different.

Yet, not everything.

Now that we were married, I told myself that all the partying was a thing of the past. We'd settle down behind our white picket fence and live happily ever, just like Mr. and Mrs. Stevens.

But the partying didn't end.

On our first anniversary, I became pregnant. I could no longer tolerate the drinking, though there were no medical warnings in those days. I couldn't smoke either. *Thank you, God! I say now about the wisdom of my body.*

But my pregnancy was not easy. Day after day, the nausea I experienced was all consuming. "Eat saltines," friends who had lived through it said. In my diary, I prayed, *"Nabisco, please come through for me."* But, no luck.

After months of throwing up into my long hair, I cut it off. When I looked at that short-haired, green tinged person in the mirror I didn't even recognize her. Who was this sickly looking married woman with the short hair and different last name?

One day in the supermarket, I was bending over the meat counter trying to choose a steak for Dan. I held my stomach, trying not to retch from the sight of all that bloody flesh, when a sweet little woman came up behind me, tapped me on the shoulder and handed me a box of powdered sugar doughnuts. "These helped when I was pregnant," she said. "It does get better, I promise."

"Thanks," I said gratefully, tears in my eyes.

I nibbled one doughnut, then another. I came home and experimented further. I found when I mixed powdered sugar doughnuts with ice cold milk they created a concrete paste that at last stopped the quivering in my stomach. Once again, it was food to my rescue!

Maybe I would get through this pregnancy after all.

And then, right before Christmas, Dad went into the hospital for a sudden gall bladder surgery. All six of us kids were gathered with Mom in the waiting room, high on vending machine coffee and Snickers bars after all those hours of waiting. When the doctor finally came out he took off his glasses and wiped his brow. "We found a spot of cancer on Jack's stomach," he said.

I watched Mom's face, as her hands went into prayer position.

"We had to remove eighty percent of his stomach," the doctor continued, but I think we got it all. Jack will be fine."

You could feel the relief in the air as we all let out our breath.

"Can he come home?" my brother Chris asked.

The doctor shook his head. "I'm sorry, but he will have to stay in the hospital for Christmas."

What could we do? We had to make the best of it, as we had on all the other hospital trips with Dad. We brought a perky little tree with tiny ornaments into the dreary hospital room. We furnished sacks of horehound candy—without his booze by his side, Dad needed lots of sweets.

It was exhausting, but gratifying, to stand by him as a family, looking out for his every need.

Then Kathy, my old high school pal came to town for the holidays. "You need a break," she said. "How about we go out for a drink?"

I was all too eager for a change of scenery outside the hospital. And the prospect of going home only meant boredom, since Dan was out at an office party that night. "Great," I said. "Anywhere but the Frontier Lounge. That's where Dan is."

"How about the Gaslight?" Kathy asked when she picked me up. "It's always a hoot. Oh, and how's your Dad?"

"Better, thank God," I said. "The Gaslight sounds good."

We walked into the blue haze of cigarette smoke and found a table away from the dance floor. The smell made me gag—but then everything made me gag. We ordered our drinks while out of the corner of my eye I saw something that made me more nauseous than ever. Was it really true? I shook my head, hoping I was mistaken.

I looked back again toward the dance floor and groaned inwardly. There was my husband, in a lip lock with another woman.

"He's at the Frontier!" I whispered, unable to tear my eyes away from the couple. Oh my God!" I cried, staggering to my feet. "He's making out with his secretary!"

Knocking over a chair with my basketball for a stomach, I stumbled to the door searching for air.

Kathy stood up, not sure what to do, while some of Dan's coworkers heard the commotion. Norman looked at me with deep pity, while Rusty's mouth dropped open in shock. "Dan, your wife is here!" he shouted.

Outside I was gasping, not sure whether I was going to throw up or hyperventilate. While Kathy was paying the bill, Dan came out and said, "Mary Pat, listen to me. It's not what you think!"

I shook my head, unable to speak. Kathy burst through the door, took one look at me, and grabbed my sleeve. "Come on, girl," she said. "Let's go."

She put me in the car and slid into the driver's seat. After we sped away in the darkness, we both caught our breath. "Do you . . . want to talk?" she asked hesitating.

I buried my face in my hands. "I don't know what to say," I said and we drove in silence.

When we got home, Kathy helped me to the house. She handed me my purse and sweater and flipped on the light. She stood there looking at me, helpless.

"I just need to be alone," I said. "Thanks, Kathy."

"I understand." She turned and closed the door.

I dashed to my closet and started pulling out clothes, searching for a suitcase. I didn't stop to ask myself where I was going. Dan had our only car and I had just quit my job. I thought about calling Mom but she had her hands full with Dad in the hospital and three kids at home.

I'd figure something out. I had to.

I went on, intermittently running to the bathroom to puke, and standing at the closet, sorting my clothes. At last I had all my worldly belongings in a big pile on our waterbed.

Then I heard the car pull up outside.

"What did you think you were doing tonight?" Dan said, stomping into the bedroom. "Were you checking up on me?" His hands were fists at his sides.

"No," I said quietly. "You said you were going to the Frontier."

He threw his hands in the air. "Checking up on me!" he ranted. "Just like a woman!"

I looked down at my pile of shirts, skirts, nylons. There was my favorite blue sweater with the pearl buttons that I hoped I could fit into again. Suddenly I felt ashamed and guilty.

It was all my fault.

Or was it?

Confusion swirled around me. How could this be my fault?

Was it a wife's fault when she discovers her husband is cheating? Was it a child's fault when a parent is blamed for sending her to school with a broken arm?

I was confused, nauseous and weak from crying. What was I to do? Where could I go?

Eventually, Dan passed out in bed after throwing my clothes on the floor. I took refuge on the couch. I curled up on the cozy green and gold brocade that had been my home many nights when I was sick or lonely. I wrapped myself in the orange and brown afghan Mom had knitted and wrote in my diary: *"Once this baby is born, I will never be dependent on a man again."*

# CHAPTER 8

## *He Gets By With a Little Help*

Mom, my brothers and sisters and I hauled all our presents to Dad's hospital room that Christmas. He laughed about the cheesy red tie with the Santa Clauses from my brothers. Then he lifted up the bottle with the bow on it and said. "I can't wait to get home to drink this 12 year old scotch from Dan!"

"Now Jack," the nurse said, stepping in. "No drinking for at least a month!"

Dad's eyes went wide as he pretended to straighten up on her behalf. "Hide the scotch!" he yelled with an impish grin. "The Ole Battle Axe is here."

"Oh, Jack. Behave," the nurse said blushing. It was useless trying to be serious with such a charmer.

Indeed, I'd always wondered how Dad could get away with these jokes with the ladies. As a six-year-old kid, when I went with him to do handyman work at the convent, Dad would pull stunts for the nuns. He'd crack jokes or pull his ukulele out of his tool box and sing, "Ain't nothin' but a hound dog, cryin' all the time." They blushed like the nurse did, and tittered. "Oh Jack!" they said. "Go back to work."

Before long, the holidays were over and Dad was out of the hospital and on the mend. He went back to work and back to drinking. Everything was back to normal. It was grapefruit season, and twenty-eight grapefruit trees encircled our house. It was a special

41

time of year, and memories came flooding back. When they were kids my brothers had set up a table and sold them on the corner for two cents each to make extra money. One day a reporter from the *Arizona Republic* came by and snapped a picture. There on the front page the next morning were Chris and Joe in their horn rimmed glasses, looking bored with their heads propped up on their arms. The headline, "Grapefruit Gripers" said it all.

Since we had moved into our house in Phoenix we had a rule. Dad could not pick grapefruit if no one was home. We said his balance was off because of the surgery, but really it was his drinking that worried us. If no one was home and he fell, he could lie there for hours. With this reasoning and this rule we could continue to tiptoe around Dad's "delicate condition."

Grapefruit season and my pregnancy wore on. Then the movie *Star Wars*, came to the local theater. Mom wanted to see it. Dad kept telling her he would take her, but never found the time. Finally, one Sunday afternoon, my brother Chris and I decided to take her. It was nice to be doing something while Dan was at the bar with his friends.

As Chris, Mom, and I were getting in the car, Dad ambled out of his shop, looking around. "Hey, I was going to take Mom to that movie," he said. He folded his arms across his chest, offended.

"No problem," I said. "Why don't you come with us?"

"No, no," Dad said. "Not today, I have too much work to do."

"OK, fine," Chris said as he shifted the car in reverse. He gave a little wave and we pulled out of the driveway. Then we saw Dad coming through the carport, dragging the ladder. Almost with a flourish, he opened it, digging each leg into the ground by the grapefruit trees. As he stepped onto the first rung, Mom watched him, her face full of panic. "Oh, Chris!" she cried. "We can't go. What if he falls?"

Chris looked straight ahead, his hands on the wheel. "That would be too bad, Mom," he looked at her sternly. "But he knows the rule. So if he falls, he falls." He drove calmly down the street. Out the rear window Mom and I watched Dad on the wobbly ladder. "Please, Chris, go back," Mom pleaded.

"Mom," Chris glanced over and tried to make eye contact with Mom while she was staring pitifully out the window. "You know he's just mad, don't you? Because we're taking you to the movie he promised. He never follows through."

"I know, Chris," I said, looking from my Mom to my brother to the precarious looking figure on the ladder in the rear view mirror. "But what if he falls?"

"Alright, alright," Chris said with disgust. "I'll go around the block."

By the time we drove past our house, Dad had taken the ladder down and gone back into his shop. Chris had been right. It was just another show Dad put on for us.

Time after time, I watched Mom be manipulated by Dad in this way. It had always made me angry. But now I was letting Dan do the same thing to me. He did what he wanted without regard for my feelings. And me, I was letting it all happen, without saying a word.

I wasn't sure if Dan was still seeing his secretary. All I knew was that he was out at least four nights a week, a lot like Dad when I was growing up. I'd always felt I wasn't good enough for Dad to spend time with me, and now sitting on my couch sobbing I had the same feeling with my husband. But in my diary I was formulating a plan: *"As soon as this baby is born I am getting a job."*

# CHAPTER 9

## *Here Comes My Son*

Getting ready for baby. This was my single focus as I dusted, mopped, scrubbed out the oven and even scoured the gas fireplace. I climbed on a ladder and wiped the fan in our vaulted ceiling. This was probably not a safe move considering the shift in my center of gravity, but I was on a mission. When I took all the light bulbs out of their sockets and washed them, it was clear that the nesting instinct was in full swing.

Then the day finally came! When they handed me my son I was transported to another place. I was at one with God, in awe of human nature. I couldn't sleep from the excitement (or was that the Demerol they gave me after the Caesarian?).

He was perfect. How could his dad and I have created such a sweet little nose and rosebud lips? His head was cone shaped from the long hours of labor, but I didn't care. I looked at him and was filled with a kind of love I had never known. He was truly a gift from heaven. Surely this would make Dan stay home at night. Heck, this baby could cure my Dad's alcoholism, or at least create world peace!

I named this beautiful boy, Heath, from Emily Bronte's love story, *Wuthering Heights*. It was also the name of one of the brothers on a favorite show of mine, *Big Valley*. Heath was the strong, silent brother.

That's how I pictured my son: full of strength even in his tiny body. God was handing me a clean slate to write the ideal formulas to mold this baby into the perfect person. My son's childhood would be so much better than mine. I'd make sure of it.

Euphoria filled me as I relaxed in my hospital room, relishing the care and attention. I chose all my meals and they were brought to me. Nurses bathed Heath and even changed him, then handed him over for feeding and play time. I rocked him in my arms and sang a song I made up: "You're the best little baby in the whole wide world and I love you, yes, I love you." This brand-new motherhood was a blast. I was in no hurry to go home.

Jim, Dan's old roommate, came to talk to me most nights of my hospital stay. He reached down and I placed the baby in his arms to hold. "Jim," I said, as we both gazed at Heath's tiny face. "You've been here from the beginning. Will you be Heath's godfather?"

Jim blinked and smiled. "I'd be honored," he said.

Not a thing was missing from the picture.

Except maybe, Heath's father.

Where was Dan, you ask? I wasn't sure, but I didn't care. I was high on life, hormones or pain killers—or maybe the fantastic combination of them all.

And it kept getting better.

I had gained eighty pounds with my pregnancy but the day I had Heath, I lost thirty. That left me with plenty of weight yet to lose, but here was the great part: the doctor gave me diet pills. Ah, my beloved diet pills!

I was SUPER MOM on those things. The feeling accompanied me as I took Heath home, and was able to get up with him each night without complaint, completing all my daytime tasks with ease: housecleaning, laundry, cooking dinner and caring for the baby.

This was it. My new role in life. Surely nothing could be better. I thought back to how much I appreciated my mother being at home. Even in college, it had been nice to know I could reach her any time I needed her.

Now, with my new baby, I was following in her footsteps.

One day Dan came home from work with his friend, Norman. He stopped in the middle of the doorway. "Where did you go today?" He said with his hands on his hips.

"Nowhere," I shrugged.

"Don't tell me that," he said moving toward the refrigerator. "I touched the hood of the car. It was warm. You drove somewhere."

"Oh, that's right." I said, nodding my head. "I went to the store for some milk."

"Don't lie to me again," he said handing Norman a beer.

Was he just showing off or was he really serious?

I knew I still didn't measure up despite all I was doing around the house. Another time Dan and I both wanted a new pair of jeans. We didn't have enough money for both pairs, so Dan said, "Well, it's too bad for you. But I get to buy the jeans because I make the money."

There was no sign that anytime soon appreciation and recognition were going to become a part of this arrangement. Rather, our marriage was all about power.

And money was power. The one who made the money ran the show.

For now I kept doing it all: the housework, the grocery shopping, the cooking, the laundry, running errands. Yet nothing I did brought me the accolades I had received at work. There were no kudos from my husband when all his expectations were met, including dinner on the table every night by 5:30. These things were only noticed when they didn't happen. It made me feel weak and vulnerable, a slave.

Why couldn't I just accept my role gracefully, as Mom had?

Mom was petite with thick auburn hair and freckles that bragged of her Irish descent. Her soft voice and sweet countenance gave her the aura of a holy person befitting the name Madonna.

She'd always been a talented artist and piano player. She didn't paint much when we were growing up, though. And now, she only played piano to showcase Dad's singing or sax playing. Who she was as a person was always secondary to the work she did for all of us.

Growing up in the 50's, on any given day I could see my Mom dangling off the roof changing storm windows or sweating over boiling tomatoes she'd picked for canning. My sisters and I were included in all of this "women's work."

Every day before Dad came home Mom would take a bath and change into a Donna Reed shirtwaist dress complete with garter belt and nylons. The table would be set perfectly for dinner, not a catsup bottle or jam jar in sight. Once, doing the dishes after dinner I asked, "Why do we use all these extra dishes?"

"Offer it up, Mary Pat. It's because," Mom paused. "Presentation is half the meal."

Mom cared a lot about how we looked. She twisted our hair onto metal rods as we blinked back tears while inhaling the unmistakable Toni home perm.

On Saturday nights she'd wind our hair around prickly rollers with spikes driven into our skulls for church the next morning. How did we sleep on those things? When we'd complain she'd say, "Offer it up, girls. We must suffer to be beautiful."

Mom had very definite ideas about the woman's role in the family. My sisters and I were a part of it. There was no escaping the pre-dawn wake up call on Saturday mornings. "It's a beautiful day in Southeastern Ohio this morning," she'd say. My two sisters and I would drag ourselves out of bed and begin the grueling task of cleaning. My three brothers got to sleep in because after all, this was "women's work."

Meanwhile, I had often wondered, what was "men's work?" They mowed the lawn once a week, but only in the summer. It wasn't like doing dishes every day. They raked leaves, but only in the fall. It wasn't like cleaning the toilet every week. They helped Dad in the garden, but my sisters and I could shovel and hoe as well as the best of them. What did men do?

Dad went off to work each day. What he did there, I had no clue. All I knew was if that was men's work, I wanted it. I grew up longing to be anywhere but stuck in the dawn to dusk drudgery my mother was subjected to.

"Girls, get your education," Mom had said many times. "You never know what's going to happen in life."

And even though she stopped short of adding, "You don't want to end up like me," we understood exactly what she meant.

Still, here I was caught up in my role. Months earlier, a secret plan had begun to form in my mind. "Be independent!" a voice seemed to say. "Find a job of your own!" Those childhood dreams of going to the work, just like Dad, had risen to the surface. But now, with my brand new baby, I was torn. Would I be able to keep caring for Heath, and work?

As I sat with Heath in my lap circling jobs in the want ads, I thought, *Yes, I can do this. Isn't this what the women's movement is all about? I can have it all. And I will.*

I came up with a strategy of working nights so I could be home with Heath during the day. This was it! A bartending job ad jumped off the page. I applied for the position and got it! I began working from 4:00 in the afternoon until 1:00 in the morning and some weekend days. Dan could take care of Heath since these were his off hours and I was able to be the perfect mom all day. Now, at last, I had the ideal life. *"This is perfect!"* I wrote in my diary. Did I forget that Doug went out a lot during the week?

# CHAPTER 10

## *Boys Just Want To Have Fun*

I went to work in a Wild West saloon. Or rather, it was a bar made to look like a saloon, weathered on the outside, dark and rustic inside, blending with the frontier-looking storefronts of old Scottsdale. Well worn red bar stools and booths made it a cozy but cool refuge from the Arizona heat. Dim shadows provided rendezvous opportunities for the occasional affair. The essence of beer and stale cigarettes met you at the front door from the parking lot. And for added ambiance, we were the bar for a bowling alley. Just outside the inner door you could hear the crash of bowling balls hitting pins.

My only objection to my job was the Danskin Disco outfit, a nude colored leotard with a wrap around skirt straight out of Saturday Night Fever. But I made the best of it, quickly learning how to mix drinks and get the perfect head on a draft beer.

Every week brought new experiences. Thursday night at the bowling alley was men's league, with a camaraderie that reminded me of my brothers' Cub Scout meetings. It was like a campout one night a week, when the guys were free from the pressures of work, wives, and family obligations. They would tease the bartenders and cocktail waitresses, and I felt like I was back in grade school. At the same time, the guys maintained a level of respect because if they didn't there was always the chance they might be thrown out of the club.

I broke up pool fights, standing as tall as I could in my silly Danskin outfit, commanding, "Take it outside, boys."

They were quick to plead in their little boy voices, "We're sorry Mary—we'll behave—please don't throw us out!" I liked this new sense of power.

I hoped that eventually this power would change the way I felt in my marriage, but for now, I took it for what it was. I was making money, and wasn't that a form of power? And at last, I had changed my name to Mary instead of Mary Pat. This was power too, redefining myself as more than a Catholic girl.

Working there I learned that the bar bordered the Pima Indian Reservation. This was an interesting fact, because even the word "Indian" made me nervous. As a kid I'd had a recurring nightmare in which Indians would surround my house, tie my family to the backyard tree and burn our house down. I still remembered the fear of losing everything I knew.

Once, in high school after we moved to Phoenix I was opening the door to a convenience store when a six-foot Indian with high cheekbones, long braids and a headband ran into me. I jumped back, wide eyed. Feeling foolish, I tried to cover my reaction, hoping he didn't notice. But that night I found myself waking up in terror from that old nightmare of losing everything once again.

Now I was supposedly grown up and used to the fact that American Indians were everywhere in Phoenix. I tried to get over my nervousness when some appeared at the bar, weary from working at the car wash next door. One in particular caught my attention. He wore horn rimmed glasses that made him look smart while they kept his shoulder length blue black hair away from his face. He was always joking with his co-workers, so I expected him to have a name like "Laughing Owl."

Sitting down at the bar one day he said, "Hi, I'm Louie."

Louie was witty and wise and quick to laugh. He was studying history at Arizona State, and even though he received a government allotment each month like the rest of his family, Louie was saving his car wash earnings to move off the reservation.

That Fourth of July, I was alone in the bar while everyone picnicked and watched fireworks. Louie stepped through the door and I waved him in with a big smile, "Happy Independence Day!"

He paused and looked at me with a stoic expression. "The day you got your independence," he said, "was the day we got penned up."

This was the beginning of my education on the plight of the American Indian. We discussed several of their problems, including "fire water," and how the Tribal Council had brought in experts to help with alcohol abuse. Louie slammed his Bud down on the bar. "Can you believe it? They are teaching us that because of our genetic makeup we should drink 'white' liquors. They say vodka and gin don't make us crazy like the 'colored' whiskeys and tequilas." He shook his head and took another sip of the single beer he would order, always drinking responsibly.

Louie talked about friends from high school who chose to stay at the family home on the reservation, lying around all day watching TV, drinking, and smoking pot while collecting their monthly stipends from the government. "It's a disgrace," he said.

"And what about you?" I asked him. "Why are you going to school and working so hard?"

"I want more of a life than that," Louie said. "I want what the white man has."

*And what does the white man have?* I thought to myself.

I was fascinated by Louie's stories of the reservation. His people shared one history and way of life, preserving the homeland of their relatives. They were a tribe of purebreds. By contrast, my family tree was far-flung and our blood diluted, and the friends in my circle were all from somewhere else. Phoenix, after all, was a melting pot—Catholics, Protestants, Germans and Irish—all of diverse religious and ethnic backgrounds from all over the U.S.

Looking at Louie, I expected him to respect himself because of his heritage. But this was not the case. He and his fellow American Indians always felt less than the white man. And I could relate. As we swapped stories day after day, I began to see that we shared an inferiority complex. In my marriage, I was always less than my husband. Just as I felt a twinge of misgiving spelling out my married name on every check I wrote, the Indians, too, felt owned like chattel by the white man who doled out their monthly allowance.

Through it all, Louie and I forged an interesting relationship. Here we were a married white woman and an American Indian man from the reservation engaging in deep conversations about our country and what was right and wrong about it. It was a time of growth, as I began to look at others different from me, discovering to my amazement how much we were alike.

One night there was a fight in the pool room. But this time, it was between two women. Two very large Indian women. They towered over me when I went back to break them up in my usual way. "All right you guys, take it outside."

One of the women with long straight black hair grabbed me by the shoulders, lifted me up and pinned me against the paneling. She was snorting as I stared into her wild eyes.

In that moment I was terrified. It was worse than the Indians who had burned down our house every night in my dream. I could feel this woman's thick arms trembling with anger as her sharp nails dug into my arms. I could smell her sweat, and the whiskey on her breath. What was I going to do?

Then to my relief Louie bolted into the room shouting, "Drop her!" Then he grabbed both girls, banged them together at the shoulders and pushed them outside.

I stood collecting myself while they flopped onto the sidewalk. As I made my way back to the bar I could hear their whining through the open door. "Mary, please let us back in," said one. "We're sorry! We didn't mean it," cried the other.

Their wailing became so unbearable I went out to talk to them—but not without Louie. It turned out the huge woman with the long black hair was Louie's sister, Marie, and she and Brenda had been fighting over a woman. "Denise doesn't love me anymore. She loves you," Marie sobbed to her rival.

"She never loved you," was Brenda's answer.

Marie's sobs lengthened into a wail like a siren as she buried her face in her hands, mourning her unrequited love. I felt so sorry for her. Even though I didn't understand their relationship,

I understood the pain these women were feeling. Some pain is universal I realized.

I let them back into the bar.

———— ——

There were interesting Arizona liquor laws in the 1970's. Back then you could actually drive drunk. When I was in college driving home on University Drive from Minder Binders one night, an officer stopped me, came to my car window, and leaned in. "Miss, you're driving a little funny," he said. "Are you sure you can make it home okay?"

"I think so Othifer," I replied, "I don't live far."

"Good," he said backing up. "I'll follow behind just to make sure."

"Thanks so much," I smiled.

I pulled my 1964 red Mustang into the parking lot at my apartment complex and waved the policeman on thinking, *what a nice guy.*

Now I was right in the thick of the strange rules around liquor. For liquor serving establishments, no gambling was allowed. No betting on football games, and no Liar's Poker.

Another strange law was that you couldn't sleep at the bar. If someone passed out on a bar stool, I had to move him to a booth until he woke up, and then he could come back to his bar seat.

Back then no bartender would ever be in trouble for letting a customer drink too much. Some bars in Arizona even allowed women in at 18, while the age for men remained 21. The rationale was that under aged women wouldn't be allowed to drink. *Yeah, right.* Like the older guys didn't figure out ways to slip us a few. In reality, it was all about the men wanting the younger women around.

The strangest law surrounding my job involved guns. Customers had to check their firearms with the bartender who locked them in a cabinet. I guessed this was so no one could grab a gun in the heat of a fight, like the outlaws on The Wild Wild West. I was never around guns and didn't care to be; Dad had scared me enough with his war stories.

To my relief, I only had to check a gun twice.

But that didn't mean I was free from the dangers of the wild, west frontier.

At the bar one morning, I was slicing limes preparing for the lunch crowd. The outside door flew open and a police officer spun around, pointing a gun right at me. I dropped the knife and fell back against the back bar.

The young officer was frantic, biting his lip and shaking. He looked like he was twelve years old. "I'm sorry I scared you," he said apologetically, "but someone just robbed several of the businesses nearby and I thought he came in here."

Then he gasped and pointed at my foot. Blood was spouting everywhere. In my shock, I had dropped the knife and sliced a vein on the top of my foot. The officer grabbed a bar rag to administer First Aid, making a panicked effort to stop the bleeding. When that didn't work, he went out to talk to the management about getting me to the emergency room for stitches.

He felt so bad he drove me to the hospital. When we got back, the regular patrons were lined up outside, upset the bar hadn't opened on time. I limped in with my bandaged foot and served drinks until my replacement bartender made it in.

As the weeks went by, the story got crazier each time it was told. I heard Louie telling another patron, "Can you believe that dumb cop? He was aiming for the burglar and shot Mary's foot."

I chuckled to myself. What a place!

One busy night some guys bluffing each other with dollar bills were playing Liar's Poker. Their voices grew louder and more feverish as the stakes grew higher, until one of them won all the money. Unfortunately, there was an undercover cop in the bar. He reported the gambling incident to the management. Rather than lose their liquor license, the bar fired me.

I had never been fired before. This was a crushing blow. This was the place I had gained power and learned so much about myself. I was devastated.

On the way home I stopped at Baskin Robbins for comfort. Mercy me, they had come up with a new ice cream. This was the greatest Wild West treasure yet: chocolate ice cream with veins of peanut butter running through it—a cold concoction of my favorite Reese's cups. I had hit the mother lode.

When I got home, traces of chocolate still smearing my mouth, I sadly broke the news to Dan.

"No problem," he said, smiling. "I've been having trouble finding babysitters anyway." With a peck on my cheek, he grabbed his jacket and bolted out the door. Now he was free to go out and enjoy his latest addiction—the dog track.

I went through the freezer, checking for more ice cream, sobbing to myself. I wished my husband would have been there for me. Ashamed and alone, I sat down with the last scoop of rocky road and gathered my orange knitted afghan around me. I wrote in my notebook, *"I have lost my freedom, my place where I feel good about me."*

# CHAPTER 11

## *Help*

I was desperate to find another bartending job. I soon found one in a French Restaurant called *The Interlude*. I could keep working nights and be home with Heath during the day, and all would be well.

This new job turned out to be a step up in the world. Opening the front door, the aroma of butter and tarragon was a treat for the senses. The black and white checkerboard floor and crisp white tablecloths provided a bistro atmosphere. I began concocting Martinis, Manhattans and Mai Tai's instead of schlepping beer and rum and cokes. And, I could wear real clothes.

The tips were much larger and the patrons more sophisticated than my customers at the bowling alley. Some of them had been coming to this restaurant for twenty years, through different owners and cuisines. They all knew each other, sharing intellectual barbs and banter. All the elements worked together to create a classy, lively atmosphere.

One of the regulars, Tim, was the perfect cross between a salesman and a professor. He was quick with a smile and a joke, but his deep, philosophical one-liners made you pause and think. He wore the gold jewelry of a slick salesman and smoked cherry flavored tobacco in a pipe. He reminded me of Mr. Stevens because of the positive way he'd talk about the government as he drank his Dewar's on the rocks. Or was it the smell of cherry tobacco?

Tim explained Reaganomics to me in a way the "trickle down" theory made sense and inspired me to vote for Reagan, my first for a Republican as president.

Tim introduced me to interesting books. One of the best ones, *The Road Less Traveled*, by M. Scott Peck, helped in my continuing quest for true spirituality. I had baptized Heath Catholic just in case what they said was true—only Catholics made it into heaven. I didn't go to church every Sunday, but I would go to confession before Christmas and Easter and attend mass on those holidays—just in case. But I was still questioning what I had learned in Catholic School. I yearned for something more and this book was exactly what I needed.

Mr. Peck questioned that if we don't grow past the religion of our parents, have we really grown into a relationship with God? That felt right. So maybe it might be okay to let my Catholic religion go, to find my own way.

Another regular at the bar was a glamorous middle aged woman, a real estate agent named Carol. She reminded me of Elizabeth Taylor with her expertly tailored suits. I was surprised the rock on her finger allowed her to even pick up her drink. But, drink she did. An hour later, the disheveled woman at the bar was only faintly reminiscent of the woman who had ordered her first bourbon on the rocks.

One night as she was fixing her lipstick, the man next to her asked her a question. As she turned her head to answer she didn't take the lipstick off her face and smeared it across her cheek to her ear and back to her mouth in a garish red line. It gave her a lopsided grin like the Joker from Batman. I slid over from behind the bar and tried to wipe it off with bar napkins the best as I could. Then one the regulars gave me the high sign. It was time to call Carol's husband to pick her up.

The incident rattled me. I was used to Dad's drinking. The men in my family always drank and acted like idiots at family reunions and funerals. And, my college roommates and I drank, but we were just silly and goofy. This was my first exposure to a woman who drank alone. Carol was different and it really disturbed me. Why was it okay for a man to be drunk, but so shameful for a woman in my eyes?

Other patrons, Ron and Carla, were a May-December couple. She was a petite blonde, newly divorced with money. Ron was fifteen years younger with a salt and pepper afro. He was a very persuasive salesman. They were a lot of fun and invited Dan and me to dinner. Soon we were playing weekly card games, and since we had Heath, we met at our house most of the time.

One night Ron came in and handed me a little brown bottle. *Ah, cocaine!* I recognized it from college. My friend Mandy had worked for an ear, nose, and throat specialist and brought home Liquid Blue, the U.S. pharmaceutical grade cocaine used for broken noses. We had used the cocaine to study all night, or at least to stay up sharing great intellectual thoughts. It made me feel like the smartest person in the world.

Ron took a mirror down from our wall and poured the white powder on it. He used a credit card to move it into four parallel lines. Then he rolled up a dollar bill and handed it to me. I sniffed half my line in one nostril and half in the other, then handed the dollar bill to Carla. The next thing I knew Ron was all over me, kissing my face and neck. I looked over to find Dan on the couch in a lip lock with Carla. I jumped up, "Get off me!" I screamed. What had happened to us? "Get out of here. Both of you!"

"What's the big deal?" Ron asked, shrugging his shoulders.

"Get out!" I repeated. I stood there catching my breath, looking from one crazed face to the other. They all made me sick.

I was disgusted. With them, but mostly with me. How could I have let this happen? I'd come a long way, baby, but I was still Madonna's daughter. I was a mother and a married woman and was going to keep my dignity. Even if it was the '70's.

I never wanted to touch that stuff again, not after I'd seen how it could make us lose control and common sense. The next day at the bar, Ron came up and pushed my elbow. "Don't you think," he teased, "you overreacted just a bit?"

"No, I don't," I said, grabbing my bar rag and heading to the other end of the bar.

Later that evening Carla took me to the side. "Mary," she said with hands on hips, "don't you think you're just a little naive? We were only partying. Aren't you being immature about this whole thing?"

"Not a chance," I said defiantly.

After seeing Dan and Carla on the couch, it had all come back to me: how Dan had cheated on me with his secretary.

I should have been used to Dan's unfaithfulness by now. But I couldn't get over it. And he too, shrugged off that night.

"It's all in fun," Dan said, siding with Ron and Carla. I was furious.

As the days wore on, he was out a lot more now with this latest obsession, cocaine. We weren't the happy family I hoped for when Heath was born. I had to do something.

One rare night when Dan was home I said, "We need to talk," as I cleared the dinner dishes.

Heath was in the family room playing with his Masters of the Universe Grey Skull Castle. "I don't want to continue this way," I said in a low voice. "We need marriage counseling."

Dan looked over my shoulder, trying to catch a glimpse of the Vikings game. "Why?"

"Because you are out most nights,' I said, reaching to turn off the television, "spending money we don't have on drinking and cocaine." I was yelling now. "And if you won't stop, I want a divorce!"

"I don't think it's a problem," Dan said calmly with a sly smile. "But you know if you divorce me, I will get Heath." He leaned back in his chair, smug, and laced his fingers behind his neck.

"W-why would you get Heath?" I stammered.

"Because I make more money," he smiled again. "And I think you should see a counselor."

"Me?' I asked, wanting to slap that silly grin off his face.

59

"You're obviously the one with the problem," he said flipping the TV back on.

How was this my problem?

I felt like I was his Cutlass being sent to the shop for an alignment. I was rusty and needing a tune-up and he hardly seemed to care. But I made an appointment the next day.

Dr. Brown was as drab as his name. His office even had a brown chair and a brown couch—how redundant. As he took the chair, I pointed to the couch, "Do I have to lie down?" I asked.

"Only if you want to," he said pulling a pen out of his shirt pocket.

I perched on the edge of the couch. Before I knew it, I was sobbing out my sad story. I ended with, "I guess I'm pretty normal. Aren't I?"

"Normal?" Dr. Brown blinked at me over the top of his glasses. "Why would you think it's normal for your husband to drink and do drugs while you work and take care of everything?"

I just looked at him. Was this what I'd been doing? Had I even noticed?

"I, um," I said at a loss. "Because Mom did it?"

"Good answer," he said, leaning forward. "But do you want to continue to do it?"

"No," I said, biting my lip in thought. "But I can. I can handle it just like she did."

"And why do you think this is okay?" Dr. Brown's brown eyebrows hovered like caterpillars above his brown eyes.

I gave a deep sigh, thinking back. "Because," I said. "Because I was born lucky, not like Annie, my handicapped sister." I stood up wringing my hands and pacing. "You see, anytime I had a problem Dad would say, 'You think you have problems, look at Ann.' So I've always thought I should be able to handle anything. After all, I'm the lucky one."

Dr. Brown shook his head, tapping a pen to his lip. "Just because your sister was born with an unfortunate handicap doesn't mean you aren't allowed to have a problem."

Allowed to have a problem. The words echoed in my head. Here I was twenty-eight years old and was finally granted permission to have a problem.

Later, in my notebook I wrote: *"No wonder Dan can always be right. I'm always wrong. Just like the nuns and priest made me wrong the day they lied to my Mom."*

# CHAPTER 12

## *I Want to Take Me Higher*

At Dr. Brown's suggestion, I went looking for a group called Al-Anon—a meeting for relatives, friends and spouses of alcoholics. The first one I tried was at a church by my house.

I walked in tentatively, taking my seat on a folding chair among women much older than I was. One had a black eye and a tooth missing. Another had an actual handprint in bruises on her upper arm. It was almost like they were wearing these bruises as badges of honor. I crossed my legs and held my purse close, keeping to myself all night. I didn't fit in there. After all, my husband wasn't that bad.

I tried another AL-ANON meeting in Scottsdale. This group was all women also. Drama queens as far as I was concerned. Why weren't there any men at these things? Weren't there any women alcoholics? Or didn't husbands of alcoholics need help? The women in this meeting hid their bruises under theatrical makeup and long sleeved silk blouses. But the stories were the same. My husband *still* wasn't that bad.

Anyway, I told myself, there were other ways of bringing about change. Heath was in preschool now, and Dan had even been talking about having more children. This might be the thing that would make him straighten up at last: another child. It could open the door to an entirely new future for our marriage.

Meanwhile, my nights were busy at the bar. The place had lost its charm for me, though, ever since the Ron and Carla incident. In all honesty, I was sick of the bar scene. I had developed a quick wit that could shut anyone down before they could slam me with their smart remarks. I had to admit my personality was becoming way too sarcastic for my taste.

Did I really want to continue like this?

Chuck was another regular at the bar. He owned a chain of carpet stores but you wouldn't know it by his cuffed, Pre-World War II trousers and crumpled jacket. Paired with his old Chevy he made you think he was one step away from the soup line.

He only spoke to me once, the first time he ordered, "Gin and tonic." He came in a few times a week but it was always me who would ask, "Gin and tonic?" and he'd nod. Then he'd sit quietly, leering at the ladies, or watching me intently. He seemed amused by my jokes.

After a few weeks he finally spoke up. "Say," he began. "Would you like to come work for me?"

"Work for you?" I asked, taken aback. "Doing what?"

"Selling floor coverings. You could make a lot more than you're making here."

I liked the idea of getting into sales. I thought back to my college counselor's remark about my sensitivity. Surely, I wouldn't be too sensitive for sales. Salesmen aren't sensitive. I could learn. To make it even more attractive, sales was a man's field, and I would be paid like a man.

The more I thought about it, the better it sounded. I would be going into people's homes and seeing how they lived and houses always intrigued me.

I decided to put another child on hold and take the job selling floor coverings. I was excited about my new career. I was even more excited about the kind of money I could make. In my notebook I wrote: *"Dan will never be able to take Heath away from me now."*

# CHAPTER 13

## *Chain of Clowns*

I looked around the floor covering store on my first day and thought, *I can learn a lot from these salesmen.* It may have been true—but in ways I never expected.

To start with, there was Mike. Mike was a small man—in both body and mind. His hair looked like it had been painted on like a Ken doll. His bravados about his latest triumphs in sales and sex could be heard throughout the store.

"You'd better buy this today or it will be gone tomorrow," Mike said about a roll of carpet we had in the warehouse. One of Mike's customers, a heavy woman with a short curly haircut, had chosen the perfect color, and he said in a conspiratorial tone, "This is the last batch of Clay Pot they are making. Just so you know. You'd better order it now."

The woman turned to her husband. "Please, can we get it? I love this color."

Next there was Gary. It was either his barking German accent or his towering physique that made you pay attention when Gary spoke. He was a guy who would switch the customer's carpet choice to a lesser grade in the same color to make more money. Most of the time they didn't object because they were afraid of Gary.

Arnie, another salesman, was the father of four. He had huge, brown eyes that made you want to take him home from the pound. His favorite way to close sales was to sigh and look down, sadly shaking his head. "It's been such a slow month," he'd say. "I don't know how I'm going to feed my kids."

Then one day Arnie changed his line to say, "My wife is really ill. Her medication is more than I usually make in a week." He really knew how to tug the customer's heartstrings.

Jerry, the manager of the store, sold carpet like the rest of us. His honey colored afro and buffed fingernails did not outdo his French cuffed shirts with the JM monogram on the right sleeve. He walked with the stiffness of a white man trying to be cool. Whenever Jerry sat down, he'd work the perfect creases in his pants while slowly crossing his legs. On his day off he could be seen sporting gold chains with an open collar on a sparsely haired chest. His jeans had the same perfect creases. With one attractive female customer, Jerry leaned forward whispering something that made her giggle and bat her eyelashes like a femme fatale. *Ewww* I thought, wondering what he had said.

Jerry thought nothing of lying to a customer about when carpet would arrive. Even though he knew they weren't making that particular color before the client's move-in date.

One day I called Jerry on it. "What are you going to say," I asked, "when the carpet doesn't make it in time?"

He shrugged. "By then they won't be able to get Chantilly Lace anywhere else." He grinned his cheesy grin. "So they'll just have to wait."

These guys provided my first encounter with the selling profession. The tactics they took in stride made me uneasy. I didn't feel right about any of it, but that's what they said you had to do to make money.

*Oh great,* I thought, *I'm too sensitive for this kind of work too.*

Yet even though the selling approach made my stomach turn, I really wanted this job to work out. I loved visiting customers' houses.

I'd always loved houses.

When I was six years old I'd built a house out of shoe boxes and hid it under my bed. The cardboard walls were carefully taped in place. I colored red and yellow roses in the bedrooms to look like wallpaper. I even fashioned a table and chairs out of cardboard and painted them brown with little lines to resemble real wood. I made a chest of drawers out of a tiny matchbox and painted it white. As a finishing touch, I dabbed peanut butter into a tiny cardboard cylinder so you would know where the kitchen was.

It was a serious house.

Not a doll house, but a replica of the house I wanted to live in someday, a place I would feel safe.

Mom, however, must have thought my "house" was garbage. She came across it while I was at school and threw it out. At the sight of peanut butter, she had suspected me of hiding food again, and had to deal with it swiftly.

My fantasy refuge was gone.

But now I could fantasize about houses once again. In this job of selling floor coverings I was exposed to every kind of home imaginable. How people decorated their homes, how they lived—it reflected so many interesting qualities.

Surely if you had nice things, and kept things tidily packaged, you were in control of your life. You were really someone.

I'd felt this way ever since I'd known Crystal.

In grade school, Crystal had the best of everything, even skin. Hers was smooth and pale as a China doll's. Her birthday slumber parties were so much fun because they gave a glimpse of a different kind of life. You knew you were "in" that year if you got invited to the party.

Driving the long winding road to her house reminded me of race horse farms in Kentucky where we vacationed one year. The bright white fences matched the white pillars of the house and transported me to a different time. White wall to wall carpeting greeted you at the front door with a warmth so different from our hardwood floors at home. Textured fabrics on the furniture and a real oil painting over the toasty fireplace made me want to cuddle up and stay forever.

For the party we had pizza from Adornetto's, the expensive Italian place on the north side of town. And we each got our own coke bottle. The birthday cake was store bought with pink frosting and a ballerina on top that looked just like Crystal.

Crystal's white lace canopied bed actually matched her dresser and desk where she could study in her room. Since she only had one brother she didn't have to share a room with anyone. *Sigh*.

I practically drooled at all the glamour. And there on her wall hung a bulletin board overcrowded with red and blue ribbons she had won riding and showing horses. It was so lavish and inviting. If I lived there I'd feel like a princess.

And now in my work I had the chance all week long to daydream about living in a variety of houses.

And yet there were still more obstacles. As Jerry the sales manager told me, "Women aren't good at math or the building trades. I seriously doubt you'll be any different. But I might as well ask: do you think you can handle a tape measure? It's important to figure how much carpet you'll need on jobs."

Self-doubt came creeping in. Growing up, I'd always heard that Linda was the smart one in our family. There could only be one smart one, and it definitely wasn't me.

Hey, wait a minute, I told myself. Hadn't math been easy for me in college?

Maybe I was smart, too.

But if I was the smart one, I couldn't be the pretty one. Because as everyone knew, you could only be one or the other.

And I was definitely the pretty one, not Linda.

Hold on again, I found myself thinking.

Hadn't Linda been selected "Junior Achievement Queen" in high school? In Zanesville, Ohio you didn't get to be queen of anything if you weren't pretty. So Linda *was* pretty.

And then I was . . .

Oh, darn it all.

I found out my child's logic didn't hold up anymore. As far as Linda and I went, we were both smart and pretty. And if Linda was good at math and I was good at math, then what Jerry said about women couldn't be true.

"No problem," I said, looking Jerry in the eye and standing a little straighter. "I can measure anything."

And it was true.

As a kid I'd gone with Dad to do handyman jobs at church and the convent. He dressed me in corduroy overhauls and a striped T-Shirt topping it off with a Cincinnati Reds cap worn backwards. Dad taught me how to use different tools. I was especially fascinated with the level. Dad let me stand on a ladder and hold it on the cabinets he was hanging.

"Isn't that sweet?" Sister Marie had said. "He's taking the time to teach his daughter."

In his shop at home Dad taught me how to read blueprints using an architect's ruler. I liked the smell of the wood and learning all this *guy* stuff. It was much more fun than washing dishes and cleaning.

Now, as I stood in the middle of the floor covering store, realizing I was the smart and pretty one, and had all the skills I needed, I looked around at Mike, Gary, Jerry and Arnie. I can do this, I thought. And that instant, I made a decision, and formed a plan.

I began studying everything I could find about selling. I read books and went to seminars to learn how to make presentations and close sales. I memorized scripts. I kept going, even when the strategies I discovered made me feel like a fake.

Then I came across *How to Win Friends and Influence People* by Dale Carnegie. I learned to treat customers the way I wanted to be treated. When I began dealing with each customer as a person, finding out what they wanted and giving it to them, I became more successful. That was what selling was to me: filling a want or a need.

I continued to practice my new skills. And I found the greatest teacher of all, right in my own home. The best salesman ever, was Heath. He was able to get anything he wanted from me. He never let the word NO stop him from asking for a treat again and again. And he never curled up rejected after being told, "No."

One night while cooking dinner I felt Heath tugging on my jeans. "Mom, can I have two cookies?" he asked, smiling sweetly.

I turned down the stove and reached for the cookie jar. "No. You can only have one."

Did I even want him to have a cookie? No. He did a perfect "ask for the moon and see what shakes down" close.

Grinning hugely, he went off, cookie in hand.

If even a child could sell without feeling fake or guilty, then surely I could do this. Salesmen were the backbone of the American economy. I could be proud to be a salesman.

I subscribed to *Architectural Digest* and bought books about basic design. I learned about lighting and balance, texture, and especially color. I worked with a color wheel to identify complimentary colors for a specific look. I studied the different effects color can have on our lives. Red, for example, is used in fast food restaurants because they don't want customers to sit and linger.

In one study, a prison had been painted Industrial 30, a greenish yellowy mixture standard in all state institutions at the time. In the prison lunchroom, numerous fights broke out among the inmates, so they decided to experiment with a pinkish rose color instead. Immediately the squirmishes stopped, because of the calming affect.

It made sense to me how some days I'd be drawn to a red blouse, adding zip to my mood, or on other days, blue to calm myself. I had been picking out the colors of my diaries, notebooks and journals according to mood for years: red for action, green for money, purple for spirituality. My fascination with color could serve me now in my new career as well.

As I grew even busier, it became more challenging to keep up at home and work. I took a seminar in time management. Already, I'd learned to start my day at 5:00 each morning to walk, write in my journal and talk to God. (After all, He wasn't as busy at that time of the morning). And I had kept up with housework and cooked dinner every night, but now I learned how to cram even more into my day.

The class fired me up with possibilities. This was the most amazing thing since *Silva Mind Control*. Every morning I'd list the things I'd accomplish that day. I shopped for groceries once a week, chopped vegetables for the week's meals (implanting ample alpha energy into them), threw dinner into the crock pot before work while doing a load of laundry, and planned every minute to the max.

Listening to sales tapes in the car, I became a master at my game. Customers remarked on how refreshing it was to have a woman salesman.

One day a lady customer was engaged in conversation with one of the sales guys. She paused and turned as I walked by. "Say," she told him. "You don't mind if I ask her opinion, do you?" She pointed to me. "Women are just better at color than men."

Eventually the guys would ask for my help with a tough client.

In a short time I had many repeat customers and referrals. I was having fun and making money. In my journal I wrote: *"There is NO way Dan can take Heath from me now."*

# CHAPTER 14

## *Who's the Lady?*

As a sales professional, I became an expert at reading women. For one thing, their clothing gave fascinating clues. Most came into the store unconsciously wearing the color of carpet they wanted to buy. What was more, if a woman's outfit had straight classic lines, her house would be tailored and minimalistic. If she wore a feminine dress with ruffles, I knew we'd be decorating with pillows and lace curtains. And women adorned with many pieces of jewelry seemed to furnish their homes with lots of knick knacks.

Every once in a while, a woman would break the pattern by dressing in ordinary, unremarkable clothing in contrast to her house, which would be a lavish outlet of all her creativity. This, too, was a type of woman I learned to read. But one afternoon, I met a customer that fit none of my rules, completely baffling me.

Mrs. Wainwright walked into my floor covering store with an air of sensuality you don't often see in an elderly woman. Even though she seemed eighty, her eyes reflected the excitement of a small child as she admired all the colors on display. She wore a classic cut pantsuit as beige as her skin. Around her neck was a wispy silk scarf in shades of scarlet and rose, transforming her business-like outfit into a bohemian ensemble.

"How can I help you?" I asked, walking up to her.

"I need help matching the colors in my bedroom," she replied, fidgeting with the carpet pile in a sample rack.

71

"Color coordinating is one of my specialties," I said. "What color are you looking for?"

"I want red carpet."

"Red?" I asked. "Do you mean burgundy or maybe a wine color?"

"No," she said pointing to her lips, the color of maraschino cherries. "I want red."

"Okay," I said tentatively. "Lipstick red. Hmmm . . . I'm not sure how many choices we have since earth tones are all the rage right now . . ."

*Red carpet?* I was thinking. No one puts red carpet in their house in Phoenix. For one thing red is too hot for the desert. For another it's hard to match reds. And red is a really intense color, especially for a bedroom. It would keep me awake all night.

I cordially smiled and guided her to my desk to make an appointment. When we shook hands and said good-bye, I was relieved I didn't have to change her mind right then. I'd have some time to talk her out of her terrible choice.

When the day came to visit her home, I threw a couple of beige samples in the car along with her red ones in hopes of making her see the unsuitability of her choice of red.

Driving down her street, I played my usual game of trying to guess which house belonged to the customer. I called upon all my rules regarding women, their dress and personality. But again Mrs. Wainwright surprised me.

Her house was a small, conservative ranch with a perfectly trimmed hedge and a lawn like a putting green. I knew this was the right address, but it didn't fit the exotic charm of the woman who had walked into my store. I had expected beds overflowing with wildflowers, bird baths and gnomes. But all the lines of the house and yard were angular and square. When she opened the door I knew without looking it was her, from the scent of gardenias.

The inside of her home mirrored the outside. It was conservatively furnished in shades of beige and brown without much embellishment. How would red carpet ever fit in this house? I thought. It was going to be tough, but I would have to get this woman to change her mind. She led me down the hall to a bedroom and when she opened the door I almost lost my balance.

There in all its glory stood a king sized bed draped with a cherry red velvet bedspread that took up the whole room. Layers of pink lace and black fur pillows were piled high on the bed. The matching gold fringed lampshades on the nightstands looked straight out of a brothel. They were surrounded by statuettes of Roman gods and goddesses—all of them nude.

The same red velvet that covered the bed swagged two walls. The only contrast was the black fringe on the edges of the swooping design.

Mrs. Wainwright must have heard my gasp when I entered. She began explaining, "All my life I have wanted a red bedroom, but my husband would never let me. He was a good man, a good provider, but he didn't feel the same way I did about . . . certain things. He had a tough upbringing. It was hard for him to relax and have fun."

I stood in silence as she continued, "He's gone now and I am 82 years old and I'm going to have my red bedroom!"

"And you should," I said, whipping out my tape measure as I let go of all my urges to correct this decorating nightmare.

Luckily we found a carpet that almost matched the red velvet that swallowed her room. She was elated. "This is exactly what I've been hoping for!" she warbled. "It's going to be fabulous!"

I received a note from her the next week thanking me for my assistance in making her dream bedroom into a reality. She said she was enjoying it immensely. I didn't ask how.

Mrs. Wainwright sent me several clients, all because I sold her what she really wanted, not what I thought she should have. I had found the perfect career at last, my place in the world. No matter what was happening at home, or what disappointments I'd faced, I could use my sensitivity to understand people. Even when my own dreams seemed out of reach, I could help others get what they wanted. In my journal I wrote: *"I'm not just in the business of selling floor coverings. I'm in the business of selling DREAMS."*

# CHAPTER 15

## *Everybody Should Shine*

When I heard the news our company was hiring a new General Manager, I was concerned. The wrong guy in charge could kill my chances of success.

Nothing was ever sure in this business—especially when you were a woman. Some women, in fact, had completely given up trying to excel in our male—dominated profession. Tired of the fight, they accepted their "lower status."

Such was the case with Jen, on our sales team along with her husband, Ron. Jen had blood red fingernails, hair that would make a Texas woman proud, and a boob job I envied. If she had more sales than her husband at the end of the month, she would write her sales in his name to be sure she never outdid him.

In such an environment I was worried. The new general manager, Fritz was huge and gruff, kind of like Gary except without the German accent. But when he talked about his wife, Joan, he turned into a big teddy bear. She had her own printing company and Fritz bragged about her business skills and accomplishments. Every chance he got he would talk about how successful she was. Seeing the respect he showed Joan, I knew this was a man I could count on. He wasn't threatened by the success of a woman.

Even more exciting, Fritz announced that he was offering a Salesman of the Month award, with a prize of $500.00. I went to work, selling my heart out.

Everyone was shocked—including Fritz—when I won. "I have to admit," said Fritz, "that when I inspected the troops my first day, I couldn't help but wonder what I was going to do with the blond girl. But it turns out you're the hardest working salesman I've found here."

It was true: I'd outsold all the guys, and it was only my fifth month in sales. I was elated.

But, I should have known that I was painting a bull's eye on my back.

It wasn't long before I heard Jerry the store manager say to the other salesmen, "So, you guys were beat out by a GIRL?" The men retaliated by making up new rules. Normally, the first to come in on a particular morning got the morning's first customer; the second salesman would work with the second customer, and so on. But suddenly they were changing the rotation and leaving me out. It was almost impossible to get new customers.

When I talked to Jerry, he sided with the guys. Meanwhile, Jen played the game along with the boys. And even if her husband, Ron, hadn't been one of the salesmen, I'm sure she wouldn't have given up her place on "the team" to side with another woman. I wouldn't, if I were on it.

In the weeks that followed, when customers asked for me, the salesmen would tell them I didn't work there anymore. Once when this happened, a customer peered over her salesman's shoulder and pointed. "But . . . isn't that Mary over there?"

"Oh, you mean Mary," said Gary, smooth as could be. He smiled and found another clever thing to say.

I worked out my frustration picking up carpet samples and slinging them back on the racks. Now I remembered: it's not safe to be on top.

Seventh grade. I was standing in the school auditorium, carefully stringing letter after letter in my mind, speaking with the strongest voice I could muster in the Spelling Bee Championship of St. Thomas Grade School. And then, to my surprise, the eighth grader missed his word. I was the new champion! I had defeated the smartest kid in the eighth grade and was going to the state championships in Columbus. Hurray for me!

Mom made me a new dress for the event. This was a big deal, since I usually wore uniforms or my sister's hand me downs. My new dress was a navy blue and red plaid shirtwaist with a red, patent leather belt. It had shiny red heart buttons fastened all the way down the front. With my black church shoes and new white socks, my outfit was complete.

The day of the spelling bee, I pranced around the living room in my new dress singing, "I beat out the eighth grader, I beat out the eight grader."

Dad stopped me with a frown. He reached over and tapped my shoulder. "You'd better be careful," he said. "Next year when you're the eighth grader, you could be beat out by a sixth grader. How would that feel?"

I blinked back at him. I had never thought about that.

It wasn't until we got in the car that the butterflies in my stomach began swarming. We drove for what seemed like hours to get to Columbus. The closer we got, the sicker I became. When we walked in, I gasped, "Oh no!"

"What's wrong?" Mom asked, grabbing my hand.

"This place is huge," I said, wide-eyed.

Mom sighed. "Just calm down," she said leading me to the registration table.

I had never seen an auditorium that big. All the kids were huge, too. And they all looked really smart.

When the swarming turned into a full blown stomachache, I began, "Our Father, who art in heaven . . ." as I counted off the rosary beads in my pocket I had brought for good luck. Luckily, this familiar chant calmed me down.

The spelling bee began and soon they called my name. I walked proudly up to the front of the stage. "Animalistic" was my first word. *Piece of cake,* I thought. *This will be easy.*

For my second word the announcer said, "Tombstone." *Ha! These eighth graders are nothin', I can take 'em all!*

My third time I pranced up to the microphone like I had pranced around the living room that morning.

"Your word is pompous."

Pompous? I had never heard that word in my life. "Definition please."

"Pompous. Having or exhibiting self importance, pompous."

I had no clue. Well here goes. "Pompous, P-O-M-P-U-S."

Buzzzzz. "WRONG, sit down."

I made my way off the stage to sit with the rest of the losers.

Here I was, just like Dad said. I had gotten too big for my britches. In my diary that night I wrote: "I will never be POMPOUS again."

So what was I thinking now, trying to stand out among the men at Baker Bros? Why did I insist on doing my best when the world was full of people who wanted to knock me down? The message was clear: Don't shine too bright!

"HA! I'll show them!" I wrote in my notebook that night.

# CHAPTER 16

## *Take the Money, Hon*

The guys on my sales team kept trying to keep me down, unable to accept me as an equal. Yet they weren't the only ones having trouble accepting females in the floor covering field. Even some customers had their issues.

David Feingold, an attorney, called the store to get information about carpeting his offices. I asked him about the color and type of carpet he was looking for, and made an appointment to bring samples and work up a bid for him.

When I stepped off the elevator on the top floor of the Valley Bank Building I was impressed. The marble entry led to the suite labeled "Feingold, Smith and Rapture" in gold filigree. Everything about the place screamed, "MONEY!"

The secretary looked like one of the lawyers in her well tailored navy blue suit with matching pumps. She led me down the long hall to Mr. Feingold's corner office. The most beautiful view of Camelback Mountain was centered on one side of the wall to wall windows, with Squaw Peak on the other.

"I thought you were sending someone to measure," Mr. Feingold said, looking down at me over the top of his tortoise-shell reading glasses. "I need an accurate estimate."

"That's what I'm here for," I said smiling. Without missing a beat I continued, "These are lovely offices. What color are you considering?"

"I'm not sure," he said crossing his arms over his chest.

"Well, why don't you look at these samples while I measure?" I suggested. "Then I can help you decide. What areas are you re-carpeting?"

"The whole floor?"

"Great," I said, doing my best to keep the tremble of excitement out of my voice. This was going to be a huge sale!

Luckily, I was wearing my most expensive suit. It was silk in a muted gray and yellow stripe with a yellow silk blouse. The skirt fell straight to the knee with a comfortable slit up the back. My gray, open toed, sling-back pumps were a perfect match.

Mr. Feingold leaned back in his chair staring at me over his glasses pretending to be looking at the carpet samples. His eyes followed me all around his office as I measured and drew a diagram with my architect scale. When I moved to the other rooms he followed me, carpet sample in hand, standing in the doorway, not saying a word. Did he think I was going to steal something?

When I finished measuring I asked, "Did you choose a color?"

He pointed to a plush commercial carpet in Steel Grey.

"Good choice," I said grabbing my calculator.

Interestingly, the carpet he chose matched my suit exactly. I figured the measurements and handed him the bid.

"I'll get back to you," he said.

"Thanks," I smiled.

I couldn't wait to get out of there and leave this anal man with no personality. But I really wanted this sale. Not only were there eight hundred yards of carpet but it was forty dollars a yard! I was too new in the business to be jaded and think I didn't have a chance. I had given him a fair price. Now I just had to wait, fingers crossed.

A week later Mr. Feingold called and when I heard his tight voice on the phone, my heart jumped.

"I have to be honest," he said. "I didn't trust a woman to measure this job." He paused. "So I had two men from two other companies come out and give me bids. The yardage you figured was the same as theirs." He paused again. "But I was really impressed with you. I want you to do the job."

I relayed the story to Jerry and he told me it was the largest sale the store ever had. Coming out of the restroom, I noticed Jerry and Gary hanging around the water cooler. Jerry was saying something about "Mary's big sale."

Gary rolled his eyes. "No kidding," he said. "Can you believe she landed a sale that big? I wonder who she fucked to get it."

I felt I had been punched in the gut. I couldn't breathe. Gasping, I turned on my heels and ran back into the restroom, where I fought back tears until I could get a grip on myself. When I got home that evening, I cried for hours with my carton of peanut butter and chocolate ice cream. It was my one sure thing in this cruel world. (Because now—life might still be worth living—they sell this blissful flavor in the grocery store!)

When Dan came home, I was pulling Heath out of his high chair. "How was your day?" I asked.

"Fine," he said heading to the family room.

"What about yours?" He asked as he settled into his lazy boy.

"Let me get Heath cleaned up and I'll tell you."

As I wiped the Mac and Cheese off Heath's face and hands, I was glad Dan was in the business world too. He would understand my plight.

I put Heath on the floor with some blocks and began relaying the story of my day to Dan. He just shrugged and went back to the TV, "That's what business is like, honey. You'll just have to toughen up."

When he turned, I stuck my tongue out at him. "Thanks a lot," I spit.

*Gee, I never heard that before,* I thought, heading to the kitchen to wash the dishes.

*Stop being so sensitive*, the world kept telling me.

In any case, I got the message: toughen up. I ignored my coworkers and went to work on making money. I didn't come to work to make friends. I had plenty of friends. I would just roll with whatever they did to me! In my notebook I wrote: "*The next time someone makes a crass comment about one of my sales I'm going to say, 'No wonder I crave a cigarette after a big sale!'*"

# CHAPTER 17

## *The Team of the Season*

At work it was all about the team. You were either on the team or you weren't. And while guys were often raised playing team sports, I was not.

Yet I'd learned a lot, watching teams. I had three brothers who played basketball, baseball and football. And the biggest sports fanatic of all was Dad. Anyone who knew us thought twice about visiting our house on Saturdays in the fall after an Ohio State loss, because the mood of the entire house would be a somber one.

Rooting for a team, being on a team—these things made you part of something bigger than yourself. This much I knew. And yet I'd never been in on that team glory. Until one night, when I experienced the greatest team win of all: John F. Kennedy's election.

The race was bitter and close. The Republicans claimed that if Kennedy beat Nixon for the White House, he would change the Statue of Liberty into a statue of the Blessed Mother. I didn't know if that was true, but watching the first televised Presidential Debate, I thought how handsome and relaxed Kennedy looked. Nixon, by comparison, had his shoulders up around his ears. Nixon's eyes darted back and forth like a criminal on trial. I couldn't understand how anyone could vote for him.

It was 11:00 p.m. on election night when the yelling and screaming started downstairs. It woke all of us kids in our beds. "What's going on?" Linda asked sitting up in bed.

"The election," I said. "That's why Mom invited all those people over."

We stumbled downstairs to find an entire party gathered around the TV. Mom raised her cocktail glass. "Kids!" she shouted. "We have the first Irish Catholic president of the United States!"

For once, we were allowed to join in the fun, talking and shouting and eating leftover chips and dip. Then, the next day at school everyone was still happy. We held a special Mass for our new president. By the mood of the nuns, you would have thought we had elected the pope as our president. But young and old, student and nun, parent and priest, we were all in this together. We were the "St. Thomas Irish," and our team had won.

After things calmed down, we continued to pray for our admired president. Then on that sad day in November, Uncle Bud, came to my classroom door and summoned my teacher, Sister Mary Margaret. I had never seen such a tortured look on my great uncle's face. Along with the other students, I gripped my desk in fear. Uncle Bud whispered something to Sister, who screamed, "Oh no!" and dropped to her knees, blessing herself with the sign of the cross.

Uncle Bud helped her up and she relayed the news to the class. We all sat frozen in our seats as she told how our beloved Irish Catholic president had been assassinated. I didn't know what that word meant before that day.

Our whole grade school convened to church to pray for the soul of John Fitzgerald Kennedy. Afterward, we were sent home. I'll never forget the sight of my mother watching TV from her ironing board, crying hysterically. Life would never be the same.

It was not the same sadness as when Grandma died, or at school when we lost a basketball game to our rival, St. Nicholas. This sadness was everywhere: in the grocery store, at friends' houses and on TV. And now, strangely, it wasn't just us Catholics on the team. Everyone felt it. We were no longer Republicans or Democrats,

Protestants or Catholics. We were all Americans on the same team, and had suffered a great loss.

Now, twenty years later, I was learning about teams all over again. One thing was clear: I wasn't considered a part of the sales team. I wasn't only left out of the rotation, now they didn't even talk to me, except Mike when no one was looking and he was flirting with me.

While my sales helped us outrank all the other stores, I was still not on the team. I'd never felt so isolated, and yet I had a tremendous sense of satisfaction. I was giving my best. In my spiral notebook, green for the color of money, I wrote line after line: *"I am the top salesman in my company. I am the top salesman in my company."*

# CHAPTER 18

## *A Horse with a Name*

I'd show them all. I'd build my own team. I concentrated on getting new customers and phoned anyone who bought floor covering: contractors, insurance adjusters and property managers. I created color boards for builders to help their customers visualize the possibilities for their new homes. I was a one-woman sales machine.

I loved going out to construction sites, tromping through the dirt in my high heels measuring for carpet. Many times the guys would stop working and look over at me critically, expecting I wouldn't know how to use a tape measure. But I would lift my chin and keep at it, penciling measurements on my notepad while taking in the atmosphere of it all. I had always loved the smell of sawdust from working with my Dad, but now I added a new smell: drywall mud. Since I usually measured about the time they were installing the drywall, that smell became the smell of money to me.

Through my focused efforts, I met Morris, a contractor who handled numerous government projects. A small man in wire glasses, Morris looked more like an accountant than a contractor. What mattered to me, though, was the business he brought. We worked together successfully on several offices, and then Morris received a contract for the Pima Indian Reservation. We were to install carpeting and vinyl in five ranch houses.

Everything went smoothly, and as always, I thanked Morris for the chance to work together. It wasn't until a couple of months after completion that I got the phone call. It was Morris. "Mary," he said, with frustration in his voice. "What happened? I thought we'd made a good choice of carpet for those houses on the reservation."

"Of course we did," I said.

"Well," he sighed, "the residents are complaining that the carpet is packing down. I thought we'd selected a carpet that would hold up to a lot of traffic."

I puzzled over this. "Yes, Morris," I told him. "We picked the top of the line. I don't understand how it could have problems so soon after installation."

"They're also complaining that the vinyl is curling up in one of the bathrooms."

"Hmm," I said. "Let me go out and take a look at it. I'll get back to you."

I lost no time in jumping into my shiny new Oldsmobile and heading out to the reservation. Driving through it, I was struck by how the new houses seemed out of place next to the weathered teepees and small adobe huts. The government agency had spared no expense on the houses or the floor coverings, so the poor carpet performance was a complete mystery.

One of the elder family members met me at the first house to tour the problem areas. His hair was in a long braid down his back with a red bandana headband. Beads hung around his neck. It was the late seventies and he looked like a cross between a hippie and an Indian straight out of a *Spaghetti Western*. Ten years earlier I would've been terrified or intimidated or at least have had my mind made up about these "Indians." But I thought of my old friend Louie, smiled, and followed my tour guide.

Inspecting the floor covering in the first house, I continued to be at a loss as to why the living room carpet was worn thin, yet only in the center. I went to the next house and the carpet looked the same as the first. Not only was the carpeting packed down in the middle of the living room, but the padding underneath had somehow been stamped flat. Strangely, the hallways were fine. It defied everything

I knew about carpet, which usually showed wear in the halls first, where people walked and turned grinding the carpet down.

The carpeting in the first four houses was worn in exactly the same way. As we entered the fifth house I stepped back in shock. There, in the living room stood a beautiful palomino, the color of the desert.

"Move, Paco," warned my guide, as he motioned me through the door. Paco gave a small whinny and stepped to one side of the living room. A kid grabbed his mane and walked him outside. "Come on, Paco, we love you, but you have to go out."

I stood there on the carpet, which was flattened like the rest. As I fumbled for words, my guide said, "Come," arms crossed over his chest. "Bathroom floor not right."

He led me down the hall. I stepped into the bathroom and jumped back. There was Paco poking his head through a cut-out in the wall, drinking from the bathtub. Water was everywhere. The floor was soaked and the vinyl was definitely curling up at the edges.

I stuffed my laugh so far down I thought I would burst. My guide stood there silently, arms crossed. It took me several moments before I could regain composure. I cleared my throat and turned to my guide, "Do you think," I began, "that it might be the horse?"

He didn't flinch or move a muscle. Arms still folded across his chest, he frowned. "Not sure."

Once I got into my car, I couldn't stop laughing. I hooted all the way back to the store. As soon as I got there, I called Morris. "Hey, you didn't tell me the carpet had to be horse proof!"

"Horse-proof?" I told him the story and we both howled with laughter.

Morris gave me another huge sale re-doing those houses. This time I recommended an industrial strength ceramic tile. I wasn't sure ceramic was horse proof, but I knew it wouldn't pack down or curl up. Morris was happy, and hopefully Paco, too. We never heard from them again, so I'm guessing my choice was good.

In my notebook I wrote: *"It's really important for a salesman to know who will actually be using the product."*

# CHAPTER 19

## *Karma Will Get You*

In my endless campaign to get business, I heard a lot of "no's." When I began feeling down, I remembered how Heath handled "no," and pressed on. I consistently sold enough to be in the top five percent of the salesmen each month.

Fritz became a great mentor. From the day I won Salesman of the Month, to the week the guys began stealing my customers, to the moment I began my new telephone campaign, Fritz watched me closely. "Do you guys see what Mary is doing?" he'd say. "She's on the phone getting business instead of waiting for it to walk in the door."

Maybe this was my chance to finally make the team, I told myself. Since Fritz was rooting for me, maybe he could help my situation with Jerry and the others. Too soon, I was to learn another guy rule: The Chain of Command. Guys know this law instinctively or from the military. It says, "You may never, ever go over your immediate supervisor's head with any problem you may have."

So getting Fritz involved made the atmosphere of my job even worse. Jerry sat me down, shaking his finger in my face, "If you ever talk to the General Manager again about the workings of my store, you will have hell to pay."

"Okay, okay," I said getting up. "I get it." I shook my head and left his desk knowing I would always be an outsider.

But then came the big announcement.

We were building a new state of the art store in Scottsdale. Fritz told us in our monthly meeting and everyone was excited. This store would have all the latest high end carpet, ceramic, wood and area rugs. And, since the homes of Scottsdale were much larger, our commissions would be larger as well.

Fritz called a meeting and pronounced ME the manager of the new flagship store. I couldn't believe it! My hard work had paid off!

But my excitement was short lived. It wasn't long before a rumor came circulating our store with a vengeance: Mary schtooped the boss to get the job.

It had been a long time since I paid any attention to the rumors. But this time the rumor reached Fritz.

Fritz called in all thirty salesmen from eight stores for a mandatory six a.m. meeting. None of us knew what was up. We usually had meetings at seven-thirty, so we could get back and open our stores by nine.

Fritz began the meeting with, "I am furious!" His face was bright red. "Some of you have been saying that Mary must be sleeping with me for her to get the new management position." He moved across the room like Hitler in front of his troops and turned sharply. "All of you know Mary has been one of our top salesmen since she's been here. And all of you know she deserves this promotion," he said, picking up an *Architectural Digest*. "I am not only angry because of what you said about Mary, but also for what you said about me. I am a happily married man and this is a slight against me and my wife. I won't have it! Do you hear me?" he shouted, throwing the magazine down on the desk.

"Am I understood?"

The meeting was over in five minutes. I left knowing, despite all of Fritz's efforts, I would be ostracized again. But this time I felt good. I was the one who would be deciding which salesmen to transfer to that big, new, beautiful store, with the big, new beautiful commissions. I was in control.

I sighed with pleasure. "What goes around, really does come around."

I had learned that lesson in grade school.

All the girls at Saint Thomas wore uniforms of navy blue pleated skirts and crisp white blouses. There were variations of course. We could wear white socks or navy blue knee socks. We could wear the navy blue cardigan with the STS badge or we could take the sweater off. We could wear the navy blue beret straight or to one side or the other. As seventh grade girls, we had exhausted all these possibilities by October first—at the latest!

So when the last school day came, and with it the chance to wear real clothes, it was as exciting as some rare holiday. This year I planned to wear the Easter dress Mom made me—blue and white striped seersucker with a yoke decorated with three white pearl buttons. A pleat from the yoke to the hem gave it an A-line shape.

Most of the girls in my class had started wearing hose to church. How grown up, I thought. I couldn't help picturing a pair of hose with my new dress. The last week before school, I rushed home through the back door. "Mom! We need to go shopping for a garter belt and nylons for me!"

"Why?" Mom asked wiping her hands on a kitchen towel, and turning to look at me with surprise.

"Because everyone is wearing them the last day of school!" I cried.

"Everyone?" she said. "You're too young. Besides, you'll get to wear them soon enough, at eighth grade graduation."

"But Mom!"

"Sorry," she said, walking away. "You know the rules."

I pulled off my navy beret, balled it in my fist and threw it on the floor of my room. Couldn't Mom see I wasn't a baby anymore? The next day, all the girls whispered in anticipation about what they would be wearing; some were even getting new shoes to complete their new grownup look. I just *had* to wear nylons that last day of school! But Mom wasn't budging.

I made a plan. The evening before the last day, while Mom was downstairs cooking dinner, I sneaked into her bedroom and tiptoed to her lingerie drawer. I opened it and took in the familiar scent of Mom: lilacs. I started to feel guilty about the crime I was about to commit, and then I reminded myself how it would feel to be the only girl in seventh grade wearing white anklets with my dress on the last day of school. Determined, I rummaged around the drawer and toward the back found an old garter belt still attached to nylons. She won't miss this one, I thought. The straps were held on with safety pins, but wouldn't show under my dress. One leg had a run in it, but I could move that to the inside. No problem.

On the last day of school Mom dropped us off and I ran to the bathroom to change. This contraption was harder to get on than I thought! I couldn't get the nylons straight and it was hard to walk. As the bell rang, I shuffled off to class.

"I have your report cards," Sister Mary James began as we all settled into our seats. "Joseph Ambrose, come get yours."

Squirming in my seat from sitting on the safety pins I finally heard Sister calling, "Mary Pat, come up."

I slowly inched my way to the front of the room. Suddenly I heard, *Ping! Ping! Ping!* My right nylon fell down to my ankle with the garter belt straps still attached. I grabbed my report card and dragged my encumbered leg back to my seat while the class laughed hysterically.

From that day on I learned never to disobey my mother. When you think you're getting away with something, you'd better watch out. But I was really surprised by how fast Karma worked.

I left Fritz' meeting that morning singing, "Instant Karma's gonna get you, it's gonna hit you right in the face, boy!" This time I was on the good end of Karma. And those disrespectful, thieving guys on the sales team were not.

That night in my notebook I wrote: *"I won! I won! Now what?*

# CHAPTER 20

## *I Have to Thank You*

Mom had pressed the beige linen tablecloths and filled the cornucopia with paper mache pumpkins and yellow flowers. Dad had assembled a huge piece of plywood over three saw horses, seeing we'd outgrown the family table. Foldout paper turkeys interspersed with orange candles ran down its length.

It was Thanksgiving, and everyone was in their most festive mood.

I stopped to admire the vibrant table arrangement, so striking against the turquoise carpet. It was my first year in floor covering, after all. Meanwhile my brothers and sisters milled around the living room with their spouses while Heath and his cousin Molly played hide and seek. Mom had invited some "strays" as we lovingly called them.

This year it was a gray haired newly widowed lady from church and an ASU college student who couldn't afford to go back to Wisconsin for the holiday. I used to think she invited them so we would behave, but later decided it was because she had a big heart. We had grown up, thank God, and most of the sibling rivalry was finally over. For one thing, my hippie brother-in-law no longer found it fun to tease my brother in the Pipe Fitters Union about "bowing down to the man."

As we gathered for our meal, Dan and I took our places across the table from Dad. He looked drawn and tired on top of his usual drunken stupor. I suddenly felt happy for all I was achieving in my life right now, and at the same time, overcome with gratitude for all Dad had taught me through the years. I couldn't help myself. I sat up, reached over and took his hand. "Dad," I began. "I just want to say thanks. Thanks for taking me to the church for odd jobs all those years ago. Thanks for teaching me about the building trades. I could never have been this successful if you hadn't taught me how to read blueprints, handle tools, and use a tape measure."

Dad pulled his hand away and grunted. Dan rolled his eyes, biting into a turkey leg. Then Dad began bobbing and weaving in his chair. His face fell smack into his mashed potatoes. Mom shouted, "John! Joe! Help your father!"

With mixed horror and humor, I couldn't take my eyes off Dad, wondering how he could blow bubbles in his gravy like that. My brothers helped him to the couch while I got up and wiped the gravy off his face. In spite of Mom's embarrassment, Thanksgiving Dinner went on.

We recovered in time for Christmas, with dinner taking place at my house that year. To all our disappointment, Dad stayed home, sick. His health continued to decline, and when we pushed him to go to the doctor, he'd mutter, "After the holidays, after the holidays."

After the holidays, he was in the hospital again, but this was nothing new. We were used to these trips from Dad's numerous surgeries over the years. Mom and all six of us kids would sit for hours in the waiting room, cracking jokes and teasing each other until the doctor came out and assured us Dad had cheated death one more time.

But this time was different. The doctor came out of the operating room, removed the mask from his face and sighed, "Your Dad is filled with cancer. There is nothing more we can do. He only has a few weeks to live."

"What?" we cried in unison as John and Chris stood up. Linda and I just stared at each other while Mom crossed herself.

I felt a strange mix of guilt and fear. Ever since I was a toddler, Dad had said, "I'm not going to be around much longer, you'd better be nice to me." He said it so often we didn't believe him. And now Dad was really dying.

---

Dad had been a good provider. He had worked extra jobs to pay for Annie's cosmetic surgeries, not covered by insurance. First, he had his regular job as an electrical draftsman then he sang and played the sax in a band some nights. He also did handyman jobs at church to help pay for our Catholic School education. With all that work, it seemed like he was always gone.

But when he was home he made the most of it. He loved to dress up in costumes, especially for the holidays. When I was in college, home for dinner on New Year's Day, there was Dad to greet me in nothing but a diaper and the year 1972 on a sash across his chest.

When I brought Dan home to meet the family, Dad emerged in his tuxedo serving drinks from a silver tray with a white towel over one arm. He told us later he wanted Dan to think we were in the chips and had a butler.

Dad was always a showman. When he sang in church, the ladies loved him. He stole the show—even at my wedding.

I had been upset with him from earlier that day. As he walked me down the aisle he turned and said, "If there's anything you want to know about sex, you'd better ask me now."

"WHAT?" I looked at him bewildered, unable to grasp the joke, as the cameras flashed. I was supposed to be the beautiful bride, not all scrunched up in the face, squinting at my Dad's stupid remark. "What did you say?"

Later, in his unbelievably smooth tenor voice, he gave an incredible rendition of *Ave Maria* just as I offered my flowers to the Blessed Mother at the side altar. In the receiving line after the wedding, Mrs. O'Brien said, "That was such a beautiful moment when your Dad's voice cracked with emotion."

"Yes, wasn't it?" I said knowing Dad had probably practiced that "emotion" for months.

As time when on, Dad's schemes and costumes became more elaborate. At a surprise party for Dan's thirtieth birthday, Dad showed up wearing a sombrero with a red and green striped serape flung over one shoulder and a gun belt resting on top. He had taken the cat's eyes out of one of those black classroom clocks where the cat's tail ticked back and forth and put them behind his glasses. He was the hit of the party while Mom and I sat in the corner, embarrassed as usual.

One of my favorite pranks involved Heath. For fun, Dad dressed baby Heath in a black and white prisoner's uniform complete with hat, wheeling him up and down Montecito Avenue in a cardboard box on a red dolly.

And now, this funny man was dying. There was nothing funny about it. Why couldn't I cure him with my *Silva Mind Control* like I did with Dottie. I was helpless.

The doctor walked slowly out of Dad's room, took off his glasses and wiped his eyes. "I've told Jack what's going on. You can see him now."

As we lined up around his bed with our white, stricken faces, we all stared at each other in disbelief.

Dad just lay there, staring at the sheet pulled up to his neck. Finally he said, "I want to die at home."

When we got him home of course Dad had to be out in the middle of everything. No discreet letting go in a back bedroom for him. We settled him onto the couch in the family room and the dying began.

Ann, Chris and Joe were still at home, so they pitched in to help Mom. Joe was home after knee surgery, so he bathed Dad and helped change his colostomy bag.

One by one, we came to find peace with our Dad.

My brother, John, was the oldest boy and had seemed to get more of Dad's wrath growing up than the rest of us. He had a nice visit with Dad and told me afterward that he felt better about his long years of Dad's belittlements.

My turn was coming next. I was hoping I would feel the same. I knelt down beside my father. "Let's see," he said, "I've talked to Joe and John, but I still need to talk to you and Annie and Chris and Linda," counting us off on his fingers.

"About what?" I asked taking his hand in mine.

"Well, is there anything you'd like me to ask St. Peter?" he smiled. "It looks like I'm going to see him before any of you."

All I could think to do was change the subject. The first thing that came to mind was my beautiful new store, where I would be the manager. I pulled construction site pictures out of my purse. He looked at one picture a moment, blinked, and pointed to the Port a Potty. "Is this your new office?" He smiled cutely.

It was a joke, I knew, but the familiar pang of not being good enough hit me hard. Once again, Dad was warning me against getting too big for my britches.

Through the years, I had learned that Dad had been raised that way himself. Born with big blue eyes and a head full of blond curls, all the relatives cooed and adored him. His mother put her foot down. "I won't have my son getting too full of himself," she declared. "So from now on, I want you all to call him 'Ugly.'"

Dad kept that inferior feeling throughout life. Returning from World War II, he came home to find his mother had spent all the savings he had sent home. Although she had put aside the money his two brothers had sent. Dad had nothing. That same unfairness showed up in Grandma's house. Visiting her as kids, we would see all our cousins' pictures lined up on the piano, while our pictures were nowhere to be found.

After the move to Phoenix, Dad lost his job to the boss's son, who had just returned from Viet Nam. He began drinking much more after that. It wasn't long before he had another job, but he was never the same.

His frustration came out when he picked on us kids at the dinner table. Night after night we wondered, which kid would it be tonight? He went in streaks. When it came my turn, he'd grumble, "You're burning the candle at both ends, Mary Pat. You're going to have to give up cheerleading since you're involved in Junior Achievement and Candy Stripers. It's too much. You need to be home helping your mother."

I sat listening, my heart sinking. Later I asked Mom if that was what I had to do. "No," she said. "He is so proud of you! When he goes to the games, he sits with his friends and brags. It's just his way of talking. Don't worry, he doesn't mean it."

After dinner one night, I heard Mom setting John straight in a similar way. "You know," she said, "your Dad doesn't mean it when he says you can't do anything right."

Mom made things right after all Dad's tirades. I'm not sure how any of us would have turned out if she hadn't been there.

Now, swallowing my pride, I put away the picture of my new store. I squeezed Dad's hand tightly, realizing this might be my last conversation with him, the first strong man in my life. Whatever his example, he was my father. And now he was leaving me. He turned to me with tears in his eyes and said, "I don't know how I could have been so stupid."

"What do you mean?" I asked as I leaned in to hear him.

"You all loved me so much," he sighed as he put his hand on his forehead. "Why couldn't I quit drinking?"

"I don't know Dad."

"I was gone too much, too," he said rubbing his head. "If I had it to do over again, I would never work an hour of overtime."

"I know, Dad, I like to work a lot, too. It's where I feel good about myself." I stroked his arm. "Thanks again for taking me on those handyman jobs at the convent when I was little." After all Dad told me that day, I vowed I would not be in my rocking chair or on my death bed with regrets about how I lived my life.

Time went on and Dad got sicker. The days turned into weeks and Dad was out of it more than he was in. His eyes were sunken and his mouth and teeth protruded like a skeleton from biology class. His skin hung on him like his white T shirt. The stench of the cancer was evident when you walked in the back door. Dad was decaying right before our eyes. I wasn't sure why he kept hanging on, since he was in so much pain.

One night as I was sobbing into a pillow on the couch in our family room, Dan came in. "You are going to have to get a grip here," he said with hands on hips. "You can't keep crying all the time."

"You have no idea what I'm going through," I said, "Your dad isn't dying."

The next day I had a long drive to measure for carpet in Sun City. I cried the whole way. Driving home, I stopped on the side of the road and took a walk in the desert looking for solace.

I had so many questions. For one, I wasn't sure how to tell Heath about his Grandpa. Dad was especially close to his only grandson. As a baby, Heath had laid on Dad's chest for hours while they both napped.

I continued on my walk. I had always found the desert to be very spiritual. The vast emptiness left room for all kinds of possibilities, and I understood why Jesus had gone to the desert for forty days and forty nights to become enlightened.

This day the desert was in full brilliant bloom. I sat on a rock grounded in the beauty. Breathing in the desert air, I came to some kind of knowing that everything would be okay. It would be alright to let Dad go.

Later that day Mom put Dad in the hospital. She and Joe could no longer care for him. He died the next day, away from all of us, where he could finally let go.

A friend sent the words from *The Prophet* in a card to me, "And when the earth shall claim your limbs, then shall you truly dance." Dad was free of his pain now and that quote made *The Prophet* one of my favorite books when I needed to find peace.

Mom, Linda and I went to the funeral home to make the arrangements. As the funeral director guided us into the coffin room, Linda said, "Holy Moley, look at these prices! Do you think Dad would be upset if we just shoved him into a pine box?"

"We need to get one big enough to fit his Knights of Columbus hat," Mom quipped.

I came back with, "Are we actually burying Dad in a costume?" Then we all looked at each other and burst out laughing.

"Perfect!" I said, hoping the funeral director was used to this kind of insanity. "One last costume for Dad." By now we were all shaking with laughter, loud and obnoxious.

Mom looked over at the director. "I apologize for my daughters," she said, shaking her head.

The funeral director smiled back. "Trust me, I'd rather have you laughing than not."

Our next stop was K Mart. Linda needed some shoes to wear to the funeral. As we walked through the door of the store, Linda yelled to the clerk, "Hey! Where are the cheapest shoes you've got? My Dad just died!"

The clerk's mouth dropped, but she didn't speak. She just pointed to the shoe section. Dad's death was such a relief that the laughter made its own kind of sense, while at the same time nothing made sense. I had never felt such release but I was empty and had no clue what to fill myself up with.

When I explained Grandpa's death to four-year-old Heath, he grasped it better than any of us. Later that day, I heard him out in the backyard. "Hey God, hey God," he yelled. "Can I come up for a second? I don't want to die or nothin'. I just want to see Grandpa one more time."

I wanted to join Heath out there, yelling at God so I, too, could see my Dad one more time.

And then, the strangest thing happened. Dad came back to visit me a few weeks after he died. As I opened my notebook one morning (purple for spirituality), I smelled the familiar odor of cancer that lingered with Dad on his death bed. It wasn't scary or sickening this time: just clear and real, like the smell of toast burning or coffee brewing. The scent announced that Dad was with me. He was okay and I'd be okay. In my notebook I wrote: *"Thanks Dad."*

# CHAPTER 21

## *Holding Back the Fears*

After Dad's funeral I walked into my brand new store and looked around in shock. I wasn't prepared for how huge it would be. Workmen were finishing up and leaving, while behind them stood Fritz. He opened arms wide to hug me. "Welcome back."

"Thanks," I said, with tears in my eyes. "And thanks for coming to the funeral."

"You're welcome," he smiled. "Are you ready to work?"

"You bet." I set my briefcase down.

"Work was the best thing for me," he said, "after I lost my dad." He handed me a floor plan of the brand new store. Each carpet rack and vinyl display was sketched out. The salesmen's desks were arranged to the right of the front door and the massive area rug rack towered on the far wall.

"Get these guys busy," Fritz said pointing to the salesmen who were joking around by the coffee pot.

"OK," I said and turned to Jay. "Can you unpack this box of inlaid vinyls and put them in the display? Paul, clip these dhurries and berbers on the area rug rack. Carl, move the wool samples over by the carpet." Without a second's hesitation, they put down their coffee mugs and got to work.

These guys are old enough to be my Dad, I thought, but they're all doing what I say.

Most of these were new salesman I had hired. They had moved here recently from the Midwest. Large grain producing companies were buying up all the farms there. These guys had inherited their family floor covering stores only to close them down as populations moved out. Many of the businesses had been in their families for years, and now these men were answering to someone else. That someone else was a woman. The men had never had a woman boss before, let alone one younger than they were. I thought this over, trying to be sensitive to what they were going through. I remembered the beating Dad's ego took, losing his job. Still, I didn't know how to be boss in this situation.

In my usual way I turned to books to figure it out. To my frustration, I couldn't find any books on helping a younger woman manage older, more experienced guys. And most books outlined management styles that were military or much too authoritarian for me.

I had seen some salesmen become awful managers and I was determined I would be different, whatever it took. I decided to fall back on my instincts and deal with each salesman individually. I hoped this would work for me, managing employees the way it had worked handling customers. Either way, I was determined to get good at this, so I made a plan.

I sat down with each salesman and let him talk about his life, family, and goals. I asked how he felt about what happened to his business. I asked for ideas on making our store a success.

Jay was the first I talked to. He wore white suits and dark T-shirts, like Don Johnson on *Miami Vice*. "I'm looking at this move as a big start over," he said optimistically. "I think my boys will have better opportunities here in Phoenix."

Another salesman, Paul, had the demeanor of Dudley Do-Right, with his straight posture and gallant gestures. "I hope I can make enough for my family to live like we did in Minnesota," Paul said. "You know I have eight kids."

"Wow, eight," was the only response I could muster.

When Carl sat down he reminded me of the Major on *I Dream of Jeannie*, dark haired and solemn faced. "I hope to retire in a few years," he explained, "but first I need to sock away more money, since my Navy pension won't be enough."

And then there was Ned, my best employee. He was a big, huggable teddy bear of a guy—sweet, loyal and totally respectful of me in my position. If I ever needed anything done, he was there for me.

Finally, there was one more hire from the Midwest, Phil, who had the white hair and clueless air of Leslie Nielsen from *Airplane*. As we were setting up the store I heard him say to Fritz, "You know I've got *years* of experience on Mary." I pretended not to hear, but stole a look behind me.

"I could do a much better job running this place," Phil went on.

Fritz raised an eyebrow. "Obviously you haven't heard about Mary's performance in sales. She is the boss here and if you have a problem with that, you can transfer to another store or leave the company."

Yea, Fritz! I loved that man.

Later that day I sat down with Phil. "So, Phil," I began. "Tell me. Do you want to stay here?"

He looked sheepishly at his polished oxfords. "I do. But I want to be a manager, in six months or less."

"Well," I said. "I can help you with that. Do you have any ideas that can make this store a success?"

"We can change our displays," he said. "For one thing, why don't we move all the Stainmaster carpets to the front, since they're on special?"

"Great idea," I said handing him the price book. "And why don't we put prices on them? It will be easier for the new guys."

"Oh, Mary, what a fantastic idea," Phil said, dramatically opening his arms. "Ned, did you hear that idea Mary had?"

I nearly puked from his condescension. But as time went on he became smoother or I didn't notice it as much.

All told, I had only been in the floor covering business eighteen months. I knew these guys could teach me a lot. I continued to press them for suggestions, welcoming their input. Slowly it came to me. Managing was a lot like being a mother. As I helped my employees reach their goals, they would help me become the kind of leader I wanted to be.

To my joy, this was exactly what happened. In two years, my employees helped make my store number one out of eight in the chain.

As I learned about managing people, I began to notice how they get stuck in their comfort zones. A worker feels okay about making a certain amount and doesn't try harder. Some workers, however, just need to be exposed to the possibilities. Alissa was a good example of this. She had been a medical transcriber making $18,000 a year. Then she began selling carpet alongside salesmen making $40,000 a year. Within six months, she was earning the same as they were.

Carl was used to living on $30,000 a year. He seemed to have that amount etched in his brain. If his sales were going well and his commission got to $2,500, he would slack off and not try so hard. It was as if he was hardwired to produce that amount and no more. I showed him how one or two more sales a month weren't out of reach; how that could get him to retirement so much quicker. He looked skeptical at first, but began putting my ideas into practice.

At the Christmas party that year, Carl's wife cornered me. "You know, when Carl came to work here he had been in the Navy. Then he was his own boss for twenty years. He told me he couldn't possibly work for a woman!" Then she added, "But I've been silently cheering you on. I knew it would be good for him and me to have a woman in authority." We shared a smile over that.

It wasn't until a few weeks later that Carl admitted as much to me. "I never told you this," he said. "At first I wasn't sure I could work for you. But now you have helped me make more money than I ever thought I could!"

Opportunities for making money abounded. All around my store, new housing developments were appearing. Scottsdale was booming, and I needed an interior designer for high end clients building new homes. Larry was one of the applicants. He had just moved here with his significant other from Hawaii. Larry's personality was as big as his six foot frame—I didn't think I could fit them both into our 10,000 square foot showroom, but I hired him.

Larry had a flair for color and didn't care how gay he looked showing off his design skills. He was more in touch with his feminine side than I was. I traded my crab dip recipe for his cheese ball recipe and soon we were like best girlfriends.

One day Larry invited Dan and me to dinner at his house. I winced and shook my head, "I'm not sure how that would be," I said, thinking about last week at my parents house when Liberace's name came up and both Dad and Dan licked their pinkies and smoothed their eyebrows in an effeminate way.

"Don't worry, sweetie," Larry said as he patted my arm, "I've dealt with lots of Dans before."

"Okay," I said reluctantly.

Larry's boyfriend, Simon, was as short as Larry was tall. He worked construction and dropped by the store one afternoon, showing off a new tattoo. "See, it's a palm tree!" he said rolling his T shirt sleeve up over his muscular bicep.

"Nice," I said, looking closely. "You must be missing Hawaii."

"I am," Simon said, lowering his sleeve and scanning the store for Larry.

"Say," I began. "Did Larry tell you he invited my husband and me to dinner Friday night?"

"Oh yes," Simon said. "He's been planning the menu for days."

I was still nervous about how this would work out. When I got home that night I told Dan about the invitation. "Larry is a really great cook," I said. "What do you think?"

"It sounds like an interesting evening," Dan said.

"I'm sure it will be," I said, still unsure. I hoped this night wouldn't ruin my relationship with Larry. If Dan were to make some inappropriate comment about Larry's lifestyle, this might be the end of things. I sighed. Larry had been such an asset helping me decorate model homes.

On Friday night we were just getting out of the car at Larry's when the front door flung open. Larry strutted down the walkway shoving me off into the grass. He grabbed Dan on both sides of his face with his massive hands and planted a big, wet kiss right on his lips.

Dan stumbled backwards as Larry said, "Good. We got that out of the way. Now let's have a drink."

Dazed, Dan laughed, "Yes please, I need one."

And so, with Larry's flair for the dramatic, his great sense of humor, and his ability to laugh at himself, he proved he really could handle the homophobic Dans of the world.

The dinner was fantastic and we all had fun. After that, we spent many nights enjoying dinners at Simon and Larry's. Larry taught me the finer arts of cooking, such as braising and reducing broths into incredible sauces for meats. One of his best tips was how a little fish sauce makes any soup taste better.

And so it happened that I had an ally. Larry wasn't a woman, but he didn't exactly fit with rest of the guys, either. Things were improving. I was finding my people.

And then a woman joined my team.

Chuck, the company owner who hired me, stopped by one day to talk about his daughter. "Jan is moving home from San Francisco after getting divorced. Will you hire her, so she can learn from the best?"

What could I say to that? "Well, of course," I answered, flattered.

The first day Jan walked in I could hear her clicking high heels all the way from the back of the store. She had on a pink silk suit with a matching lace blouse that caught everyone's attention—including mine. I hadn't worn pink since the feminist movement began. My suits were man suits with skirts in masculine navy or gray.

But Jan was blatantly female. One morning as she sat down at her desk she opened her black patent leather purse and pulled out a Midol bottle. "You guys had better be nice to me today!" she said rattling the bottle teasingly, then setting it on her desk.

"Nooooooooo!" I screamed as I slid across three desks to grab that bottle. The guys were staring at me with dropped jaws and I could feel the heat rising in my face. I tossed the bottle back to Jan, stood up, smoothed out my suit jacket and cleared my throat, trying to be nonchalant. "Um, put that away, please, Jan."

I never wanted to call attention to the fact that we were women. Deep down I was afraid they would suddenly realize I was not a guy and stop paying me the same as them.

Since women had been freed from garter belts with panty hose and were unencumbered thanks to Tampax, we had been able to keep up with the guys. This was fine by me. I liked being a woman in a man's business. I didn't mind tromping across construction sites in straight skirts and high heels to meet my builders. But, at the same time, I hated when salesmen accused me of having sex with a customer to get a sale. On the other hand, I didn't hesitate to jump in and give a woman color advice. As I always said, women were just better at it. Then again, I resented the stereotype of men being more skilled with a tape measure. Was I selectively using my femininity when it served me? Where did I draw the line? Being a feminist was more complicated than I thought.

In the meantime, I kept learning from Fritz about how to run a business. At the time there were four hundred carpet manufacturers. Fritz decided to work with only ten. "That way," said Fritz, "we become much more important to each manufacturer. We receive better pricing and we'll have faster shipping."

The strength of partnering in business became evident when we ordered from these carpet mills. They would drop everything to produce a carpet for us. Their reps were on call for us twenty four hours a day. They gave us special pricing and treated our salesmen to spiffs. They invited us on lavish trips to their facilities in the south.

On the receiving end of those trips, I was happy to learn that Southern hospitality was everything I'd heard it was. From the grits every morning to the Everclear moonshine every night, we were treated like royalty. On one trip we had a special valet, Andrew, who left a snifter of brandy by our beds and a chocolate on our pillow every night.

Even so, it was rare for a woman to be in management, especially in the South in the 1980's. When I arrived with the other seven managers, the president of one mill complained to Fritz about all the trouble he had gone to, arranging "bunking" for a woman in the guest cottage. Fritz puffed out his chest, leaned into the man's face, and said carefully, "I'm glad you did. She's one of my key people."

By my second year of management I earned a $10,000 bonus for my store's production. I was finding success at last. In my journal I wrote: *"I'm making more than Dan now."*

# CHAPTER 22

## *Pour a Little Sugar on It, Grandma*

With my management bonus, I planned a family vacation for Dan, Heath, and me, including a Disneyland adventure for Heath. Mom was having a hard time coping with Dad's death, so I invited her and my handicapped sister, Annie, to join us at our rented beach condo in San Diego.

This was Heath's first trip to the ocean. Every morning he couldn't wait to run down to the shore. With arms in the air, daring the waves to splash over him, he made me think of Rocky Balboa, running up the steps in Philadelphia.

One morning Mom slowed Heath down long enough to eat breakfast. As she sweetened his bowl of Cheerios and placed it in front of him, I said, "Mom, I don't put sugar on his cereal."

"Are you kidding?" Mom said, looking at Heath. "He can't eat Cheerios without sugar."

"He gets plenty of sugar in other treats, Mom."

I watched Heath take his first spoonful. His eyes got wide and I immediately knew the look—the sugar high. Darn, I was trying to save him from my plight. I hoped the food addiction wasn't going to start with him, too.

After breakfast Heath took Mom aside, "Grandma, when we get home can you buy me a pack of sugar?"

"Don't worry, I'll talk to your mother, Heath," Mom said patting him on the back.

Great, I thought.

Later we all walked down to the beach. I wished Dan would get out of the snit he was in. I wasn't sure if he was acting like a grump because I had planned this vacation, or because it was my bonus that paid for it.

After a few more hours of him snubbing me, making smart remarks and generally being disagreeable, I got an idea and discussed it with Dan. He agreed that we should both leave the rest of the family for a day and take a cruise to Ensenada, Mexico. Maybe the adventure would help our relationship. In any case, I hoped Dan would start enjoying himself.

And enjoy himself he did. No sooner had the ship left shore, than Dan was off buying drinks for some skinny little blond from California. Meanwhile, I sat with an older couple I had just met, Bonnie and Bill from Colorado.

Bonnie watched my face as I nervously tracked Dan's movements around the ship with Miss Barbie Doll. Bonnie seemed to see what I was going through. "Honey, Bill used to do the same thing," she said leaning forward and touching my hand. "But look, I stuck it out, and I'm the one who has him thirty years later."

I looked at Bill. He hadn't shaved that morning and his gut was hanging over his rodeo champion belt buckle. Great, I thought, what a prize. And it only took thirty years?

Later, I spent some time with my journal, reviewing the trip, my life, and all that happened to me in the past few months. Things were great at work, and Heath was amazing, but my marriage was another story. Remembering my conversation with Bonnie, I pictured her with her "dreamboat" husband, drink in hand. The two had hardly said a word to each other. I sighed as I wrote, *"So this is what I have to look forward to?"*

# CHAPTER 23

## *Living in the Fast Lane*

Mom and I had always been close. We talked on the phone every day since I left home after high school. Now with Dad gone, she needed a lot of help. "I don't know anything about finances," she said one day. "Your Dad took care of everything. I'm so confused. Can you help me figure it out?"

"Sure, Mom," I said, and the next chance I got, went over to help her balance her checkbook. She was so helpless and lost, having never learned how to do anything on her own. I vowed I would never be in that situation.

To my relief, Mom learned quickly what she needed to do to carry on for the family. Even though she kept saying we should have picked out her coffin when we picked out Dad's.

"Mom, you're only 58," I told her. "You'll remarry."

"No way," she said emphatically.

Then a wonderful man from church came into her life. John was tall and handsome and reminded me of Ronald Reagan (if Reagan had gone grey). He was recently widowed and had a gentle demeanor. Quietly reverent, John still liked a good joke. Mom and John were soon inseparable. They married and began traveling the globe. Yes, it did happen that fast.

It was shortly after our family trip that Dan received a job offer he couldn't refuse. He was asked to run a garbage company in Tucson—and the benefits were great. But how could I leave

Scottsdale? Long ago, after the devastation of crying into my pillow for an entire year in high school, I swore I would never do a major move again. I had hated saying goodbye to family and friends. But here I was, facing the same scenario, to follow my husband. Why was his career more important than all that I had promised myself?

*Never mind Mary,* I told myself. *You already earn more than your husband. It's not what a wife should do. You can't be better than your husband.*

At least I had reassurance about one thing: Mom was taken care of. Maybe it was a good time to go, after all. My husband would get away from all of his cohorts who drank and used drugs. And wasn't a wife supposed to go where her husband went?

It took a lot of effort, but I mustered a little enthusiasm for the move.

I started putting the word out that I was looking for a job in the Tucson area. Soon I had several opportunities. I was deciding between a sales or management position when an offer came to be general manager of three carpet stores. It had a great base salary and good bonus potential. It was exciting to look forward to a new challenge.

My last week in Scottsdale, the guys threw a big party for me. As I poured a glass of wine, Carl's wife, Ruth, pushed him toward me. "Tell her, tell her," she said.

"Okay," he said shyly, "Mary, I just had to say . . . you were the best boss I ever had." He practically blushed.

I almost did too. "Thanks, Carl," I said, quickly adding, "but is that really a compliment when all your bosses were in the Navy?"

We all laughed and Carl and Ruth both hugged me. "You'll do well whatever you do," Ruth said. "You inspired me, too, you know. You helped me realize that I could get my driver's license. Now I have my own job at the grade school by our house!"

"That is so great!" I said, hugging her again.

Jay came up and put his arm around me, "Wow," he said, "Now you're going to be a General Manager."

"Yes, I am," I said, clinking wine glasses with him.

Later that night at the party, Phil came up, hugged me goodbye and said, "Well, you said you'd help me get a management job. I just didn't think it would be yours."

"Aw, come on, Phil. You've wanted my job since the day I hired you."

We laughed as he looked down. "Yea, I guess you're right."

---

It wasn't long before I came to think of my new home as a cosmopolitan cow town. Driving into Tucson gave me a real Wild West feel—more relaxed than Old Town Scottsdale but the same idea. The University of Arizona attracted many intellectuals with its well known medical school. And it was only a two hour drive home to Phoenix. I could still enjoy my early morning desert walks and the magnificent turquoise and coral Arizona sunsets. This would be okay.

Dave was my new boss and the owner of the three stores I'd be managing, but you wouldn't guess it from his appearance. He wore shorts and T-Shirts everyday, not like the white shirts, suits and ties the owner of Baker Bros. had worn. He was my age and we even had the same birthday. He seemed young for such accomplishments.

I helped customers as they came into the store, but noticed how boring the store looked with rows of carpet racks lined up on one wall and rolls of vinyl on the other. When Dave dropped by I casually pointed out the unfriendly look of the place. "Women are interested in the feel when they walk into a store," I said. "Since mostly women are buying carpet, couldn't we focus on ways to make the store more attractive?"

"The store is fine just the way it is," he said.

On another day, I was explaining how to partner with certain mills to gain the greatest benefit in pricing and services. "Listen, I don't want any of your ideas," he said. "I only hired you so you wouldn't go to work for the competition."

I couldn't even answer. I stood there, digesting his words. Finally I caught my breath. "Great," I said, plopping down at my desk. Thanks a lot, Dave.

After that, I sat around, collected my big paycheck and tried to stay awake.

Even with work losing all its challenge, it surprised me how much I was enjoying Tucson. Heath was playing football and soccer. Dan had his company sponsor Heath's soccer team and we both became really involved. Like my brothers, Heath was excellent in any sport he tried. At one soccer game he had scored all of our team's five points. As I was getting in the car after the game one of the mothers ran up to me and said, "What do you feed him for breakfast? He's amazing!"

"That's my boy," I smiled. "It runs in my family," I said proudly.

The other good thing about moving to Tucson was taking a break from my family. Out of six kids, I was the one Mom relied on to get the family together. I was also the peacemaker when it came to family disputes—which happened more often now that Mom had remarried. Mom's new husband didn't set well with some of my siblings. It was complicated. At the time of Mom's wedding, for example, my brother Joe was living at Mom's house recovering from knee surgery. Chris sort of lived there using Mom's house as a stopover to shower and change clothes while cranking up *I am Iron Man*, on his stereo. And Annie was working but still lived at home.

Now things were changing. Joe could get on with his life, I hoped. Annie was getting an apartment with a deaf friend. Chris seemed to be outgrowing his visits and was moving on. But the marriage had happened so fast, we were all reeling. As for me, I was glad to be gone.

Dan's new job was to run the Tucson division of SCA, a large garbage company. The company dignitaries flew in weekly to wine and dine the local politicians making sure their latest acquisition would thrive. I was amazed at how much money there was in garbage.

That football season, Dan and I were invited to join the mayor of San Diego in his box at the Holiday Bowl. Arizona State was playing the Mayor's alma mater. Dan and I always had season tickets to the Sun Devil games and were thrilled to be going to a bowl game. The mayor and his wife welcomed us as we arrived, meeting up with some of our other SCA friends.

It wasn't long before the mayor's abrasive sense of humor showed up. "What's the matter with your Sun Devils, Mary?" he asked as we watched them struggle on the field. "Can't they hold onto the ball for even one down?" The mayor slammed down the last of his Johnny Walker Red. "Aaahhh, there they go again," he added in my direction. "Another fumble."

I had a few scotches myself and was feeling kind of cocky. His remarks only added to the effect. "So, Mr. Mayor, what do they REALLY call you?" I asked, going straight for the jugular. "Your Most Ass Holiness?" I paused. "Or Your Royal Hiney?"

Dan about dropped his drink but the mayor laughed and his wife came over and put her arm around me. "You know, I like you," she said. "He needs that once in a while."

It was a great reminder that I could hold my own. I didn't know it then, but in the coming months I would need those reminders of strength, with all that lay ahead.

Dan's garbage company was bought out by the largest garbage company in the world, Waste Management. Their headquarters were in Sacramento, so we spent a lot of time in the San Francisco area. At one charity event we dined with several thin, bejeweled socialites—the "emaciated ladies of society" is how the movie *Bonfire of the Vanities* referred to such people. I had caviar on toast points, oysters on the half shell and sorbet to cleanse my palate between courses. There were dinner wines, dessert wines and aperitifs. Garbage people really knew how to party.

On one trip we were picked up at the airport in a limo and dropped off at the St. Francis hotel while the limo waited for us to change to take us to a dinner I'll never forget. There I was in my peach silk dress with shoulder pads thick enough for a football player, sipping a white wine from Napa. When the lobster bisque was set down in front of me I felt like a princess. Before I could finish my soup, a watercress-cucumber salad appeared. I wish I would have known Pesto linguini with pine nuts was next, because I surely would have saved room. By the time the duck with a cherry glaze was served, I was stuffed. Each course was accompanied with a different wine and by the time the Baked Alaska was ablaze on the table I still had four full wine glasses in front of me.

When the bill arrived, I gasped, "$1,145.00 for six people! The meal was good, but . . . ?"

It was a time of ridiculous excess, parties, and coasting along at work. Meanwhile, Heath was growing up and the years were passing us by. Deep down, though, I knew there were problems neither of us wanted to confront.

At all these shindigs, Dan and I made a great power couple. I had my quick wit polished from my bartending days. I could talk to anyone about anything. Meanwhile, Dan was doing well in his job and the company was noticing. He was out a lot of nights, "entertaining."

I didn't want to see the truth for what it was. But when he started being out until three in the morning, I knew I couldn't ignore the evidence. Dan was back into cocaine.

*Still, it couldn't be that bad, could it?*

When an offer came for Dan to run the Oregon division of his company, I wrote in my journal: *"This could be good. We can move to Portland and get away from all these drugs in the desert. Besides, I'm tired of sitting around the carpet store with nothing to do but think about my next meal."*

# CHAPTER 24

## *The Rain is to Blame*

As we prepared for our upcoming move, I glanced out my kitchen window one afternoon at the glorious Tucson sunlight. Had I really agreed to be uprooted once again? I hoped this wasn't a big mistake.

All I'd ever known of Oregon was a TV news blurb I'd seen in college. The then-governor of Oregon, Tom McCall had said in an interview, "Please come visit, but don't stay!" Candy and I shook our heads and said, "How rude." I suppose it was his effort to protect the pristine landscape.

I pictured Oregon women wearing red plaid flannel shirts and wool socks canning green beans. I could see them sitting on the front porch macraméing wall hangings, with their hair in one long braid down their back.

After two major moves in a year, this didn't sound all that bad. If I was to stay home and play the perfect wife and mother in that wholesome green environment I pictured as Oregon, then surely it would finally be enough for Dan to be the perfect husband and father.

A short time later, Dan took me to get my first glimpse of Oregon. As we drove up the Columbia Gorge with Mt. Hood in the distance, I kept thinking, this picture isn't real. It was the kind you only saw on postcards. Portland, Oregon, looked to be one of the most beautiful places in the world.

I was lucky to have family there. I had a new stepsister in Oregon now that Mom had remarried. Chrissy had John's kind and gentle nature, and was happy to meet me when I came to town looking for a house. She patiently drove me around several Portland neighborhoods. But nothing popped out.

That night, I went down to the piano bar at the airport hotel where we were staying. Two women, Charlotte and Donna were singing along with the piano player to some old time tunes. I was delighted with their bold fun. After a 1940's Hollywood rendition of "Singing in the Rain," Charlotte turned to me and asked, "Say. What are you doing in Portland?"

"Looking for a place to move," I said ordering another glass of wine.

"What area?" Donna asked.

"I'm not sure. I don't know the area well. Somewhere close to my husband's work . . . near the airport."

"Camas on the Washington side is only a 12 minute drive," Donna said.

"And," Charlotte chimed in, "taxes are better on the Washington side of the river."

"We have no state income tax and property taxes are lower than in Oregon," Donna continued.

They were selling me pretty quickly. Turned out, they were both realtors. "But what about the sales tax?" I asked.

"Yes, we do have that," Donna said. "But you can drive across the river to Portland for all your big purchases."

"Interesting," I thought, playing with my wine glass.

"I have some time tomorrow morning and I can take you on a tour," Charlotte said. "What do you think?"

"Sounds great, can you pick me up?" I asked.

The next morning Charlotte drove me into the cozy little community called Camas. I immediately fell in love with its two lane main street lined on both sides with fruit trees. It had quaint shops and restaurants and an old time theater that had been there forever.

"You know," Charlotte said, "our schools are the best in the area." That was all it took. I found a house that day and soon we were putting all the details in place.

Waiting for our furniture and my car to arrive, we stayed at the Brass Lamp, the only motel in the area. Even in their largest room it was a snug fit for three people. Heath wasn't anxious to go to his second new school in a year and I wasn't ready to be at home alone, so we took some time for ourselves, exploring as much of our new town as we could on foot.

Every morning Heath and I would stop at Smitty's for two eggs over easy, hash browns, toast and a side of country gravy (because, naturally, such a meal wasn't fattening enough). Then we walked to downtown Camas, passing the baseball park. I was mystified by the giant trees. Were they Redwoods or Sequoias? The only trees I knew were palm trees and Saguaros. Except of course for Christmas trees.

Each year Christmas trees were flown into Phoenix in two varieties: bushy and full, or blue-green with limbs at ninety-degrees. But here, the pine trees were all so different. Some had limbs turning up, others bowed down. Some had feathery branches and others lacy branches. And some had downturned limbs that flipped up, like a cheerleader's hairdo back in high school.

Everywhere you looked, the landscape was layered in shades of green. There was lawn green, moss green, leaf green and every green in between. The ivy actually grew up the tree trunks and around the branches. Ferns flourished wild in the park. So this is where houseplants come from, I thought.

We'd admire the landscape, visit the shops downtown and be back at Smitty's for burgers and fries for lunch. As the days passed, Heath and I were getting to know Jean the waitress, quite well. "Are you splitting the Mt. St. Helen's Sundae today?" she asked.

"What do you think, Heath? We'll be swimming at the motel this afternoon. Is it too much?"

"No, let's do it," he smiled, "I can still swim."

"Heath," Jean said a hand on her hip. "That's an interesting name. Where did you get that?"

"Umm, my mom got it off a cowboy," Heath said.

Jean's eyes went wide. "I'll have to think about that one."

Choking on my pickle, I felt my face turn bright red. "Uh, uh, what he means is I got the name from the TV show *Big Valley*," I muttered, laughing.

"Oh yeah," Jean said, smiling with recognition. "I liked Heath on that show, too."

Finally after a few weeks our house was ready. I was surprised at how the daylight in our new climate had suddenly dimmed. I had heard about the dark, rainy winters of the northwest, but I was not prepared.

I shivered and turned up the heat, and raised the blinds to cloudy skies. Then I got on the phone and whined to Candy in Phoenix, "There are so many trees here. It's depressing."

"Since when don't you like trees?"

"Well, of course, I like trees," I said. "It's not the trees. It's the shade from the trees that makes the darkness. It's like the dead of night here, all the time."

In Arizona, I would get up early with the sun every morning. I was still conditioned to that habit—but here it was plain ironic. It didn't matter that I had all day to write in my journal, do the laundry, clean and fix dinner. I would get up every single one of those cloudy, miserable mornings at five a.m., as if that was the only time God might have time to listen to me.

In my journal of gray, the color of the northwest sky, I wrote, *Okay God, since you aren't sending rain today, could you please get rid of the clouds?* I waited. Nothing beamed down on me. *I'll give up chocolate for a week,* I went on, *just for one full day of sunshine.*

No answer.

Alas, God had better things to do.

As soon as Heath was off to second grade each morning, I began my day's schedule as the perfect mom. On top of my list was baking. I made cinnamon rolls, chocolate chip cookies, brownies, white cake with vanilla frosting, chocolate with chocolate frosting and carrot cake with cream cheese frosting. Mmm. And of course I added the alpha energy before I sampled everything. In between baking I kept in touch with friends and family in Arizona. I wrote letters and wrapped them in plastic so they wouldn't get soggy in the mailbox before the mailman arrived.

I tried to go on walks like I had loved to do in the desert, but somehow not being able to see through the gray screen of wetness made me lose my enthusiasm. I was always cold. Soon I had a closet full of flannel shirts and wool socks, just like those of the macraméing ladies I had pictured as true Northwesterners. But I never seemed to get warm enough. There was nothing for me to do but wait for the oven timer to ding, curled up in my orange and brown afghan while the smell of chocolate chip cookies filled the house. I couldn't wait for Heath to get home from school.

One day I even made him dance with me in the kitchen to *The Chair* by George Strait as we were making dinner. Earlier I had heard on a cooking segment of the *Today Show* that you could throw a strand of spaghetti to the ceiling and it would stick if it was done. I told Heath about it. He threw one. The white, sticky noodle came sailing back to the floor.

"I guess it's not ready yet," I said.

In a few minutes I pulled out more spaghetti strands after filling the pot with alpha energy and we launched them upward. These stuck to the ceiling tiles with their ends dangling. Heath threw a few more while I was draining the water and soon our ceiling was a mass of coiling, hanging worms. You had to find entertainment wherever you could get it around here.

I wasn't the only one struggling to make adjustments. Heath was having a hard time in his new school. He missed his friends in Phoenix and the sports he was involved in. He especially hated having to wear long pants now. In the mornings as he ate his Cheerios—with sugar now, since I'd given in—and watched *Power Rangers* on TV. I tried my best to get him to laugh like I always could in Phoenix. I'd hunch over, swinging one arm and scratching my head with the other, like a chimp making an insane monkey cry, "AH, ah, ah, ah . . ."

He turned one eye my direction, grunted, and went back to watching his show. Damn. I couldn't make him laugh like I used to. Maybe he was growing up. After all, he was in second grade.

But soon he had friends, who not only added interest to his life, but to my desperate plight as well. "Heath," I'd beg. "Can you please bring Brian and Will home after school today? I'm making rocky-road brownies. You know how you love those!" At least they could help with all the eating.

Yet I knew it was silly to think they could be my entertainment. Those kids would grab the brownies and off they'd go to Heath's room to play with his Matchbox race track all afternoon. There I'd be, alone again with a dirty kitchen.

After the house was clean, the laundry and shopping done, what else was there? I was way too good at time management after my years of working and doing everything at home. What did other northwest housewives do all day when the kids were in school? Maybe they met on each others' front porches to whittle, drink strong coffee, or can peaches.

I realized I could watch soaps for four hours and if I added the *Today Show* and *Oprah* I could actually lie there in a semi-comatose state all day. Did I mention it rained every day?

Dan kept talking about having another baby. Maybe that would keep me busy. I was so alone, without friends or family, that I started thinking a baby could keep me company. Then I thought about Dan saying he would get Heath if I divorced him, because he made more money. If that ever happened, how would I support two kids? Maybe another baby was not such a good idea.

*The Young and the Restless* and *All My Children* provided some relief. The characters made me feel better; they were a lot worse off than me. At least I wasn't pregnant and in jail for killing my husband . . . yet.

The nights were even longer than the days. Dan was out most of the time. His American Express bills were averaging $4000 a month with all the entertaining he did on the job. The company picked up most of it, thank God, but in the late '80's that was a lot of money chalked up to entertainment. It still is. I learned later that he was buying the drinks and the others were supplying the drugs.

As for me, I had the job of paying the bills. Calling the creditors was more like it. Once I tried to talk to American Express in an effort to have them accept a smaller payment that month. "We can't talk to you," they said. "The card is in your husband's name."

"Great, don't talk to me," I said, shrinking down in my chair. *Just Another affirmation that I'm not as important as my husband.*

When we moved, I had thought our northwest adventure would bring us closer as a family. In my imagination (outside of pot grown in the pucker brush) I couldn't picture alcohol or drugs in Oregon. After all, how many drugs could you get a hold of, when everyone lived in a log cabin?

Then, I had told myself I would make the perfect home, baking cookies and being a "Stepford Wife" and mother. But this wasn't fixing the problem, and I wasn't happy.

If only Dan could get away from all those people at his job, I thought. For sure THEY were the problem, making him stay out late, drinking and doing cocaine.

I started having dreams about whether the soap opera character, Nikki Newman would leave Victor for her lesbian lover, Erica Kane. When they became the latest topic of my journal, I knew it was time to go back to work.

# CHAPTER 25

## *Stranger, Goodbye*

I put on my navy blue pinstriped suit, white silk blouse, pearl earrings and was good to go. Driving to my new job, I was so glad to be out of the house I almost didn't notice the daily drizzling madness. My new position sent me calling on downtown architects and designers for Sound Floorcovering, the Portland distributor of Armstrong floors. Until now, I hadn't realized all the things I missed about the work world. For example, my at-home wardrobe consisted of plaid flannel shirts, wool socks and jeans. It had been dragging me down, and I hadn't even realized. On a recent visit from my brother, the first thing he'd done was to stare at my feet. "Mary Pat, what happened to you? Why are you wearing . . ." He looked up, puzzled, "men's socks?"

"Because it's cold here, Joe!" I said with exasperation. But deep down I knew I wasn't being myself.

And now I could break out the girl clothes once again. That was easy. The hard part was struggling with my Thomas Guide trying to find which bridge would get me to NW or SW Portland. The wrong bridge would end me up in NE or SE, and I had no clue how to get back. There were rivers to go over and hills to climb. It was baffling, after the easy grid pattern of Phoenix where the choices were East, West, North or South, a flatlander's dream.

In spite of my confusion, I did love the architecture in downtown Portland. The brick and stone buildings had carved wooden staircases and old refinished wood floors. In Phoenix everything was new and modern, while these buildings had character. I enjoyed their rustic elegance—until I had to lug samples up five flights. The elevators made groaning noises like an old man getting out of a chair. I didn't trust them. I took the stairs.

Which meant I was always exhausted.

If that wasn't enough, the sound of the pounding rain on my commute was interrupted every time I went under one of those Portland bridges! That brief moment of silence drove me crazy.

*Was I losing it?*

I sent out Christmas cards showing a snowman pelted with rain above the caption "Seasons Greetings." When you opened the card, a skeleton of a melted snowman said, "From the Northwest."

Candy could always read between the lines. "Are you OK?" she asked after receiving my card. "I just had to call you. That card looked really depressing."

"I know," I sighed, "but it *is* depressing here."

There was nothing I could do but take it one day at a time, as the dark, gray winter went on.

One day I slammed ceramic samples onto the table at one of my design accounts. The owner, Celeste asked, "Are you all right?"

I slumped into a chair and shook my head. "I don't know how you do it," I said looking at Celeste. "You moved here from California. How do you handle the rain, the darkness?"

"I found a light box," she said.

"A light box?"

"You can rent them from medical supply places." She scribbled on the back of a card. "Here, read this book." She handed me the information. "And I wrote the number of the place where I got the light box."

I blinked back at her. Could there really be an answer to my light-starved moods? "Thanks, Celeste." I didn't know whether to cry or hug her, so I did both.

The book gave me a name for my depression, SAD. How redundant was that? The book explained the science behind *Seasonal*

*Affective Disorder*, and how light deprivation affected humans. It made sense. As Celeste suggested, I rented a light box.

The first day I plugged in my new gadget, I felt like I did when Heath was born and I'd gotten that first shot of Demerol. Euphoric. Every morning I would sit in front of that light box for forty-five minutes, wrapped in my afghan, writing in my journal, watching the rain. Soon I was me again.

Shortly after that, we moved into a brand new home overlooking the Columbia River. On moving day, I reached up with a broom and knocked the spaghetti down from the kitchen ceiling at the old house. Heath and I had fun there, in spite of it all.

Our new home had an amazing view of Mt. Hood. I enjoyed the scene every morning that summer, white-capped peaks showing against a pink and yellow sky. It was nice not to have to use my light box. I sat mesmerized by the tugboats flowing up and down the river. But the happiness I felt was overshadowed by my worry about Dan. Every night when he came home—not exactly in his best form—he had to take the winding, treacherous road to our house. What if he hurt or killed himself? What if he killed someone else?

By day, there didn't seem anything to worry about. Dan held everything together during work hours. One of the duties in his new job was to build a landfill in Arlington, Oregon. When the Fourth of July came, this small town invited us as special guests for their festivities. The townspeople treated us like conquering heroes, since Dan's company had created a lot of jobs for that small, depressed area. For our part in the parade, we hung off the sides of garbage trucks, throwing candy to the kids. Celebrities for sure.

Two of Dan's employees joined us in the celebration, bringing their wives, Kerry and Julie. We all checked in at the local Motel 8. After the parade we joined the mayor, Ken and his wife, Penny, for the town barbeque. Steaks and salmon sizzled on the grill, while huge pots of corn on the cob boiled on several camp stoves. Each family had brought their special recipe of potato salad, macaroni salad or Cole slaw. It all made me homesick for big families—my family—gathered together for the holiday. But they were a long way away.

The next day the guys played golf and the ladies lunched. When we all met up in the local bar that afternoon, the mayor recounted their golf game. Dan had gotten drunk on the golf course, and the joke was, "Hit the ball, drag Dan. Hit the ball, drag Dan."

I almost choked on my Cobb salad. "I'm so embarrassed," I said in a whisper, glancing around at the other women.

"Oh, don't worry, they're all drunk," Penny put in. "But it's pretty hilarious. I mean—can you imagine them sitting there watching *us* drunk like that?"

"That would be grounds for divorce," Kerry remarked.

I just shook my head, unable to get rid of my shame. "I'm really sorry," I said.

"But Dan *is* funny," Penny reassured. "And it's not the first time. Remember when he fell down the steps at that Portland restaurant and got up with that quirky smile, acting like nothing happened? Kind of like the way he's smiling now?"

Suddenly this all felt familiar. I remembered what people had always said about Dad. "He's so funny," people joked, recounting the stories of his drunken antics in conversations with Mom. Now I understood how she had felt. There was nothing funny about it.

I had never realized before how Dan was so much like Dad in his alcoholic behavior. I remembered one of Joe's basketball games, where Dan and my Dad got so drunk together that they were thrown out. When they got home, Joe could barely look at them in disgust. He was steaming. "Can you believe those two?" he shouted. "They were actually thrown out of the game!"

Mom and I just looked each other and shook our heads. There were no words for our disappointment, frustration, and hopelessness.

So here I was again. Together with the other women, I played the good little wife, sitting there charmingly, laughing with the men. And we women were drinking, too. For my part, it was self-defense; I wondered if the other wives felt the same. In these situations, the only way to survive was to drink, to be as stupid as the company I was keeping.

That trip showed me I needed help. In the years when I had tried Al-Anon, I'd never thought Dan was *that* bad. Not as bad as the other alcoholics, surely. Not as bad as the husbands of the other women who told about their drunken escapades. Was Dan *that bad* now?

*Help me, God,* I prayed. *What do I do?*

The next week as I was hauling carpet samples into an architectural office, I noticed a sign in the lobby for an Adult Children of Alcoholics meeting, scheduled for noon. It was eleven o'clock. I swallowed my pride and took a deep breath. *I'm going to try it,* I told myself. I would go in there, focused on healing old issues over Dad's drinking. There would be no need to bring up the present, with Dan. Surely that would be enough. Tackling memories of Dad seemed somehow easier than dealing with Dan.

I finished my appointment and took the elevator down to the second floor. I walked sheepishly into the room crowded with folding chairs. I slipped into a chair in the back row. When the meeting began, a petite blond woman stood up. "Hi, I'm Sara," she said in a soft voice. "I'm an adult child of an alcoholic, married to an alcoholic."

I felt my heart pounding faster. Could the people next to me hear it, too?

"Hi, Sara," the group droned in unison.

"Last week my husband of twenty-two years forgot our anniversary and blamed me for not reminding him. Can you believe that?" she sighed. "After twenty-two years?"

Everyone shook their heads in disbelief.

"Normally I would have accepted that it was my fault," Sara continued, "but now, after coming to these meetings I was able to stand up for myself."

I shrank down in my chair, fidgeting with my wedding ring. Dan had forgotten my last birthday. In fact, he'd only remembered when he heard a message on our home recorder from my Mom wishing me a happy birthday. The memory played out in my mind. When I'd gotten home that night, Heath jumped up from the couch. "Mom!" he yelled, "Why didn't you tell dad and me it was your birthday?"

At that instant I'd felt guilty. I'd believed it was my fault. But now, I heard my faulty logic, played back through Sara at this meeting. I had found the truth. I'd found a home.

One by one, I learned the steps of the program. Right off the bat, I liked step one: surrender this problem to a power higher than myself. It was such a relief to let it all go.

At my next meeting another woman stood up. "Hi, I'm Sylvia. I'm an adult child of an alcoholic."

"Hi, Sylvia," came the response.

"Well," she said with a big sigh, "I've been coming to these meetings for over two years and at my first meeting, I heard this story:

'When you start going to meetings and your alcoholic comes home drunk and passes out in the front yard, you try to drag him into the house. But when you can't, you bring him a pillow and a blanket and build a tent around him for the night.

'After you've gone to these meetings for a while, your alcoholic comes home drunk, passes out in the front yard and you turn the sprinklers on him and go to bed.

'But if you keep going to the meetings, your alcoholic comes home drunk and passes out in the front yard and you just turn out the light and go to bed.'"

Sylvia continued, "I went through those stages: over-caring for him, being angry at him, and finally reaching the last phase of not focusing on him at all. Wow, do I feel great!"

I wanted what Sylvia had. I longed to sleep through the night whether Dan made it home or not. I didn't want a divorce. No one in my family had been divorced. I had taken my marriage vows seriously. And I knew it was a mortal sin in the Catholic Church to get divorced. Besides, I was still scared Dan would take Heath from me. All I wanted was to survive.

At the next meeting a tall, thin man stood up, "Hi, I'm Mac." He smiled and shook his head. "You know, my wife was never happy when I took a job in the Bay area. I thought her drinking was because she missed her family. But now that I've moved her back to Portland, her drinking is even worse. I don't know why I thought moving could help."

I dropped my face in my hands for a moment, stunned. It sounded all too familiar: the desperate hope that my moving would end Dan's drinking and drug abuse.

At another meeting I met Rebecca, the president of a bank. She had perfectly coiffed chestnut hair in a shiny bob. Her dark neutral suits were always perfectly tailored with crisp white blouses shining underneath. She had made it in a man's profession—just like me.

Week after week I'd hear about Rebecca's husband, Ron, who drank away most of the family's money. Ron had a responsible job and had been doing somewhat better, until she started making more money than he did. That's when cocaine was added to his drinking. As I listened to her stories I thought, *Look at you, a capable, professional, with-it woman. You can support your two kids! You don't need him! Get some self respect! Get out!*

As with all the other testimonials, my own situation came to mind. More and more, as weeks went by, I saw myself in each member.

Then one morning Dan called after having been out all night.

"Where are you?" I asked.

"Multnomah Falls," he said. "I just didn't make it home."

"That's it," I said, dazed at the words coming from my own mouth. "Come get your things. I want you out."

In a trance-like state, I toasted waffles for Heath, dropped him at the sitter and made several sales calls on the way to my noon ACOA meeting. I had told the fringes of my story over the last months. This time as I stood up I was shaking. "Hi, I'm Mary, I'm married to an alcoholic and drug addict."

"Hi, Mary."

"Thanks to all of you, I finally had the courage this morning to get out of my marriage."

Suddenly there were people hugging me amidst rousing applause, "Way to go, Mary. We're proud of you!"

I stood trembling as tears welled up from the depths of me. I was so humbled by their support.

The rest of that day was a blur. I was emotionally exhausted. I knew I couldn't support Heath in the big house on the hill with my income. But I had such a sense of calm, I knew I'd be okay.

I picked Heath up from the sitter and when I entered the house I saw Dan's suitcase and duffle bag piled in the entry. His custom-made shirts were thrown on top still in the dry cleaning bags. The DJO monogram on the cuff jumped out at me.

"What is your problem?" shouted Dan. "I've left messages for you all day."

I was fixated on that monogram, the same navy blue as the stripe in the shirt. I was remembering when Heath and I went to the tailor in Scottsdale with Dan where he had them made. As Mr. Chan was measuring Dan he kept saying, "Big nick, big nick." Dan and I looked at each other trying not to laugh about which body part Mr. Chan was talking about. We decided he meant Dan had a big neck.

Dan snapped me back to reality with, "Why didn't you call me back?"

"I have nothing to say."

"Heath, did your Mom tell you she's throwing me out?" Dan yelled as he leaned on the wall with one arm cocked on his hip.

"NO! Mom, is it true?" Heath pleaded with his eyes.

"Yes, Heath," I sighed. "It's true."

"Why, Mom?" He grabbed my hand.

"I just can't live like this anymore," I said turning to go upstairs.

"Mom, tell Dad you don't mean it!" Heath screamed.

I said nothing. I was done.

Dan turned for the door. "Dad, don't go!" Heath cried. "Take me with you!" He threw his arms around his dad's leg and Dan bent down to hug him.

I kept walking upstairs knowing everything would be fine. Dan never intended to take Heath. He wouldn't want the responsibility. I repeated it to myself over and over, though this had been my deep-down fear for so many years.

Sure enough, Dan left, by himself. Heath ran upstairs, hurled himself on my bed and we both sobbed until he fell asleep in my arms. *OK, God, now what?*

That weekend, Jim, Dan's old roommate and my dear friend was coming to town with his wife, Kathy, and their son, Andrew. *What should I do?* I thought with one finger on my Day Planner. *Should I ask them not to come?*

I took a deep breath, and decided not to call. I wanted the diversion for Heath *and* me. Besides, maybe it would cheer me up to have friends around.

We had planned for the four of us to see the musical, *Cats*. "How about I stay home with the boys?" Jim said when he arrived. "You two girls can go to the play."

Driving across the I-5 Bridge to Portland I said, offhandedly to Kathy, "So, can you believe Dan cleaned out our bank accounts?"

"You have no money?" Kathy asked.

"Just $35.00 until payday next week," I said.

"I can't believe Dan wouldn't care enough about Heath to leave you *some* money."

"I know," I sighed. "The drugs have taken him over."

I was so calm. It was like watching my life go on, but was outside of all of it. Was this the detachment they talked about in the meetings?

*Cats* was a hazy mystical experience with old cats, young cats, fancy cats and sickly cats. It took my mind off things until the main cat character began singing, "Memories, all alone in the moonlight . . ." My face fell in my lap and I sobbed until the final curtain.

The next day Jim played golf with Dan, anxious to talk some sense into him. Jim had to pay for golf and lunch because Dan had no money. *Where had all his money gone?* Jim might've wondered.

Jim understood the answer when Dan came out of the bathroom with white powder on his nose.

After their golf game, Jim came back shaking his head. "Mary Pat," he said. "I don't even know who Dan is anymore."

In my journal I wrote: *"Dan is no one I ever knew."*

# CHAPTER 26

## *Promises, Nothing but Promises*

Before Kathy left town, she loaned me $400.00. I'm grateful to her to this day. I had a tough road ahead of me, including finding an affordable place to live in Heath's school district.

Leafing through the local newspaper, I found a duplex for rent. I knew it would go fast. "Heath, finish your Top Ramen," I shouted to him in the kitchen. "I found a place for us!"

We jumped in the car. "This could be our new place, Heath," I said. The windshield wipers were swiping hard against the rain as I strained to see the address on the mailbox.

"Heath, does that say 2011?"

"Yeah Mom, take this road!"

I turned up the gravel driveway, then we jumped out and ran to the door where Ralph, the landlord, answered, broom in hand. He looked just like Gilligan without the hat. "Welcome," he said holding the door open.

There were piles of drywall, coke cans, and paint stained newspapers in a big pile on the living room floor. You could smell the paint and drywall mud, but the overwhelming smell was more like moth balls and cat piss. Had old people lived here? It was hard to see very much since the only light came from the kitchen.

Heath looked around, aghast then slumped against the wall by the front door while Ralph went into the kitchen. "Mom, things are really bad, aren't they?"

"No honey, we'll be fine," I said, putting my arm around him. Luckily, the floor heaped with all that garbage was only cheap vinyl, not carpet. "And once this stuff is gone I'll clean and the smell will be gone. I'll bring in plants and a touch of color will bring out the charm of the fireplace. Just wait, Heath I can make this place look great."

Yet inside I was scared, and had never felt so alone.

Ralph heard our conversation. "We're not done yet," he said. "There's more to see . . . like the kitchen."

He had installed new oak cabinets and a dropped ceiling with lighting throughout the kitchen area. "Just beyond the back yard are woods where my girls used to build forts," he said. "They can show you sometime, Heath."

He turned to ask Heath how old he was.

"Eight."

After that every time Heath would say "eight," Ralph would tickle him.

"So Heath, what did you do before you got here?"

"We *ate* dinner."

"Ate?" And Ralph went in for the tickling which continued anytime Heath said "eight."

Heath squirmed. "Stop it! No! Please!" By the time we left Heath was laughing and having fun.

Ralph was kind enough to let me pay the deposit and the last month's rent in multiple payments over the next few months. We packed up the old house and once again I scraped a batch of spaghetti from the kitchen ceiling. I said a long goodbye to the view. Some friends from work helped us move while Dan was off with his latest squeeze—who I lovingly called Bambi.

Bit by bit, we negotiated the terms of our separation. Dan agreed to pay me two hundred per month. But soon his company grew tired of him dragging in late every morning and leaving early every afternoon. One night he called me with the news. "My company thinks I need to go to rehab."

"Rehab? Oh, really?" I said. *As if I'd never told him that.*

"It's going to be big news to break it to my employees," Dan went on. "Would you mind helping out? Could you come to the meeting?"

"Me? Why?" I asked, puzzled.

"We need to show a united front," he said. "Please?" In his voice there was a pleading, like a little boy.

"But why? We aren't even together anymore."

"I know, but it would show that you're behind me in this."

I agreed, though I still don't know why. Over the years as I've seen political wives standing next to their husbands in times of scandal, I can identify with the looks on their faces: a painful mix of shame, shock, and "stand by your man." Still, it's what we as women do. Is it for the children or just a result of automatic pilot?

So that was that. The meeting went better than I expected, with all of Dan's employees taking it well. And then Dan was in rehab.

A day later he called. "They're having Family Day this weekend," he said. "Will you come—and bring Heath?"

Would it ever end? Would I always be called upon to support the man I no longer wished to be married to? "I guess," I sighed.

Heath and I got up at 4:00 a.m. that Saturday morning to make it to "Family Day" with Dan. *Now he cared about family.* It was infuriating. This was the first time he had reached out to his family in years—but it was too late. I tried not to show my anger in front of Heath as I slammed the car door.

"Buckle up, Buddy, it's going to be a long drive," I said, fumbling with the cassette. "How about this one?"

"Good one," Heath said as we began singing, *Caribbean Queen* on our way to the Oregon town of Seaside.

"Serenity by the Sea" was the name of the place. *Ha, it sounds more like a spa resort. Why don't I ever get to stay in a place called "serenity" instead of having to work and worry about bills and taking care of Heath?*

I let out a big sigh, pulling into the parking lot of the large house on the beach. Walking in I smelled the familiar dampness of coastal towns. The '70's style wood beamed ceilings and orange shag carpet gave it a cozy feel. Outside, the soothing sound of the ocean made it feel more like a vacation than a rehabilitation.

Heath ran into his Dad's arms as soon as he saw him. Then suddenly we heard a school bell ring. "Gotta go," Dan yelled. "We have a crisis."

Heath looked at me, "What?"

I shrugged as a heavy set counselor showed Heath and me to a large room full of chairs. There were well worn lazy boys in blue crushed velvet, orange stripe and fuzzy brown. There were mismatched kitchen chairs in metal, plastic and wicker interspersed with folding chairs. *They must be expecting a big crowd*, I thought.

"I'm Betty," the counselor said. She pointed to a vending machine. "Make yourselves at home."

I got some coffee as Heath pulled the knob for a Snickers bar. More families were herded in as we took seats in the back.

Dan lumbered in with one of his inmates. "This is Donna," he said putting his arm around a stringy haired blond stick with sunken eyes.

"Hi Donna," I said, thinking, *How can you be so young and have no teeth?*

"Donna had a crisis," Dan whispered pausing. "She wasn't expecting her whole family to be here, so we had to calm her down."

*What about me? You never worried about me having a crisis!* I let out a deep breath.

Dan led us to seats in the front of the room and Heath climbed up on his lap. When the meeting began, Dan was the first to talk. "Hi, I'm Dan and I'm a cocaine addict."

Heath's head whipped around as he looked at his Dad in shock. He knew drugs were bad from what he was taught at school, but I had never told him his Dad had a drug problem.

The rest of Family Day was a blur. I was worried about Heath. We headed for the beach at break but before I got to the door, I was approached by Betty the heavy set counselor we met earlier. She reminded me of Dad's nurse, "Ole Battle Axe." She and another counselor cornered me, and I saw Dan wink at them as he took Heath outside.

Betty introduced Wanda, who looked like a starving child from BiAfra, with the ravaged look of a former drug addict. "Please sit down," she said, as she scooted three chairs together.

"You know, Dan is making great progress here," Wanda smiled.

"Great," I said.

"Do you think you could give him another chance?" Betty asked.

"A chance for what?"

"To come home and be a family again," Betty said wistfully as she folded her hands on her lap.

Obviously Dan had charmed these counselors into doing his dirty work. "Are you kidding?"

"He really wants a second chance," said Wanda.

"I'm sure he does," I said. "But I'm sorry. I am done." I took a deep breath. "I asked Dan to get help for his drinking, then his gambling and then his cocaine addiction. But he refused every time." I stared at my clenched hands on my lap. "I'm sorry, I have nothing left to give to the cause."

With that, both counselors sat back resigned. I was glad they could see there was no way I could change my mind.

By the time we left, Heath had a huge headache. I stopped at Walgreens for aspirin. "I think we can still make it back to Portland for that birthday party you were invited to," I said handing him the pills. "Want to go for it?"

"Yes!" Heath shouted as I lowered the passenger seat for him to lie down. He slept the full two hours until I pulled into the parking lot at Chuck E. Cheese. As soon as I turned the engine off he sat up.

"How's your headache?" I asked. "Are you sure you want to go to this party?"

"Yes, for sure," he said jumping out of the car.

The birthday boy's parents met us at the door. They had always been supportive of me. I told them about our day at rehab. "He'll be fine," Will's mom said. "We'll keep an eye on him and bring him home tomorrow."

"Thanks," I said. "I can use the rest."

A few weeks later Dan came home, settled into his new place with Bambi and went back to work. Just when I thought he was getting it together, his company drug tested him. He tested positive for cocaine and was fired immediately.

I was shocked at the strange mix of feelings I felt in response. In a way, I was still hoping he would straighten up, and that this might be the blow he needed. He had lost his family but that wasn't enough. Now that he had lost his job maybe that would be the catalyst for him to turn his life around.

But it wasn't. Wives of employees told me he was living with a drug dealer. Heath came home from visitation, telling stories of staying up all night playing Nintendo for money with his dad's buddies. Sometimes his dad would drop him at a skating rink in Portland when he was going out for the night. His dad was often late picking him up and he'd wait, scared, outside the rink with "all kinds of weirdoes around." Still, Heath wanted to go with his dad every chance he got.

That news terrified me. I lost no time in talking to my attorney. "It's not safe for him there," I declared.

The attorney shrugged. "Sorry," she said. "There's nothing on the record to make a judge disallow his dad's visitation rights."

I was powerless. There was nothing I could do but try to relax. At least Heath wasn't acting threatened. If anything, he enjoyed the relaxed atmosphere. All things considered, it was a lot more fun for Heath at his dad's than at my house, with homework and a strict bedtime every night.

*Relax,* I told myself again. *I* had *to relax.*

So, after Heath's Dad would pick him up for the weekend, I would stop by the video store, pick out several movies, mostly comedies, and head to the Pizza Palace. I'd get a large pizza with Canadian bacon and pineapple on one side and sausage, mushrooms and onions on the other. (Hey, it was healthy. It had fruit and vegetables on it.) And then it was on to the grocery store to choose doughnuts:

three glazed, three cinnamon glazed, and six maple frosted. And of course, I had to pick up a half gallon of Tillamook Peanut Butter and Chocolate ice cream. Then I'd be set for the weekend. I'd eat, watch movies, go comatose, sleep, eat, watch movies, go comatose and sleep. If that wasn't relaxing, I didn't know what was. I couldn't tell day from night until Dan brought Heath home on Sunday evening.

I put on twenty pounds. (Most people lose weight when they get divorced, right?) I thought of moving back to Phoenix. I even called Fritz to see if there was an opening. "Anytime," he said, "I'll make room for you. I'd love to have you back."

But Heath had been through so much in the last year: three different schools and now the divorce. I couldn't take him away from his dad on top of all that. I decided to stay put.

I received this letter from my Mom:

*Dear Mary Pat,*

*Have been thinking of you since we talked this morning. Must be very difficult for you as it was for me after Dad passed away. You and Dan I'm sure had good times and it's sad it has to end because of a man's refusing to get some help. You cannot look back. You have all our support.*

*Always pray for guidance, as I know you do. The good Lord is always with you and <u>only</u> through him anything is possible.*

*We love you.*
*Mama and John*

Her words made me feel better, but still I was so alone, with no family or friends close by. It was hard to meet people as a rep on the road, without the camaraderie of an office to go to each day. My only friends were the parents of kids on Heath's soccer team.

One day when Heath came home from school he threw his backpack on the couch and sat down. "Mom, what's a blow job?" he asked.

"What?" I stood up staring at him.

"I heard some kids talking about blow jobs, so when I was at Will's I called his brother a 'blow job.' Their mom got really mad at me."

"I see," I said, and took a seat next to him on the couch.

It was one of those precious parenting moments and all I could do was curse his father under my breath for not being here to handle this. But I was on my own.

*How do I explain this to an eight year old boy?*

I had promised myself I would always tell Heath the truth. I'd been told so many "untruths" growing up.

*Oh well, here goes . . .*

I stammered out what a blow job was, through my terrified face.

"YUCK!" Heath said, got up, grabbed his basketball and dribbled out the door.

I sat there bewildered. So that was that. Over the years I often wished everything I had to tell Heath would be accepted that easily.

And every weekend he visited his dad, I worried. All I could do was pray, "Okay, God, take over."

Through it all, I knew I had done the right thing leaving his father. I found solace in the Kenny Loggins song, *The Real Thing*.

> I did it for you, and for me,
> Because love should teach you joy
> And not the imitation,
> That your momma and daddy tried to show you.

I wanted more for Heath. I mourned the loss of the dream of a happy family. I felt guilty for of all the lies I told at the altar: to "love, honor and obey in sickness and in health." Who was I to leave this marriage just because my husband was an alcoholic and drug addict?

Yet, once again, I felt this calm assurance that I was in the right place. I remembered the lies my husband had told. It started with the broken promise to "forsake all others"—women as well as drugs. We had been through "richer and poorer" and "better or worse," but the hardest lesson to learn was that just loving him enough wouldn't make everything okay. With my heart aching I reread my journals, where over and over I had written, *"Love can conquer all, right?"*

# CHAPTER 27

## *The Time Has Come to Pay*

They herded us single file into the courtroom just like in Catholic School. A chill came over me. The benches were stiff and unforgiving like the pews in church, except the kneelers were missing. The wood paneling could never warm the icy marble floor. All you could see from the high windows were barren trees and gray sky.

There were young white women, black women and brown, middle aged white women, black and brown, and old women, white, black and brown. Didn't guys file for divorce? Or did they just put all of us women together?

The door swung open as the judge came in. The bailiff said, "All rise."

"Well, we have a large group this morning," the judge said. "Let's get started. Mrs. Gonzales, four children, $100 a month, dissolution granted," and the gavel came down.

"Mrs. Jones, two children, $250 a month, dissolution granted."

Name after name was called and then I heard mine, "One child, **$640** a month?" the judge questioned.

"But—but, you don't understand," I started to say. "I'll never see any of it." Then the gavel came down and it was over. I was divorced.

Dan got his BMW and the payments. I got my Oldsmobile and the payments. The remaining bills were split down the middle, except for the divorce, which cost me two grand.

But when Dan couldn't be found for his part of the bills, the debt started pouring in. Funny how American Express would talk to me now.

How was I going to make it?

Heath and I went to Phoenix that Thanksgiving, where I was embarrassed to see my family. No one in our history had ever been divorced. It was an unwritten rule not to disgrace the family in such a way. I knew Mom understood, despite this, but I was ashamed and afraid of what my brothers and sisters would say.

My oldest brother, John came by the day we arrived. He hugged me and said, "Well, Sis, we wondered when you were going to dump that asshole."

I couldn't believe it. As the conversations unfolded, it turned out they had all watched my struggle for years, hoping for a change for the better. And I thought I was keeping up such a good front, just like Mom had. This was how I had stayed in my marriage for eleven years: worried what my family would think and believing Dan would take Heath away. These two "truths" guided all my decisions.

On Sunday I went to Mass with Mom. When it came time for communion, I realized I couldn't receive that sacrament anymore. I was divorced—excommunicated from the Catholic Church.

While Mom went up for communion I sat in that wooden pew feeling just like I had in the courtroom, cold, sad and alone. I bent my head in shame and quietly cried into my hands. I hadn't been going to Mass for years, yet this felt like a humiliating, shameful blow.

I knew stealing and killing people were sins. They were listed in the Ten Commandments. But why was divorce a sin? There should have been some wiggle room, I thought. But sins were sins and that was that. And while we were on the subject, was this the real reason nuns and priests wore black and white, to remind us there was no gray in the sin department?

I went home and poured out my thoughts in my journal: *Why should I feel so ashamed? What do I have to feel guilty about?*

As the days went by, I continued to turn to pen and paper as an outlet. I wrote to Dan expressing how I felt. My anger came through the pen and at times sliced through the paper. I never mailed any of these letters, but they were part of my healing process.

I loved the empty feeling that followed my rants. Once I had said whatever I wanted to say, I felt an open space where all the good could come in. It was meditation at its best.

As usual, I found solace in books. From *Emmanuel's Book, A manual for living comfortably in the cosmos*, I learned how to approach life more gently than Catholic School had ingrained in me.

*Emmanuel's Book* posed the question, "What can I do concerning my deteriorating marriage?" And it answered, "Let it deteriorate. Marriage is another word for relationship and when a relationship no longer serves, if you have scraped the bottom of the barrel to find the meaning, to find the lessons, to find the essence of why you have come together, and this has not brought forth what you are seeking, what more can you possibly do?"

I decided to try going easy on myself for a change, letting go my rigid standards. If I didn't focus on the past, with all its guilt and shame, I was okay for right now. If I didn't worry about the future, getting out of debt and providing for Heath, I was okay for right now. We had enough food—right now. Heath was fine—right now. If I focused on what was in front of me, everything was manageable.

Yet day to day, it was all too easy to panic. There was the day I had a huge presentation for one of my largest accounts. I had gained weight and nothing fit. I needed a sharp looking jacket, but how could I afford one? I stopped in at the local Goodwill, and found a fitted black jacket with plenty of polish for five bucks. It fit perfectly! Later that day I slipped it on, and inside the pocket was a five dollar bill. At that instant, I knew that I would okay.

That five dollars in my jacket pocket became a reminder of how I was being cared for. I found that in the darkest of times, a simple thing could change my outlook forever.

There was another time, when Heath and I had been eating beans and Top Ramen for weeks. Talking to Angela, one of the moms at Heath's soccer practice, she mentioned redecorating her home interior. When I told her of my design background she said,

"Why don't you and Heath come over for dinner? Then I can pick your brain on what colors to use."

"Great. When?"

"Tomorrow night?" she suggested, getting in her car.

"Perfect," I felt a smile break out on my face as I dug for my keys.

The next night we sat down to dinner with Angela's family. The roasted garlic chicken smelled fantastic. Heath and I scooted up to the table, our mouths watering as we barely contained our excitement. "Mom, check out all the side orders!" Heath said in a hushed shout, eyeing the mashed potatoes and gravy.

When Angela brought out chocolate cake with ice cream I thought Heath would burst with delight. It had been a long time since we had eaten such a glorious meal. It happened at the perfect time, keeping our spirits up and our bellies fed. To this day I'll never forget Angela, even though she probably never knew what a godsend she was.

Like Angela, so many angels appeared in those scary times. I began to see that there was someone bigger than me running the show. When I relaxed and marveled in these little signs of being taken care of, more good things flowed my way.

Not that the bad stuff stopped coming. At times I felt like Mongo in *Blazing Saddles*. With his limited vocabulary, he expressed it so well: "Mongo just pawn in game of life."

When Dan's BMW was confiscated for trafficking narcotics in Hillsboro, First Interstate Bank came after me to pay the $18,000 left on the loan. I had been a cosigner. When would these "left hooks from heaven" end? Why didn't my attorney in the divorce tell me to get my name off his loan? I took a deep breath and thought, *Oh well, what's another bill?* I felt the same sense of calm as when I had made the decision to leave Dan. I would figure it out.

The attorney for Hillsboro was a single mom, too. I explained my situation and she returned my call a few days later. "Don't worry about paying off the loan, honey," she said. "I'll talk to the bank. We can auction the car."

In my journal I wrote: *"Saved again."*

# CHAPTER 28

## *Try a Little Compassion*

I proved myself at Sound Floorcoverings and got a sales territory just like the big boys. I had accounts all around Portland, the coast, Eastern Oregon and Eastern Washington. I was finally making as much money as I had in Phoenix, with the potential to make a lot more. The pounds of shame I had gained from my divorce were coming off and I was feeling like me again.

My boss, Tom, was 6'4" but had the impish twinkle of a five year old. His Tennessee drawl had been Northernized, but you could tell he was a Confederate son. He bragged about his days playing basketball at North Carolina. "But, that was a long time ago," he sighed stroking his pale chin, "when I was young and black like Michael Jordan."

There were only two women on the sales team and Tom loved us. "You women work harder and you're meaner than the men," he said. I didn't understand that until much later.

I fell into step working for Tom; it came easy, as he had a similar philosophy to Fritz. Tom had me choose one carpet dealer in each of my small towns and build a partnership. It was a great way to strengthen my territory.

Traveling with Tom was part of my job. He was easy to joke with and brought out the zaniness in my sense of humor. On one trip Tom rode along in the passenger seat of my Caravan from Yakima to the Tri-Cities. I pointed to the hills on either side of us and heard myself asking, "Do they call them buttes because it's French for butts? They look like butts to me."

Sure enough, Tom started cracking up. The mood was broken, though, when my cell phone rang and I found myself screaming into it, "What do you mean Dan can't pick Heath up?" It took me a moment to calm down, but thankfully, Ken on the other line understood. He was a single father of one of Heath's friends and offered to keep Heath at his house. "Thanks, Ken," I said, "I owe you one or two."

I slammed down my three pound car phone and missed the receiver on the dash. I tried to collect myself. "I can't believe Dan," I said through gritted teeth. "I can't count on him for anything. Thank God I have a great family where Heath can stay." Outside the car windows, those buttes were still rolling along.

"You know, Mary," Tom said in his quiet southern way, "I've decided that exes are like dog shit on your shoe. No matter how you shake 'em, they just never go away."

"So true," I giggled.

Suddenly, a semi in front of us swerved. I put on the brakes until it moved out of my lane. "Whoa!" The air was filled with feathers.

"Hey—it's a pheasant!" Tom shouted, "Or at least it *was*. Stop the car!"

I pulled to the side of the road, and before I understood what was happening, Tom had jumped out, run into the middle of the highway, grabbed the bird by the feet and sprinted back to my van.

He opened the door. "This is some gooooood eatin'," he said, sticking something into my face. A moment later I could make out a ratty looking bird with bugged out eyes.

"No way," I said. "I don't like my food looking like *that* before I eat it."

"Just wait," said Tom, throwing the bloody carcass on the floor. I caught a glimpse of it as I pulled onto the highway. *Oh, well,* I thought. *I have a red interior.*

After we checked into our hotel rooms, Tom said, "Come get me for dinner in half an hour." He grabbed his suitcase with one hand and the ragged bird with the other.

*My boss certainly has his quirky side*, I thought. But I soon forgot about it on the way to my room, thinking about the work ahead. I had several phone calls to make, setting up appointments for the next day. Before I knew it, it was dinnertime.

Knocking on Tom's door, I heard, "Hold on."

And then Tom opened the door, wiping his bloody hands with a towel. Behind him in the sink I could see the remains of that stupid bird, and deep red blood all over the counter. Even the mirror was smeared with blood.

"I uh . . . dressed the bird," he said with the pride of a child making his bed for the first time. With a bloody hand, he gave me two pieces of meat the size of golf balls. "The best meat you'll ever taste," he said. "Just slow cook it for about eight hours. You'll see. Go put them in the cooler while I clean up the place."

"Yuck!" I said, walking to my van. No doubt he was going to miss some spots. I could just imagine what would happen the next morning, the maid finding blood stains and calling the local sheriff.

I breathed a sigh when we finally drove away the next day, feeling like some kind of criminal. I cooked the pheasant when I got home. It was tougher than shoe leather so Heath and I had his favorite—grilled cheese and Top Ramen instead. But I never see pheasant on a restaurant menu without thinking of Tom.

At last, I was having fun—at work anyway. In my first year at Sound, I won the award for the largest sales increase out of thirty salesmen. I was thrilled when they handed me my trophy—a little businessman dressed in a suit, carrying a briefcase.

As we talked after the sales meeting, Ted, one of the managers, reached for the trophy. "We need to get that changed into a woman."

"No, I like it the way it is," I said, pulling it close. I wasn't letting anyone touch my little man. Hey, I was proud to be on top in a male dominated company.

"I insist," said Ted. "We can't be giving you a trophy with a man on it!" No sooner had he said it than he pried the trophy from my hands. "You'll see."

A couple weeks later I had my new and improved version. The trophy was now topped with a Dolly Parton look-a-like. She carried a briefcase and wore a miniskirt that would make even Madonna blush. Madonna the rock star, that is. Madonna my mother would've died seeing the statuette on my shelf. I hid it from her.

So much for the women's movement.

Time went by. I sold carpet, wood and ceramic tile. Then Ted, the head of the Armstrong division, told me I could sell vinyl floors in the outlying areas. "You will be the first woman in the Northwest to sell Armstrong products." I wasn't sure what the big deal was for Armstrong to let a *woman* sell their stuff. But by the way he lifted his chin and gave me the solemn news I could tell it *was* a big deal.

In any case, I loved my job. When all the salesmen got together we had amazing synergy. We weren't in direct competition with each other and our meetings were always filled with great sales ideas.

The salesmen themselves were as different as their territories. Chad was what would now be called a "metro-sexual male." He was handsome, well groomed and very metropolitan—perfect for the city area he covered. Chad was the smoothest salesman I had ever witnessed. You wouldn't care what he was selling; you would just buy it and thank him for the pleasure.

Another salesman, Sam, looked like an old hippie who no doubt grew pot on acreage out in the pucker brush. His long hair and beard fit his laid back approach. He matched his territory in rural Oregon.

Ken was the salesman for Idaho. He was built as strong and rugged as the Marlboro Man. He didn't talk much, but when he did his words always seemed amazingly profound.

The Portland territory was manned by Ron, a man of character, the kind of man who made Christians look good. He was a genuinely good husband and father and I learned I could trust him at a time when there weren't many men I felt I could trust.

One of the owner's sons had the charisma of a snake charmer, loved by both men and women. Ed had known all my accounts for years so he was great to take along on sales calls. Like all the management, he was helpful and supportive.

I also enjoyed the fact that I didn't have to be personally involved in every sale to make money. While I was out selling, the sales desk was taking even more orders for me over the phone. Not to say they got it right every time. Tom called them "The Sales Prevention Department," when they messed up an order. But all his criticism was in fun. We all loved working for him.

And then another woman came on the scene. Alice. For me, it was love at first sight. We met in the office parking lot. She was blond and bubbly wearing a bright pink suit trimmed in black with black sling back heels. *Great style,* I thought. *Like me,* I added mentally. We became immediate friends. We were both single moms without child support trying to provide for our kids. She had the job of calling on architects and designers in Seattle, but soon she had a territory, too. We talked every day.

Alice and I bunked together on all the trips our company took. Once in the Atlanta airport, I stopped to buy a book just after Alice had gone through the line. The clerk said, "Weren't you just here?"

"No," I said. "That was my sister."

From then on we played it up, how we looked and acted alike. We were such kindred spirits, everyone confused us.

As I peeled back the pages of my Day Planner, Market Day was coming closer. We had Market every year in January. All of our accounts would travel to Seattle to see the new floor covering styles and buy rolls of carpet at discounted prices. I was really excited about this. Many of my accounts were making the trip for the fun weekend.

We decorated the warehouse in a carnival theme and supplied food, booze and prizes. Tom's philosophy was, "Keep the people having fun and make sure to feed 'em every four hours, so they won't get surly on us."

We wore chartreuse and fuchsia plastic leis advertising our bonus trip to Hawaii for our accounts.

A few days before Market, all the salesmen gathered in Seattle to learn how to pitch the new carpet lines and specials. Then we set up the showroom with the carpet samples and tagged the rolls in the warehouse. After the long days we'd go out drinking and dancing. We had such camaraderie!

Most of the owners of the carpet stores brought their wives for the weekend, so I got to know them even better. This relaxed atmosphere was perfect for learning how to do even more business together. After wining and dining all day, we went out drinking and dancing with our accounts every night. By the end of the weekend I was so exhausted I could barely drive the two and a half hours home.

The week after Market, I was in the Portland branch office talking to Ed about my success that weekend. The credit manager, Shirley, came by. "Mary, when you're done with Ed, come into my office."

No doubt she needed credit information on all the sales I had made. I slipped into her office, surprised at the serious look on her face. "Close the door and sit down," she began.

My breathing became tight as I took a chair, crossing my legs.

"I have to tell you," she said. "Some of the salesmen at Market have informed me that you propositioned them." She tapped her pen on the desk. "They were worried you were doing that to our accounts, also."

"What?" I sat there, perplexed. *Propositioning them? Propositioning? What an odd choice of words.*

I didn't know how to respond. I clenched my hands. I had always prided myself on being professional in the "whore mongering" carpet business. I got up and left her office feeling like I had been punched in the gut. Words came back to me from my first sales job: "Who'd she fuck to get that sale?"

But this was worse. This had come from a woman. I expected the occasional putdown from men. But why did Shirley say what she did? She wasn't even my boss.

Still confused, one thing I understood was my chain of command. I called my boss Tom in Seattle. When I told him what

Shirley had said he burst out laughing. "You'd have to do a whole lot more to disgrace *this* company," he said. "Have you seen the owners in action?" It was good to be laughing again. I could breathe easier, knowing Tom was on my side. Then he said, "I told you the women were meaner than the men."

Next, Tom called each salesman, looking for the source of the slander. Later that evening, I got a call from Chad. "Hey," he asked. Why didn't you proposition *me*?" And then I was laughing again. Similar comments, supportive and funny, showed up in my voice mail from the other salesmen. "The propositioning" became a big joke. This time the guys I worked with were on my side.

"Don't worry," Ed said. "Shirley's just jealous."

It was such an awful truth to swallow. I had always known men were competitive but now I understood that women were the worst. We're socialized that way: lined up to be picked by the best men. We each had to be the prettiest, the smartest or the something-est. It wasn't as easy as it sounded. There was a fine line to walk, for you couldn't be *too* aggressive or *too* smart or *too* successful or—God forbid—you'd be *better* than the man you were trying to attract.

And so, we women resorted to discreet means of manipulation. No punching. No yelling. We did what we had to, to get what we wanted.

Still, I was taken by surprise whenever a woman hurt me. I never expected it from my own team.

I remembered how my older sister Linda had been the first female to hurt me. She was an inmate in the same asylum I was in growing up. How could she be so mean?

In high school, Linda was quick with the putdowns. In our room at night after a game she would recap what I did wrong, cheer by cheer. "You really screwed up the landing on that second cheer at half time."

"Gee, thanks for pointing that out, Linda."

And though I didn't realize it at the time, she was competing with me for guys. When Mike, from her senior class, asked me out, I could hear her downstairs telling Mom, "But he's too old for her."

"That may be true. But your father is two years older than *me*," Mom said on my behalf.

Dating Mike made Linda even worse with the putdowns. She started calling me "Thunder Thighs" and "Massive Ass." Mike was a really nice guy, and though he kept asking me out, I only went on one date with him. I couldn't handle Linda's backlash. It just wasn't worth it.

My competition with Linda extended to our weight. Sometimes I would be fat; sometimes she would. We teeter-tottered. What I noticed was, Linda was easier to be around when *I* was fatter. Then she didn't pick on me as much. I started thinking maybe skinny wasn't worth it either.

Dad tried to lighten up the competition. "This is why you're so short and round, Mary Pat," he said. "When you were two years old, you crawled under the fridge. We didn't find you for three years."

"You didn't look for me?" I asked in a hurt voice.

"Why would we want to do that?" he asked, chuckling. "It was one less mouth to feed."

Dad teased Linda just as mercilessly, but she wasn't as sensitive. She had a pair of straight leg pants in large stripes of orange, gray and red. One day I heard Dad yell to her across the backyard, "Hey Linda, Barnum and Bailey called and they want their big top back!"

Linda just glared at him and went into the house, her typical response. I, on the other hand, would've been crying in a heap in the corner of the yard.

As sensitive as I was, the fat/thin dichotomy affected my relationship with other women, too. Many times I discovered women were nice when I was fat. When thin, I was treated differently by both sexes. At times I would rail against the injustice. *I'm the same person inside!* Other times I would try to ignore the whole thing.

Which brought me to this moment—performing at my peak. Thin again, confident and attractive.

And here I was again, being hurt by a woman.

From that day on, I steered clear of Shirley whenever I was in the Portland office. But more than once when hiding from her,

I found myself at the vending machine, pulling the knob for my bright orange wrapped friend behind the glass, Reese's Peanut Butter Cups.

My only safety was in extra padding. My only comfort was food.

As the months went by, we got ready for a trip to one of our suppliers in the south, where most of the floor covering manufacturers were located. Tom would hold great business brainstorming sessions. From time to time in these ventures, there were culture shocks.

Once, an Arkansas restaurant owner felt the need to entertain us. He began with, "I had a nigger come by the other day and ask if we served niggers. I told him, yes, sometimes we serve them fried."

We all sat there, stunned while he smirked to himself. This was the late 80's, twenty years after race riots and segregation. If the south was stuck in the fifties regarding race, it made sense why the women's movement hadn't made any strides either.

On another mill trip south we had a lovely dinner at a guest cottage. The peach tablecloths matched the peach silk draperies. The whole room glowed in the soft light of chandeliers accented with candelabras on three round tables. After the waiters (all of them black) poured our brandy and handed out cigars to the men, they left the room.

Tom stood up lifting his snifter in a toast and said, "You know if you Northerners hadn't fucked this up, we'd all be livin' like this."

I swallowed. How could any intelligent person—let alone my terrific boss, Tom—think that he was better than another? It must have been his southern upbringing. We all looked at each other then laughed but very nervously.

Back at work I pushed myself to make more money to pay off the bills. I was exhausted when I went to the doctor about a disgusting, red rash seeping across my face. "What's going on with you?" he asked after he did a test. "You have a strep infection. Didn't you notice your throat was sore?"

"Yes, I guess," I said sheepishly.

"Well, since you didn't pay attention to it, your body put it in a place where you would!" he scolded, "don't ever do that again!"

*Why do I always end up with doctors who yell at me?* I wondered. Doctors just like my Dad.

After a few days of penicillin, I was back to normal, working like a maniac. That year I won the largest sales increase award again. I was getting my debts paid off and moving forward. Heath was doing well in middle school and was an exceptional basketball player. I scheduled my days around his games and loved it. In my journal I wrote: *"Life is getting good but something is missing. I want a man in my life—someone to complete our happy family."*

# CHAPTER 29

## I Need a Lover That Won't Drive Me Batty

When Heath would visit his dad on weekends, I'd put on my skinniest outfit and go out on the town with Nikki, a friend I met calling on hotels for carpet business. We laughed so much we always drew others to our table. I loved the male attention, needing to feel like I wasn't washed up. After all, I was 35. Not to mention I had a son. I had brief stints with two married men, somehow thinking this would get back at Dan for all his affairs.

Eventually I came to the realization I wasn't mistreating anyone but myself. I didn't feel right having sex without a relationship. The feminist movement brought out the idea that a woman could be just as cavalier about sex as a man. I wasn't sure anymore if this was what women wanted or needed. All I knew was that it wasn't working for me.

I was ready for a man in my life. Someone to make us into a real family. In my journal I wrote:

*Dear God,*

*Could you please send me someone who is physically attractive, who can help me lighten up and not take life, work and me so seriously?*

*Someone who will support me and help raise my son. He must have a great sense of humor and want to commit to only me.*

*Love,*
*Mary*

Within two weeks John appeared. Nikki knew him and one night he joined our table merging into our craziness. He had rugged, masculine good looks that made my heart flutter. Every time he'd see me he'd say, "Wow, you look great, Ruby Lips."

John and I could take time to get to know each other since Heath went to his dad's most weekends. After a long day of lugging carpet samples around in high heels, I'd come home to have John rub my feet. He saw the humor in every situation, and helped me see it too. One night after several exhausting days on the road, I tried to talk. My lips were moving up and down really fast like a parrot, but no words were coming out. John looked at me with eyebrows raised and said, "Yes?"

I burst out laughing. The parrot mouth became our sign that I was too tired to talk.

We were always joking around. I tied a knot in a used Bounce dryer sheet and stuffed it in the toe of his cowboy boot. The next morning I heard, "H-e-e-y-y-y, what's that?" as he pulled it out of his boot.

Later that morning I opened my day planner and found the same dryer sheet stuffed in the side pocket with my business cards. "H-e-e-y-y-y, what's that?" I could almost hear him laughing right beside me.

Fumbling with my briefcase one morning, John said, "Let me carry that for you." He opened my car door. "And since you're going to be late tonight, let me take care of dinner."

As time went on, Heath got to know John, too. Then one night we sat down to discuss John moving in with us. "Did you say you had a really big TV?" Heath asked.

"Yes, I do," John said.

"You are bringing that with you, right?" Heath's eyes lit up.

"Oh yes," John said. "What do you think?"

"Then its fine with me," Heath said, grabbing his basketball and heading outside. So much for that big transition.

I sighed with happiness. At last I'd found a relationship where I could be an equal, not subservient. A relationship where we could share the household chores and both contribute monetarily. I felt Heath was my financial responsibility since I wasn't receiving child support, but it was great to have John's contribution. He was in real estate, a businessman with tremendous earning potential. Not to mention his creativity and sense of humor.

One day we ran into one of his real estate clients at the grocery story. Mona, an elderly lady, thanked him for finding her home. Then Mona quickly pointed out, "You know John, you only showed me two houses and asked, 'Which one do you want?' I'm glad I liked one of them."

John smiled in his charming way. "Well, Mona," he said. "I didn't want to waste your time. After all, you *are* getting up in years."

"Oh, John," said Mona, blushing.

He could get away with teasing the ladies. He had the gift—just like Dad.

It wasn't long before John confided in me a little background info. "Just so you know," he said. "I'm going to outpatient rehab. Just a little problem I'm working on." Good thing he was getting that fixed, I thought. I certainly wasn't getting involved with another addict.

That Thanksgiving we all went to Phoenix. Mom was concerned that John and I were living together and went to her priest to ask about sleeping arrangements in her home. The priest said, "Oh Madonna, just sprinkle holy water around the room and let 'em go at it."

But Mom wasn't entirely convinced. To make things more appropriate, Mom had Heath share the room with us. John entertained my family and friends with his corny jokes and Mom remarked how much he reminded her of Dad.

When we got back from Phoenix, my company celebrated the opening of our new Portland facility with a black tie affair. I chose a black silk dress with huge shoulder pads (It *was* the 80's). The skirt had five ruffles from waist to knee. With black leather stiletto pumps I felt like Crystal Carrington from *Dynasty*. John looked handsome in his tux with his black cowboy boots. We melded together on the dance floor to *Someone to Watch Over Me*. We were both thrilled to have that someone in our life. As we walked back to our table, Judy from the order desk said, "You guys look just like Barbie and Ken."

All the salesmen from our company had come into town for the party. My gal pal Alice had heard about John—I'd even told her about our dryer sheet game, and she was anxious to meet him. She came dressed in a gorgeous low cut white silk dress with black polka dots. Her hair was swept back with combs to show off her diamond earrings. "Where's John?" she asked looking around.

Just then Tom, our boss, interrupted and told everyone I said the Yakima hills looked like butts. Then I told the story of him murdering a pheasant in his hotel room. Soon more salesmen joined our table with all the laughter.

As Alice and I were touching our lipstick in the restroom, she said, "You look so happy. You can tell Johnny loves you so much. And I'm really glad to know we can still find someone like that at our age."

"I know," I said as I pulled a dryer sheet out of my evening bag. "Hey, what's that?"

Alice and I both broke into giggles.

The fact that John had been to rehab and was now having a few drinks didn't matter. The fact that he had cleaned out my liquor cabinet within a week didn't matter. He had been heavily into cocaine in the past, but that didn't matter either. He wasn't doing it now. He had been to rehab. Everything was under control. It was good to have John sharing the responsibilities of the household. We lost no time in getting married.

In my journal I wrote: *"Thank you for sending John to me."*

# CHAPTER 30

## *Sweet Surrender*

With my new husband at home, I could enjoy traveling to my accounts in the deserts of Oregon and Washington, knowing Heath was taken care of. The brightness of the sun was a welcome relief from the darkness of most of my sales territory.

Carpet stores in smaller towns relied on companies like mine that offered a wide variety of floor coverings. Yet some accounts weren't used to a female sales rep. On my first visit, one owner said, "I guess the days of going out drinkin' together after a business deal and gettin' hookers for the night are over."

"For sure." I shook my head. "That part is o-ver."

On my next visit this same store owner told me he was beginning to like doing business with a woman because he didn't have to do the male dance. "The male dance?" I asked.

"You know," he said standing up straight. "Where the guys size up their body parts and see who backs it up. With women we just get the work done. There's no macho to it."

A receptionist at another account said, "Do you mean your husband *lets* you travel over here all alone?"

*Lets me?* These people were something!

I was assigned a new account sixty miles off my usual route down the Columbia Gorge. One particular day, pulling onto the desolate road heading south, I was led over giant sand dunes, reminding me of the family move to Phoenix so long ago. My cell phone didn't pick up in the area and for the first time on the job, I was almost scared. My thoughts took me back to an old childhood fear.

In grade school, I had been terrified of being left alone. With the Cuban Missile Crisis a constant threat, Dad sat us down and laid down a family disaster plan. If there was an attack, the city buses wouldn't be running, so all of us kids were to meet at the corner of Sixth and Main. Then we were supposed to walk as fast as we could the three miles home.

"Since Aunt Alberta's house is on the way home on Pine Street," I put in, "can't we just stop there?"

Dad thrust his hands on his hips. "If you would rather die with Aunt Alberta than us," he said. "Then just go ahead."

I felt a horrible panic stab through me. I didn't really get it—dead was dead. But I guessed dying without your family was not good. It did scare me just thinking about it.

The same illogical fear was reinforced when I spent the night with a friend. "Don't stay away too long," Dad said. "We might move while you're gone."

I hope dad didn't plan on those words haunting me all night long. But they did. Many a night at Martha's house, I would begin sobbing into my pillow at the thought of what might happen. Martha's dad would crawl out of bed in his blue and white striped pajamas. "Okay, Mary Pat. Let's go home," he'd say, pulling on his coat. "I'm sure your parents haven't moved, but let's get you home so you can see for yourself."

*What a silly fear to hold onto,* I thought now, putting my attention back on the road. I was perfectly safe. The desert butts were beautiful this time of year. My mind at peace again, I was thinking about which carpet samples I would show at my upcoming appointment when I had a flash. My customer wouldn't be there when I arrived.

*But, you just talked to them yesterday and they were looking forward to seeing the new carpet lines,* I argued with myself. But I still had the nagging knowing that I should turn around and not waste my time.

For the next sixty miles, my intuitive mind fought with my logical mind.

*You shouldn't drive all this way. You won't make it to your next stop in the Tri-Cities until after dark.*

*But I told them I'd be there at 9:00. Even if I went back to a phone and called, they wouldn't be in the store this early.*

*You should have asked for their home number.*

As the debate continued, I didn't even enjoy the warmth of the sun.

I drove into John Day. It looked like all the other small towns in the northwest desert. The carpet store on the main drag was easy to find, and I was right on time. But the store was dark. I waited fifteen minutes, then stepped into the diner next door. I heard a nervous rustle, then the sudden pause in conversation as all the locals turned to stare at the foreigner in their town. I could smell coffee brewing and bacon frying. "Has anyone seen the McCaffery's from next door?" I asked.

"Oh, yeah," a waitress said, "Mr. McCafferey's mom died suddenly last night. I doubt they will be in today."

Driving back to civilization I tried to enjoy the desert scenery between bouts of kicking myself for not listening to my intuition. I had used it all my life. It used to be a put down calling it "women's intuition" and I kept quiet about it for that reason. But it never let me down. I just needed to trust it.

As I drove across the desert that day I decided to pay more attention to that inner voice.

Heath had his own kind of intuition. He called it "being in the zone" when he played basketball. A point guard, he had a magical way of maneuvering the ball between players. He could actually feel where his teammates would be on his next pass.

I remembered an interview with Mickey Hart, the drummer for the Grateful Dead. He sat in playing drums for the Allman Brothers and was surprised how differently they approached their music. The

Allman Brothers were well rehearsed and precise in their amazing guitar performances where the Grateful Dead played off each other and just let it flow. The music created was the magic of the Grateful Dead.

I began dusting off my intuition, using it more and more. That winter, traveling over the mountain passes to the coastal areas of my territory was a crap shoot. Sometimes the roads were icy and sometimes clear. As I trusted my inner voice, I always seemed to make the right decision about when and where to go.

On one trip I was driving to the song *Hold On* by Simply Red. I was admiring the light dusting of snow in the forests along Highway 26. I stopped at my usual gas station to get coffee. An added bonus was that this station had the cleanest bathrooms for miles. Before I jumped out of the car, I changed tapes so I could listen to Garth Brooks' *I've got Friends in Low Places*, when I continued my trip.

The red haired woman behind the counter said, "Sure you don't want a lottery ticket, Sweetie?"

"Not today," was my response for the fifth time in the five times I'd stopped there before.

"Not feeling lucky?" she asked.

"It's not that," I said. "In fact, I'm feeling quite lucky lately." I felt an inner nudge of something—confidence, premonition, I didn't know what. I smiled and shrugged. "Oh what the heck," I said. "Give me one of those."

Heading outside, I rounded the corner of the station and the cold wind about knocked me down. I looked around the empty parking lot. *Where was my car?* I must have parked it somewhere else, I figured. No, this was where I always parked. Did someone steal it? Oh no, where was my car? My purse was in there with the rest of my money, my credit cards and my license!

I took a deep breath deciding not to get upset and said, "Okay, God, take over."

As I became calm, out of the corner of my eye I saw my gray Aerostar in a field of snow. It had somehow missed a telephone pole when it rolled backward the length of a football field, stopping three feet from the road. I couldn't believe it. I must have had my attention on the tape player and didn't put it in park. I ran to my car and unlocked the door. "Thank you God!"

Whatever lessons I still had to learn, I knew I was being watched over. At the hotel that night I wrote in my journal: *"There is no need to ever worry. I am always taken care of."*

# CHAPTER 31

## *Riders of the Storm*

Sunday night after a weekend with "Disney Dad," Heath came slinking out of his room. "I need a new bed," he said with a serious face. "My waterbed is leaking."

"Leaking?" I asked, following John into Heath's room. The royal blue top sheet was wadded into a corner, soaking wet. I pulled the other sheet back to find the mattress punctured in several places. "How did that happen?" I asked, running my hand over the holes.

"I dunno," Heath answered, jamming his hands in his pockets.

"You did it," John said. "Didn't you?" He moved toward Heath.

"No." said Heath, backing up.

John narrowed his eyes at him. "You're lying."

I couldn't believe John accusing him like that. Why would Heath do something so destructive? He said he hadn't, and I believed him.

"I know he's lying," John said, turning to me. "I was just like him when I was a kid." Looking around the room, John set his beer down as he picked up an ice pick lying on a shelf. "Is this what you used?"

Heath turned away, saying nothing.

We had to ground him. The deal was: he had to come home immediately after school for a week. This punishment could work under our roof, I knew, but I was afraid his dad's influence would make our efforts worthless. Because the next time he would visit his dad, there'd be milkshakes and Fritos, all-night video games, and no homework. Basically, he could do whatever he wanted. He loved going there.

The next week I got a call from Heath's math teacher, Mr. Fulton. "Could you please come to school?" he asked. "Heath is acting up, and I am at the end of my rope."

My Heath? I couldn't believe it. When I got to the classroom, I looked inside the open door at a whole class of slouching bodies sitting with ball caps on backwards in that unmistakable adolescent hormonal stare. Mr. Fulton came out and closed the door behind him. He looked exasperated. "Heath was one of my more well-behaved students. I don't know what's happened to him. He is disrupting the class every chance he gets. Will you please take him home and talk to him?"

"Okay, Mr. Fulton," I sighed. "Send him out."

When we got in the car I turned to Heath. "What is going on with you? You've never been in trouble like this."

"Nothin'," he replied under his breath, slouching down in his seat. I shook my head and started the car.

Another day after school, Heath's bus driver called. Barely containing her laughter she said, "Heath mooned the school bus."

"He what?"

"Heath mooned the bus and I have to punish him," she said still giggling. "He can't ride the bus for a week."

I tried to keep a straight face as I told John. But we both laughed. When Heath got home I said, "Heath, we have to ground you this weekend for mooning the school bus."

Then we all burst out laughing.

"I'm sorry but you aren't going with your dad this weekend, and you can't have friends over."

"Fine! I'll just fix up my room!" Heath slammed his door.

By Sunday he had moved his bed to the opposite wall, put up his new Guns and Roses poster and even hung his all-black wardrobe in the closet. By the clothes he was wearing, I didn't know if he was going goth or just depressed. But I could see he still had his positive attitude, emerging in a different form. He could turn a weekend of grounding into a redecorating extravaganza.

The next weekend Heath came home from another fun-and-games trip with his father. "Mom," he said. "I tried this stuff at Dad's."

"Stuff?"

"I think it was cocaine. What does cocaine look like?"

"Uh, uh . . ." I stammered.

"It was in this box with all this white powder in it," he went on. "Kind of like that stuff you put in my basketball shoes. And there was a round thing with a little screen door over it."

"What did you do with it?"

"I put some on my tongue. But it was no big deal, it just burned."

"Huh," was all I could say.

When he went to his room I ran to call his dad. "What are you doing?" I demanded. "Leaving drugs around for Heath to find?"

"He has to grow up sometime," Dan said nonchalantly.

"He's only 10 years old!" I screamed, slamming down the phone.

I called my attorney. But there was nothing she could do. There was nothing on record to make Dan look like a bad father. I made an appointment with a counselor for the next day.

"I don't need to talk to anyone," Heath said. "I don't want to go."

"You're going," I said.

Karen, our counselor, talked to Heath in her office while John and I waited outside. Then she called us in. "There is nothing to worry about," she said folding her hands on her lap. "Heath learned in school that drugs are bad, and he knows his dad does drugs. He's just trying to prove his dad isn't that bad by trying them himself. He's acting out at school because he's confused. With his dad in the picture, I need to work with you and John to help blend your new family."

At our next appointment, John and I were given a five page questionnaire about what we wanted for our family.

The next week, Karen went over our answers. "This is good," she said. "You both want exactly the same things. To create a happy family and grow old together, laughing all the way. This is a good start."

"What about Heath?" I asked.

"Heath will be fine," Karen said.

*"Thank you, God, that Heath is okay,"* I wrote in my journal that night.

# CHAPTER 32

## *Love Songs Make the World Go Round*

One week when Heath came back from his dad's, he told one of his usual stories of staying up until four a.m. watching movies. John had just come home from the Moose Lodge. As he popped a tall beer, he slurred, "Go clean your room, it's a mess."

Heath stepped forward with his chest held high and glared at John.

My breath was tight in my chest while I looked at Heath, then John as he chugged his beer. When had John started drinking so heavily? Was it a gradual thing or something new? I felt numb with this awareness.

"You can't tell me what to do," Heath snapped. "You're not my dad."

John came toward Heath menacingly. "You little cunt!" he shouted. "Get in there!"

"Fuck you!" Heath screamed.

John raised an arm. "Don't kill him!" I shouted, jumping in between them.

I got Heath into his room and closed the door behind him. I shook my head at John and went down the hall to our bedroom. *This is not how the happy family is supposed to be.* I thought we had figured out the rules in counseling. But when John was drinking, the rules didn't matter. *How could I have brought this man into our family? What was I thinking?*

I headed back to Al-Anon, but this time with Heath in tow. There was an Ala-teen meeting across the hall, but Heath only lasted a few times before he got tired of drawing pictures. I continued the meetings, trying to get a grip on my life.

Even so, there were some aspects of John's drinking that were useful. For instance, I always knew where he was from 4:00 to 6:00 each afternoon: in the bar. Another good thing: he was out of it most of the time, so I made all the decisions about our lives.

I talked to John about getting help for his drinking. He said he'd curb it. And he did. For a week or two.

One night when John had been drinking he came into the kitchen. "Heath should be home by now," he yelled. "Where is he?"

"Out for pizza with Kit after practice," I said, drying a glass.

"He should be home," John huffed. "It's a school night."

"Since when do *you* care?" I asked.

"I God Damn care!" he yelled.

"Just stay out of it!" I screamed. "Do you hear me?"

"No, I won't," John screamed back.

"I've had it with you!" I yelled throwing down the towel. "Just fuck off!" I turned to walk away. "And, and—" I turned back around. "And **stay** fucked off!"

With that, we both burst out laughing. At least our sense of humor was still kicking.

The morning after that fight, I handed John a cup of coffee when he walked into the kitchen. "Sit down," I said. "We need to discuss your drinking."

Reluctantly he took his place at the table. "Here's the deal," I began, "No matter what you say, you are drinking heavily again. So for my sanity, I am making you a deal."

John looked at me intently. "Okay," he said tentatively.

I took a sip of coffee. "When you have been drinking, I don't have to talk to you, and you will leave both Heath and me alone."

"Okay," he said.

"I don't care how much you *say* you've had to drink. I don't care how drunk you think you are. It is always MY decision whether we will talk to you or not. Agreed?"

"That's it?" John said relieved.

"That's it," I said. "Will you honor that?"

"Sure," he said readily. "No problem."

John stuck to the deal. I'm sure he thought I was going to insist he stop drinking, so whenever I said, "I'm not talking to you," he'd be quiet and leave me alone.

After all this time, I still didn't understand the hold alcohol had on people. There was my Dad who basically died from drinking and was sorry on his death bed. There was Dan who lost his family, his high powered job and his BMW. And now, there was John slowly killing himself.

I was never enough for any of them. Always, I was second best to the drinking and the drugs. But I held onto the idea that if I could just love them enough, love could conquer all, right? That's what all the songs said. In my journal I made of list of songs that urged me to keep loving.

> *"Love Will Keep Us Together*
> *Love Makes the World Go Round*
> *What the World Needs Now is Love Sweet Love. It's the only*
> *thing that there's just too little of."*

# CHAPTER 33

## *My Brown Eyed Pup*

A series of events moved us to yet another house. It started when John, burned out in real estate, took a job sandblasting at the shipyards and suffered an eye injury. He was compensated with a large settlement. Then, with help from John's mom, we bought a rustic ranch home with a view of the Oregon lights.

The slate entry reminded me of the desert in deep teal and coral. The bank of south-facing windows welcomed the daylight (if you could call it light). The huge Camas rock fireplace could be viewed from both the living and dining room. A family room adjoined the bedroom in back, perfect for Heath and his friends. He even had a kitchenette and refrigerator.

*Things will be better in the new house,* I thought.

One night, fixing dinner in our new kitchen, it was just Heath and I. "Spaghetti's almost ready!" I called.

When Heath came in, I held out the wooden spoon dripping with strands of spaghetti. Heath took his cue and began throwing them on the ceiling, one by one. "Not sticking yet," he said. "Keep boiling."

"Do you miss your dad?" I asked. Dan had gone to jail for his escapades, and couldn't take Heath on weekends.

"Sometimes. But sometimes it was scary at dad's."

"What do you mean?" I asked, wiping my hands on a towel.

"Well, one time a friend of dad's came by and gave dad this paper all folded up. Dad stuffed it down the side of his TV chair and gave the guy some money."

"O-kay," I said slowly.

"When dad went to take a nap, I reached down into the chair and took it out. It looked just like a magazine page folded up. So I opened it up and this white powder blew all over the place."

"What did you do?"

"I freaked out." Heath handed me the spoon. "I tried to brush it off the chair and carpet. It must have been the same stuff I tried that one time, so I stuffed the paper in my pocket. Do you think it was cocaine?"

"Sounds like it," I said. "What happened when your dad got up?"

"He tore up the chair looking for it," Heath said, "throwing pillows around and swearing."

"What did you do?"

"I just sat real still on the couch and then finally asked, 'What are you looking for?'"

"'Nothin',' he yelled at me, and took off to his bedroom. I was scared he'd find that paper on me," Heath continued, "and be mad like the time he sent me to the store for butter and I came back with margarine."

"What happened that time?"

Heath let out a big breath, "Dad was so mad he made me walk all the way back to the store in the dark. It was scary."

"Hmmm," I sighed, grabbing him in a hug.

When he went back to his room, I whispered, *Thank You, God, for keeping him safe*. What a relief he wouldn't be going to his dad's anymore. He was twelve now and I was relieved Dan wouldn't be an ongoing example of what a father should be.

But then there was John. A good dad . . . when he was sober.

I had to admit, things had improved between Heath and John. Maybe it was because we could all spread out now. Or maybe it was the fact that Dan went to jail. I didn't examine it too hard, just hoped it all would last.

Heath wanted a dog and John was all for it. As for me, between work, worrying about Heath, and keeping up this big house, I didn't want another thing to take care of. Still, they persisted.

So I drew up this contract:

> *Heath will be responsible for the new dog. He will feed it, make sure it has water and keep the doors closed so the dog will stay out of the main areas of the house. We will put in a doggy door so the dog can go out to the back yard but if it has an accident Heath will clean it up.*

Heath gladly signed the contract and we were off to the pound. Both he and John fell in love with a sweet, fawn colored dog, fox-like except for a long, bushy tail that curled up over her back. Heath named her "Foxy," but one day he called her "Poochers," and the name stuck.

When Heath came home from basketball practice the next day, Poochers was lying next to me on the living room couch. Her water bowl was full and her coat brushed. Heath burst out laughing. "What happened to our contract, Mom?"

I laughed, too. I couldn't believe what I felt for this dog. It was different from all the kinds of love I'd known. There was the love for Mom, Dad, and all my siblings. There was the passion of first love, and then settling in as a couple love. There was the true awe I felt when they handed Heath to me for the first time. But my love for Poochers was different. In my journal I wrote: *"When Poochers meets me at the door at the end of a hard day, I feel that maybe, 'Love really can conquer all.'"*

# CHAPTER 34

## *Freedom*

I looked across the river just as evening fell on another rainy day in the Northwest. The Oregon lights weren't twinkling yet, even though it had been dark all day. John was passed out on the living room couch with Poochers curled up at his feet. I was as unclear about my future with John as I was about the sun setting. Who could tell behind all the clouds if the sun was coming up or going down?

The tea kettle whistled and I reached to open the tea box. Tucked inside with the tea was that damn dryer sheet. I'd hidden it the night before in John's jacket pocket, so he'd find it this morning. He knew I'd be having tea tonight and planned this to make me smile. How could he withdraw into his drinking and still leave little signs he was thinking of me?

I shuffled down the hall to my bedroom, sat down on my bed and scooted back against the headboard. It was all too confusing, too overwhelming. "Okay, God, take over," I sighed.

My stomach churned as I began deep breathing. I sought my favorite place of not thinking, that place of peace, my only comfort. As I kept breathing, I was transported to a magical place. I felt peace in my stomach, in my heart, everywhere in my body. It was similar to the love I felt for Heath the first time I held him. But this was much bigger. It was huge. I felt my entire self expand to be part of everything. I was part of every person, animal and plant on the earth. I was part of the earth, the stars . . . and really, the whole universe. *What the heck was in that tea?*

The expansion I felt carried an amazingly warm, loving acceptance of all of creation. I felt at one with everything but at the same time, separate. How could that be? It was a sudden, beautiful shift. Could this be what mystics called "enlightenment"?

As I continued to revel, the word "detachment" flashed in my mind. THIS was what they had talked about at Al-Anon and Adult Children of Alcoholics meetings!

I had resisted detaching for years because it just didn't seem Christian not to keep loving. I felt detaching would leave me devoid of sensibility like I had had a lobotomy. But this feeling of detachment was different. I still loved John but I didn't have to be emotionally sucked into all of his drama. I no longer had to worry about whether he was drinking or not.

After this experience, all of life became like watching a movie. I could be separate, not emotionally dragged down from all of it.

Then I realized I had been using detachment off and on for years. I detached from Dad when I left home at 18 with an ulcer from the craziness. ACOA helped me detach from worrying all night about Dan making it home. Then I permanently detached from Dan by divorcing him.

But this detachment was different. It had remnants of the *Serenity Prayer's* "Accept the things you cannot change," but it was more. It wasn't a resignation to just live with the way things were. It was a way to start *LIVING* with the way things were.

I started applying this newfound freedom to all aspects of my life. It wasn't long before Heath's thirteenth birthday arrived. He was so independent, playing basketball, doing chores and homework. I noticed how he needed me much less. *He's growing up,* I thought. *Soon he'll be leaving me!*

I stopped myself. *Detachment,* I remembered.

When I took the emotion out of it, I was able to watch him grow into the person he was supposed to be, and applaud him. I stopped worrying about Heath being scarred for life from the actions of his father or John. I knew somehow that he'd be fine. It was all in the plan. Not my plan for his life, but THE plan.

Work became easier when I saw that most of the problems weren't mine. They weren't personal, just pieces that needed to be figured out, like those of a puzzle.

When I started looking at what *was* my concern and what *wasn't*, business became a game, challenging, but fun. I was amazed at how many situations really had nothing to do with me.

Ultimately, I realized I could only be responsible for myself. I couldn't do anything to get John to stop drinking.

And then, two days after my amazing *detachment,* John checked himself into rehab. This time I hoped it would work. In my journal I wrote: *"I wonder if they have found a cure for that thing called alcoholism, now that it has been labeled a disease?"*

# CHAPTER 35

## *Learning from the Ladies*

As a company sales rep, I missed working with individuals. Mostly, I missed the creative rush of helping them fix up their homes. I toyed with the idea of opening my own design business. Since I knew how to sell, the basis for any business—moving products, I thought I could do well. All my trophies boasted that I knew how to grow a business and sell at a high profit. I knew advertising from my newspaper days. I had sold floor coverings both retail and wholesale, so I understood this business from the inside out. I could do this.

I was tired of building up my territory and have management take pieces away. Then when Tom left the company, it just wasn't fun anymore. I tried all the usual things to liven up my job: focusing on a new product or new group of customers. But when the new boss took my Eastern Washington accounts and gave me Salem, that was it. I made plans to start my own business—to control my own destiny.

My Mom and stepdad were great, loaning me the money to open a store. Every morning, I'd jump out of bed, anxious to start my day. I enjoyed making the decisions for everything in my business. I had made a lot of money for companies; now it was my turn to reap all the rewards.

I reveled in going out to customers' homes once again. I read design books, learning about the interplay of light, and how to mix textures and colors. I especially loved the chills up my spine when a room turned out exactly as I had envisioned.

As before, I excelled at reading women. My clients were amazed when I pulled out the perfect wallpaper or drapery fabric for them.

At that time, wallpaper was popular and all window treatments had to be custom made. Cornice boxes were a trend and I contracted a local carpenter to make them to order. Then I covered them in wallpaper or fabric for the effect I wanted. I sewed simple curtains and valances myself, using the limitless fabrics available in rich, lush colors in sheers, damasks and moirés. I especially enjoyed looking at a window treatment and figuring out how to make it. I was using my talents, and having fun.

Several builders asked me to create color boards to show combinations in floor coverings, countertops and wall colors, helping buyers to create the homes of their dreams. Soon I had to hire someone to watch the store while I was out measuring and selling.

My store had a small town feel where people stopped in to have coffee and talk. Customers appreciated not having to drive to Vancouver or Portland for wallpaper and drapery fabric. Soon I needed a bigger place. I moved the store to the downtown street of Camas I had fallen in love with years before.

Heath and his friends painted the walls and I laid the marble entry myself.

One of my first customers, Colette, reminded me of Barbara Stanwyck in *Big Valley*. Her posture hinted at regal descent. The first time I heard from Colette was on an afternoon she wasn't playing bridge.

"Could you come over today?" Colette asked. "I'm thinking of replacing the drapes in the master bedroom."

"Sure," I said. "What time is good?"

"Now?"

"On my way," I said, grabbing my briefcase.

The view from Colette's house was amazing. As I got out of the car I could see Mt. Hood and the Columbia River from east to west.

Before I could knock, Colette opened the door. "How about a drink?" she asked, as I hauled the drapery fabrics into her family room.

"Sure. What are you having?"

"Vodka on the rocks," she said, moving behind the bar. "What about you?"

"That'll work." I pulled up a bar stool and looked around at her spacious rooms.

"What a great picture of your family," I said. "Do they live around here?"

"Yes," she said handing me my drink. "Sally, my daughter, lives here in Camas, but she's always busy with my grandson, Matthew—not to mention her jerk husband."

"What about your son?" I asked, wincing as I took a sip.

"Is that too strong?" Colette asked.

"No, no, it's good," I said setting my glass down. "Does your son live around here, too?"

"Yes," she sighed, "he's supposed to take over the business if he could just stop the drinking, the drugging and the women long enough to learn it."

"What kind of business is it?" I asked, wrapping both hands around my drink to melt the rock-hard ice.

"My husband bought this damn concrete company when we moved here," Colette said, taking a big gulp. "It's been nothin' but trouble." She slammed her glass down. "Years ago when we started our business we worked side by side in a Dairy Queen. Then we opened a pizza place." She picked up her glass. "Then a miniature golf course," she said, rattling her ice. "I miss those days," she sighed. "All I do now is go to lunch, play cards and read trashy novels."

"That sounds good to me," I said, thinking about my hectic life.

"Say, why don't you take some of these books?" Colette said, rising to indicate the novels on a shelf. Some covers showed muscled pirates gripping swooning women. Others were of cowboys embracing girls in braids whose breasts were over-spilling their gingham shirts. "They're a fun read."

"Thanks," I said, hesitantly taking the bag from her. I had always turned to books before, but this reading wasn't exactly what you called enlightenment. "Should we go look at the bedroom?" I asked.

I spent many afternoons with Colette, re-carpeting and drinking, recovering sofas and drinking, redoing the living room and drinking . . .

And although she was the greatest kind of customer, her life was sad to me. From the outside it looked incredible, but once inside, not so great.

Another great client, Suzanne, was a true Southern Belle. She was adding white pillars and a brick façade to her northwest home to get the plantation style she grew up with. Suzanne taught me the difference between "old" money and "new" money.

Suzanne recovered furniture that had been in her family for hundreds of years. She chose the best fabrics in traditional colors to last forever. She was sweet and very kind to all the maids, landscapers and farm hands she oversaw each day.

When I arrived one morning, she was meeting with a tailor, "Can you mend this for Richard?" she asked, handing him a beautiful cashmere jacket in a soft, camel color. The jacket was nice, but I was sure they could have afforded a new one. Still, that wasn't the point. They took great care not to spend foolishly.

This was in stark contrast to the attitude I had seen in Scottsdale. Everyone had flocked there in the eighties because of depressed conditions in the East and Midwest. These people had made a killing selling their houses and were determined to show it. In every driveway were Mercedes, Jaguars and Bentleys. Women wore rocks on their fingers so huge I thought they had to be gag rings from a gumball machine.

When someone from humble beginnings came into a lot of "new" money, they had to show it. I thought of Graceland, where the grand piano in Elvis' living room looked gold-plated. It stood behind stained leaded glass doors, with blue and green peacocks overlaid on each side. His plant-filled jungle room was furnished with huge carved chairs upholstered in fur. The TV room walls were upholstered in expensive matching fabrics, with three televisions side by side. Amazing.

But Suzanne with her old money knew better. She was one of the warmest, most gracious women I had ever met. I was convinced her life was that of a princess, and wondered if it could all be attributed to her breeding. She had gone to Radcliffe and then her father found her husband, Richard, for her. But even though it was an arranged marriage of sorts, I could tell she truly loved Richard.

After months with Suzanne, we finished decorating the main floor. Then we began working on the guest rooms. "Wouldn't this make the perfect nursery?" Suzanne asked, as we stood in a doorway one day.

"Yes," I said. "The way the morning light comes in, it would be great. Are you thinking of having a baby?"

Suzanne sat down on the bed, folding her hands in her lap, "Oh, I can't have children," she said.

"Gosh, I'm so sorry, Suzanne," I said, sitting next to her.

She let out a big sigh. "I was raped at thirteen by one of our farm hands."

I looked at her with sympathy, trying to hide my shock.

"Rory was a like a father to me," she went on. "He taught me how to ride from the time I was five, how to hold the reigns and how to jump. Then one day he had been drinking and . . ." Her voice was a whisper.

"I've had to let it go," she said. "He wasn't the Rory I knew and loved that day."

On the drive home I thought about Suzanne's "perfect" life. The depth of her warmth wasn't something she was born with, but what she had lived through.

I learned even more lessons from watching Suzanne. One day our appointment ran over into the afternoon when the phone rang. "Oh, that must be Richard calling to tuck me in."

"Tuck you in?" I asked as she answered the phone.

"Yes, Richard, Mary is still here," she said, and handed me the phone.

"Hello, Richard," I said.

"Mary, could you please come back in the morning?" he asked. "Suzanne needs her rest."

"Of course, Richard," was all I could say.

Richard insisted Suzanne take an afternoon nap. He wanted her to be fresh when he came home from work. At first, I thought, *what a controlling ass.* But as I spent the next several months with them I began to envy Suzanne's marriage. One morning on the way out of the house I heard Richard say, "Suzanne, that landscaper you chose is fantastic. Our lawn has never looked so good."

Another day he dropped in just as my installers were finishing hanging the curtains in the breakfast room. "That looks terrific, Suzanne," he said. "That yellow you chose really brightens up the room."

Richard was always like that with Suzanne. *Ahhh, what would that be like to be appreciated for my feminine role in the family,* I thought.

They brought to mind *Gone with the Wind,* where Rhett, with all of his masculine sensuality, grabs Scarlet and carries her up the stairs to ravish her. That's the way it was in most of those trashy novels Colette gave me. Being intensely desired by a man . . . wow!

I wondered what it would be like to be totally cherished. In my daydream I went on to think of all the ways I could be "ished." To be cher "ished", rav "ished" and lav "ished" with love.

Back to the reality of my life, I wished I had been appreciated in my first marriage for doing all the domestic chores and raising Heath. Most likely, I would have enjoyed staying home. I loved cooking and decorating and being a mom. But I was treated no better than a slave for my efforts. In my journal I wrote: *"I guess I've had to get my "ishes" from work."*

# CHAPTER 36

## *I've Watched All Good People*

It was the era of enormous, heavy, black televisions and mammoth speakers, with every family room boasting macho technology. Carol, one of my customers, gave her television a slap as we stood nearby. "How do we deal with this monstrosity?" she asked. "Can't you just have a talk with Fred, using your designer voice? You know, 'Oh, Dahling, that simply won't do!'"

I laughed at the tease, glad she appreciated my sense of humor. This was just another of the challenges that made me love my job. Not every decorator could laugh off clients with decorating disputes however. One friend of mine told her clients, "I charge extra for marriage counseling."

"Well, Carol, I can do that," I answered after giving it some thought. "But Fred lives here, too, you know. Why don't we design around it?" In my notes I wrote, *ask Fred—TV in FR not LR?*

I knew most men could live in caves, eternally happy with a TV in front of them, a pizza in one hand, and a remote in the other. I also knew they hated spending money on decorating, so I had to tread lightly. I thought back to how important the TV had been to Dad and my brothers. Even before Elvis, my Dad had three TV's blasting all weekend long in his shop: one showing golf, one baseball, and the other with any additional sport he could find.

Placed in the middle of many husband and wife wars, I had become an expert at peacekeeping. Hadn't I learned long ago, from the master? Mom made everything right with us kids after a dose of dad's berating. All the while keeping him calm.

As a decorator I was learning a lot about male-female relationships. One of my customers, Sandy, decorated her living and dining room in peach silk draperies. When I gave her the bill for over five thousand, she handed me a check for five hundred, with forty-five hundred in cash.

"Can you make out another bill for five hundred whatever?" she asked. "We won't tell Terry how much these really cost."

I understood this behavior. I had hidden many a purchase in the bottom of my closet, only to pull it out a few weeks later and act like I'd had it for years. I thought of Suzanne, and bet she never had to do that with Richard.

Meanwhile, my business was doing well and the local community education program asked me to teach design classes. I developed one class on color and basic design. It filled up fast. The next week I gave a lesson on window coverings; the class overflowed with students. My third class, painting techniques, was a packed room as we sponged, rag rolled and stuccoed. By the last class on installing ceramic tile, I wasn't sure the classroom would hold the crowd. The classes provided great exposure for my business.

Paging through an *Architectural Digest* one day I read about an ancient Chinese art called Feng Shui. It provided a way to arrange a home to create harmony with nature. I bought every book I could find on the subject and took several classes. I learned how each area of a room and a home had a special significance relating to Career, Wisdom, Family, Prosperity, Fame, Relationships, Creativity and Helpful People. This art also taught how to achieve balance in a space using the elements: wood, fire, metal and water.

I realized I did much of this instinctively as a designer. For instance how adding a plant (wood) to a corner would balance the dramatic mirror (water) with the pewter frame (metal).

Removing clutter is one of the main tenants of Feng Shui. Cleaning out even one closet can bring instant benefits to someone's life. I incorporated these principles into my design practice regularly and offered Feng Shui consultations to my services.

That year the Southwest Washington Parade of Homes was in Camas. Another designer in town was decorating one of the models and asked if I would make the selections for the window coverings and wallpaper. What a fun project and great exposure for my business.

The kitchen had a wine motif so I made a burgundy cornice over the kitchen window and patio door. I inserted wallpaper with a grapevine in greens and purples. We cut out the vine in the wallpaper design, trailing it off the window treatment, down the wall. Everyone loved it.

But when the bedroom wallpaper border didn't arrive in time for the opening of the show, the other designer was upset. "Don't worry," I said. "I'll figure something out."

I went to the fabric store, found beige fabric trim and glued it around the room between the taupe paint and the matching fleur de lis patterned wallpaper. "Necessity is the mother of invention," I said. Or was creativity the mother of invention? However it was, my idea received a lot of great comments.

The model had an alcove in the upstairs hall with a beautiful white on white striped overstuffed chair. I created a luxurious window treatment with the same fabric in a sheer that puddled on the floor in perfect scallops.

After the show, the Board of the Chamber of Commerce asked me to join, and I immersed myself in various fundraising events. As I became more involved in the community, more customers came to my store.

Hour by hour, I'd chat with a single customer, hang her pictures, or take great care shopping to exactly match her favorite color. Unfortunately, I wasn't careful how my time was compensated. Sometimes I would spend hours with clients giving design advice; some would take that advice and then buy carpet and mini blinds at huge chains like Home Depot. These stores could buy in such large quantities that a small dealer like me could never win the price war. I was beginning to wonder if I could truly compete in this business.

On the positive side, I was blessed with energy but I was suffering from backaches from the physical part of my job. Nikki called one day and said she just took a class on Reiki and need someone to practice on.

"Reiki?" I asked.

"Yes, it's a hands-on healing technique for aches and pains but it also relieves stress," she said.

"I can sure use that," I sighed. "How about tonight?"

"Okay!"

When I arrived Nikki opened the door with such a flourish I could tell she was excited.

"Let's get started," she said rubbing her palms together. "Follow me."

Nikki led me down the hall to her guest room. "Take off your shoes and lie down on the bed."

Following her orders I relaxed onto the bed. She began laying her hands on my shoulders, then over my eyes and then ears until she had gone up and down each side of my body. When she finished I was left with a contentedness I hadn't felt in years. I was extremely calm without any pain mentally or physically.

I had to know more so I took the first degree Reiki class and then the second. It was great to take charge of healing myself. I hung the *Spiritual Precepts of Reiki* on my wall:

*Just for today, do not worry.*
*Just for today, do not anger.*
*Honor your parents, teachers, and elders.*
*Earn your living honestly.*
*Show gratitude to every living thing.*

These were great words to live by and being able to perform Reiki really came in handy with Heath's basketball injuries. One weekend he was in a tournament and bought new Michael Jordan shoes. The last pair they had was a half size too small but Heath bought them anyway. At the end of the first day his socks were bright red with blood from his toenails being pounded back into his toes. That night we bought shoes that fit and I Reikied his black and blue toes. The next morning his toenails fell off and he was pain free for the rest of the tournament.

Another time Heath twisted his ankle coming down from a jump shot. When we got home I began doing Reiki on his foot. At the end of the treatment he had no more pain and said he felt there was a gold cord attached to his heart reaching to a gold ball in the sky.

"That must be your link to God," I said. "What a great visualization to hold onto whenever you want that connection."

I had experienced many of these spiritual connections in Reiki treatments when I was the giver and the receiver. This was also a new way to infuse my food with love through my hands with this wonderful God energy.

Since Heath was in high school during this time, he didn't need me as much. I enjoyed spending a lot of time working since coming home to a drunk husband hadn't been much fun.

What I didn't know about my business was the financial part: how the money worked. If I had read *The E-Myth*, by Michael Gerber, I might've paid more attention to the business side of things. As Gerber points out, you start a business because you're good at something and love doing it. But there's a lot more to running a business than reaping the profits an employer would otherwise retain. A business owner has numerous, hidden factors to consider. Such as bookkeeping. I didn't like it and I wasn't very good at it. Thousands of dollars were running through my business but with paying taxes, subcontractors, and employees, there wasn't much left over. John's real estate sales didn't provide a steady income. There was no money for any extras. I couldn't even afford senior pictures for Heath, since making the bills was becoming a crap shoot.

I remembered when I was a struggling single mom and Angela, the soccer mom, fed Heath and me that glorious meal. Here I was, counting on those miracles again.

Still, Dad's famous complaint kept ringing in my ears, "I'd have my own business if the government didn't take all of it in taxes." Once again, Dad was telling me that I was doing things all wrong. I must've been crazy to be in business for myself.

And yet, as I thought about it, I realized Dad's opinion had a basis in his childhood. It wasn't the truth for everyone.

During the Great Depression my grandfather owned a grocery store. Dad watched as Grandpa gave out food on credit that customers were never able to pay back. The business eventually went under and the family suffered.

"You just can't make it in business anymore," Dad would say, shaking his head.

Now, could I prove Dad wrong? I wanted to try. I hung in there, month after month, though we were on the brink of losing our house, refinancing it at every possible chance. When things looked their worst, John's mother stepped in and saved us. To the outside world our life looked fine, but inside everything was collapsing.

Alice, my friend from Seattle came to look at the houses I decorated for the show. "Wow, Mary, you are so creative," she said. "I love what you've done. You *have* to help with window coverings for my new house."

On our way back to my house she asked, "Will Johnny be home or is he at the Moose?"

"What do you think?" I sighed.

"Mary, what are you doing?" she asked. "You know Johnny's drinking is getting really bad again."

In my journal I wrote: *"I think there is a thin line between detaching from John's drinking and denying that it really is a problem."*

# CHAPTER 37

## *I Don't Know Where My Soul Went*

I sat shivering in the conference room of a high rise in downtown Vancouver. Why did they make these law offices so cold? My teeth chattered as John and I waited for Wendell Gable, a well known bankruptcy attorney. Finally he lumbered in, a large man with brush-like eyebrows and a fleshy face. Just his size put the fear of God in me.

Mr. Gable, Esquire, sat down, took out his pen and began volleying questions at us, quickly scribbling the answers. After a bit he threw his pen down and gruffed, "Well, it's up to you, now or later. How long do you want to keep the balls in the air?" He sat back in his chair and loudly cracked his knuckles. "It's all gonna crash."

I knew my business was in trouble, but I still thought I could make it work.

But I was exhausted. The money worries and long hours had done me in. Bankruptcy seemed the only answer.

Work was the one place I always shined, and now it was falling apart. I had failed . . . big time. I knew John blamed me for not running the business well. But then, I blamed him for not bringing in enough money selling real estate.

My bankruptcy would be printed in the local newspaper. It was a small town and people talked. I was so ashamed I just wanted to hide out and eat, but I went back to my store and sadly began stacking carpet samples in my trunk.

It was June, but the rain was still pouring. When I arrived home even Poochers' greeting didn't make me feel better. I began setting up a temporary shop in the small bedroom, but then slumped down on the floor and sobbed while Poochers looked on wagging her tail, helpless. I went into the kitchen, took my peanut butter and chocolate ice cream out of the freezer, dragged myself into the living room, grabbed my favorite peach afghan, sank into the couch and began grieving for all I had lost. Gone was the basis for who I thought I was. A successful business woman? Now that was a sham and it rocked me to my core.

I felt more alone than in college, losing my fiancé and my speech therapy career. I felt more alone than when Dad died, because this time I was losing part of my own self. And even through my divorce, all alone in the Northwest, I'd never experienced such unrelenting loneliness. Then, I'd had my work. Now, I didn't even have that.

All through life when I couldn't be perfect I would work harder, eat junk food or smoke. One of those addictions would usually bring me relief. But nothing worked this time. My little trick of detaching and saying "Okay, God, take over" simply felt hollow.

I didn't know who I was anymore. I could hardly climb out of bed in the morning. I'd shuffle to the kitchen, get my coffee and slump on the couch with Poochers at my feet. Day after day I'd write in my journal, sob and pray.

After what seemed like years of this painful aloneness, I finally realized a truth: I was still the Mary I projected to the world. But that wasn't the real me. I was much more than that. There was Mary the daughter, Mary the wife, Mary the mother, Mary the scared little girl. There was the lonely Mary and the happy Mary. All of these were Mary—but not the real Mary. All were facets on the surface of the diamond that was the real Mary. Underneath it all was a bright shining light, a part of God. I began to feel that incredible peace I'd experienced during detachment.

Eventually my hours of soul searching on the couch helped the truth to gel in my mind. It was really okay not to be perfect all the time. I no longer had to put myself in little boxes of the perfect wife or perfect mother. It was okay to be me—whoever that was—and that's all that really mattered.

In my journal I wrote: *"My ego has died. Thank you, God."*

# CHAPTER 38

## *Sliding into Darkness*

One August morning found me in the driveway with Heath and his friend, Tyler, packing a U Haul with all their prized possessions. Tyler's Mom and I stood sobbing. I didn't even notice the sunshine and gentle breeze of the Northwest's most beautiful season. Heath was leaving.

Since Heath was born, every decision I had made in life had been influenced by him. I worked nights as a bartender to be home with him during the day. I didn't move back to Phoenix after his dad and I divorced, because I didn't want to take him away from his father. I married again because I wanted him to have a real family. I always chose for him the best family babysitters, and became a sales rep so I could attend his basketball games. I opened my design business close to his school, so I'd be around if he needed me.

And now, he was leaving.

He was off to college in Phoenix—a decision I had encouraged because I wanted him to experience more diversity. Our little town of Camas was a great place for young kids, but a young adult like Heath needed exposure to all kinds of people, just as I had needed and benefitted from this exposure when I moved from Zanesville to Phoenix.

Mom and my brothers and sisters were all in Arizona if Heath needed anything. But deep down the truth was, I hoped Heath would love Phoenix and want to relocate there. That way I could move back one day. Even Mom was in on the plan, as she and my stepdad were paying Heath's out of state tuition.

Now, my empty marriage was glaring at me. John passed out most evenings after dinner. I prayed he would do something. Or that I would. I began checking out rehab places, however, most wouldn't take our insurance. When I finally found one, the waiting list was one week. *Great. A whole week.* At that time, it seemed an eternity.

Most nights John would be home by six, but that week before rehab he stayed out until nine or ten. I guessed it was his "last hurrah." Just like all the times I'd eaten a batch of brownies Sunday night before starting my new diet Monday morning.

I was worried sick about him driving home drunk and getting in an accident. In my journal I wrote: "*Dear God, please let him live to be rehabbed one more time.*"

Finally the day came. I couldn't wait to check him in and turn him over to be someone else's worry. We went outside for a goodbye cigarette. As I lit up I looked down into a bucket of cigarette butts by the door. There, floating in rainwater were the remnants of many nasty habits. White filters bumped up against brown filters. Cigar butts swirled in a circle, and was that a roach? I was so repulsed by the swimming butts, I vowed right then to quit smoking.

On the way home, I stopped at Walgreens, bought a box of nicotine patches and slapped one on my arm. By the time I arrived home I had a new determination. I began mopping and dusting. I moved furniture in every room and vacuumed underneath. I scrubbed down walls, unscrewed light bulbs from sockets and washed them. I hadn't had such a nesting instinct since before Heath was born.

I sat down and wrote this letter in my journal:

*Dear friend,*

*You have been with me for twenty-five years. Anytime I needed you, you were there. As long as I had the money to buy you, you were there. You helped me keep my weight in check when my eating was out of control. You helped me through the trials of my first marriage, motherhood, moving to foreign cities, divorce, single motherhood, many a rehab with husbands and bankruptcy. The only time without you was when I was pregnant and you made me sick (thanks for that).*

*I know there were times I gave you up before and the sweet smell of your charm lured me back. But this time is the last. I am sorry to let you go. You have been a dear friend, but you are no longer good for me. Thank you and goodbye.*

*Love,*
*Mary*

The first night on the nicotine patches I had a dream of Indians burning down my house, but this time instead of being scared, I was staving them off with a sling shot like David with Goliath. The next night I dreamt about a large auditorium like my seventh grade spelling bee. I walked up to the stage and realized I had no clothes on below my waist. Normally I'd wake up in a panic with this kind of dream. But, this time I walked to the podium without fear and realized the whole audience was naked from the waist down. I woke up thinking, *what is in these nicotine patches?* I was high on them like I'd never been on cigarettes.

*All right,* I decided. *That's enough of those.* Feeling that high couldn't possibly be good.

After the bankruptcy I worked out of my small home office. Then I landed a contract for two model homes—a designer's dream! Decorating houses from top to bottom with OTHER PEOPLE'S MONEY! This would be the most fun I ever had.

I turned Heath's bedroom into a workroom to make drapes. In his family room I stored my purchases for the models. Every day I went shopping for furniture or sconces or designer pillows for my latest creations. This should have been fantastic, but between every stop, I cried. I'd dry my tears, go in the store, buy what I needed, then cry all the way to the next stop.

What was wrong with me? I was tired all the time and drank pots of coffee to keep going. The bitter taste helped when I craved a cigarette. But wasn't I supposed to feel great after quitting smoking?

One morning on my way to pick out drapery fabric in Portland, I saw a dead raccoon on Highway 14. It was hardly recognizable with its guts spilled across two lanes. I thought, *Oh well, he served his purpose on this earth and now it's time for him to go.* Maybe my purpose was served, now that Heath was raised. *Why prolong my misery?* I thought as I eyed the next telephone pole.

Later that day I received a visit from Brian, the builder of the homes I was decorating. I was arranging the furniture and accessories in the great room when he paused and examined the effect. "I think that thing would look better lying straight rather than thrown," he said with his hands on his hips.

"You mean the afghan?" I asked. "It makes people feel more at home when it isn't perfect."

"Change it," he said, walking away.

I slumped down on the couch, sobbing into my hands. I could feel him looking at me from the door. Dumbfounded, Brian ran to get his sister, Jan who worked in the office. Jan came out running "Mary, are you all right?" I couldn't even answer. She sat down beside me putting her arm around me while I continued bawling.

How embarrassing. I had always been able to take criticism—God knows, I grew up with enough of it. But now, what was wrong with me?

Was I missing Heath? Was I alone again in my marriage or was it our money problems and bankruptcy? Perhaps it was having John home from rehab, with a "new plan for his life" which I had little faith in. Or could it have been my usual depression, or seasonal affective disorder. I just didn't feel like myself.

On the way home I stopped at the nutrition center for St. John's Wort. Linda, my sister, had told me it helped with depression. I dusted off my light box. But neither seemed to help.

My blood sugar was out of control so I couldn't find freedom in ice cream because I'd just pass out from the sugar. And, it's really hard to work when you're passed out. Whenever I went for walks, my blood sugar plummeted and I would get nauseous and shake.

Later that evening as I chopped carrots for soup, I began crying again as I blessed them and flowed the Reiki energy into them. Maybe there was something medically wrong. I needed to go to the doctor.

The next day on the examining table I laid out my sad story between sobs. I tried to recount all the things I had tried: meditation, walking, yoga, journaling, the light box, vitamins and finally St. John's Wort.

The fresh faced, Canadian doctor straight out of med school looked at her notes then looked at me intently. "Honey, we are way past the St. John's Wort," she said. "When you stop polluting your body with all those chemicals from cigarettes like you've done for twenty-five years, you need a little chemical balancing."

She prescribed Prozac. I wrote in my journal: *"I really hope this works."*

# CHAPTER 39

## *Rarely Breathing*

My designs for the model were a hit. The master bathroom had a sunken tub with sand-colored tile steps, surrounded with plants and brass candle holders. A white sheer with shiny ribbons swooped from the window. I could hear people sigh when they walked in and imagined relaxing into that warm candlelit tub.

I designed flouncy white lace curtains in the little girl's room, adding to the mood a local artist had created with a garden path mural.

The little boy's room was done in a cowboy motif. I hung bandanas in red and navy blue, using a lasso for a curtain rod. Now that I was feeling better I had a way to take back control of my life. It was simple. I could keep up with regular design jobs while finishing the models. I could salvage my marriage, and solve John's drinking problem. I could do anything. I'd found the key years ago, back in sixth grade.

*She who is organized has the power.*

My friend Crystal had come to school with a cream colored leather notebook. Three rings held paper in place while a gold zipper ran around the outside to keep books and papers from falling out. It had handles to be carried like a briefcase.

When Crystal unzipped the notebook, the whiff of fresh leather filled our classroom. Inside were pockets to hold small papers and bands to hold pens and pencils. My own notebook was a blue cloth three ring binder and I carried my books by hand. Every time I saw Crystal's amazing bookcase, I couldn't take my eyes off it.

Each night, I dreamt about Crystal's notebook. Then one night I dreamed Mom had bought me the exact white briefcase. I slowly moved the zipper around the outside of the notebook and breathed in the unmistakable scent of real leather. I adjusted my papers in sections for each of my classes. I filled out the identification card in the front pocket with my name and address lest, God forbid, I should lose it. I placed my favorite pen in the elastic band and was ready for school.

The next morning I woke up and ran downstairs to grab my case. It wasn't there. I searched under the dining room chairs, on the kitchen countertops, and behind the sofa pillows. I marched upstairs and turned my bedroom inside out, hollering, "Hey, Linda! Did you steal my briefcase?"

She looked at me like I was crazy. Then I realized it had all been a dream. Sadly, I sat down on my bed and remembered one last Hershey Bar hidden in a drawer.

But now that I was grown up I didn't have to be a victim of a shoddy notebook or haphazard organizers. I didn't have to envy Crystal anymore. At last I could realize my dream of the perfect system.

I bought new briefcases.

I found a black one with cordovan snakeskin trim that I packed with a tape measure, architect's ruler and graph paper for new design jobs. I loaded another larger red fake leather one with a hammer, nails, an electric screwdriver, scissors, a glue gun and a small tool kit for working on the models.

There was hope for me yet.

The days were filled with long hours of work, trying not to miss Heath away at college. While sewing draperies one afternoon, I found myself itching fiercely. I scratched to no avail. After a few more days, I broke out in a rash. I could hardly breathe when I ironed the fabric. Red blotches appeared on my neck and chest. When I was away from the fabrics, I would feel better, but I coughed nonstop, wherever I was.

When the models were done, John was drinking heavily. I refused to get sucked into his drama. It was easiest to be away from him, so I took a job in a carpet store in Portland. It was sure to be an easy way to make money and get caught up on bills.

In my second month I broke the store record selling $93,000 worth of floor coverings in one month. I was shooting for a hundred thousand but the closest salesman only did forty-five. I was back on top and it felt good.

But my success was short lived. In a few months I could hardly breathe. The doctor said I had a cloudiness in my lungs that looked like pneumonia. He gave me antibiotics for a few days; I was better and returned to work. Then, I had trouble breathing once again, and the doctor prescribed stronger antibiotics. I recovered, went to work and after a few more days, couldn't breathe again. For the third time, the doctor gave me antibiotics. While the doses grew stronger and stronger, I became weaker and weaker.

I thought I was allergic to something in the old building I worked in. When I staggered to my car, gasping for air, I knew I had to quit.

For three months I lay in bed, exhausted. Walking to the kitchen wore me out. I'd have to rest for hours after that small trip. I became sicker and sicker.

All my focus had to be on me. Each breath was a chore I couldn't get away from. Conventional medicine was getting me nowhere, but what were my options? I'd always used herbs, vitamins, massage, meditation and Reiki for illnesses since my hippie days, but I didn't have the money to spend on anything insurance didn't cover.

Money was a worry but all I could focus on was me. Each breath brought me back to the present moment. This time I couldn't run away. I couldn't hide out in work or ice cream. I had to deal with my life that was smothering me.

One morning as I lay in bed wondering if I would ever be well again I said, "Okay, God, take over."

I picked up the remote and began flipping between Jerry Springer and Judge Judy. There I saw an ad for the Naturopathic

College in Portland. They were offering patients' office visits for two cans of food as a special promotion for the annual Oregon Food Drive. This was it. I had to go.

I was excited to be out of the house as John drove me across the I-205 Bridge to Portland. But as I looked at Mt. Hood at the far end of the Columbia River, I felt sad. I realized from the lack of snow on the mountain I had missed the whole summer. The most beautiful time in the northwest and I had been in bed for all of it.

In the waiting room I labored with my breath for over two hours with hordes of sick people holding two cans of food. Finally, two kids looking younger than Heath ushered me into an examining room. "Sit down," one said. "How long have you been this way? What kind of treatment have you been on? When was the last time you worked? What do you do for a living? What is your work environment?"

For forty-five minutes the questions kept coming then they left me for another forty-five. I was drained by the time they returned with a doctor. "We think your problem is environmental," the doctor said, adjusting his glasses.

"Environmental?" I gasped. "What does that mean?'

"We think you are suffering from the off gasses of the carpet and fabrics you have worked with for so many years." The doctor sat down looking at me intently. "You are going to have to change professions and get away from all the toxins."

"Huh?" I straightened up. "You have to be kidding."

"No, we're not," he said, rubbing his forehead. "This is serious." He handed me a brown bottle with a stopper. "Take this and stay away from new carpet and fabric. Okay?"

"But, but, it's my livelihood."

"Sorry," he said, getting up and moving to the door.

On the ride home I sat in disbelief, too tired to think. How could this be?

Later at home, I thought about my twenty years working with carpet. I thought about driving around in the hot Phoenix sun with my car filled with carpet samples straight off the presses. And then peddling carpet up and down the Columbia River where I had even more carpet samples in my Aerostar. Then there were all the samples from my design business. I guessed ironing drapery fabrics gave me my final dose of toxins.

"*What now?*" I wrote in my journal.

# CHAPTER 40

## *A Change has to Come*

What do you do when you can't do what you did for twenty years?

You go into real estate.

And so, I threw my last carpet sample into the garbage can. I cracked open the books to study endless terms like "leasehold" and "fee simple estate," for the real estate exam.

Meanwhile Heath had his own career to figure out. He came back from Arizona, unsure of his future. Whatever the reason for his return, I was thrilled to have him home. He had taken basic classes but hadn't decided on a major. Maybe he should work for a while and figure it out, he decided. He was hired by Wubben Brothers to dig trenches for excavation projects.

One day he burst through the door and said, "Mom, they're paying me thirty-two an hour! More than twice what I used to make!"

"That's great, Heath," I said, thinking maybe he had found his niche.

Every day he drove to Longview to direct bulldozers on a landfill—an easy job, but boring. After three months the project ended, and Heath went back to making twelve dollars an hour cleaning sewer pipes.

Then one night I could tell something was wrong by the way he dragged himself out of the car and peeled off his Carhartt and boots by the door. He walked in and plopped down in a kitchen chair. "Mom, can you believe I had to polish a manhole cover until it was shiny enough for the inspectors? The inspector said there was still mud on it, and I had to clean it again. I can't believe it. What a jerk!" He pounded his fist on the table, "for a sewer pipe that's going to have SHIT running through it by next week!"

I sat down across from him. "Well, have you thought about going back to school?"

"For what?" he sighed.

"Maybe a business degree? I always wished I had done that. You can apply it to anything."

"I'll think about it," he said, getting up and shuffling down the hall to his room.

"The spaghetti will be ready soon," I called after him.

"Thanks, Mom, I'll be out for the ceiling test."

The next week Heath was breaking up concrete with a sledgehammer on a construction site. A Mercedes pulled up and three men in business suits got out.

"Who are those guys?" he asked his supervisor.

"Oh, those are the rich developers."

"Hmmm." Heath leaned against a fence post, watching the three men roll out blueprints on the hood of their car.

That was all it took. At the end of his shift, Heath handed in his resignation. He took a few classes at Clark College to finish his AA degree, then went on to Washington State in Pullman. I was so proud of him.

As for me, I had my own career to figure out.

After passing the Real Estate Exam I began working in the same real estate office as John. The first requirement was to take their class called Sales Skills.

Todd was a new guy at the office. A mammoth man about my age, he looked like a retired football player. He had left Spokane to settle here with his new wife he met on the Internet. Phyllis was nurse with two daughters. That winter through rain, sleet and snow,

Todd and I drove to our Sales Skills Class in Portland. I heard all his stories about how happy the girls were to have a dad. And then these stories gradually changed, and the outcry of the girls became the cliché: "You can't tell me what to do! You're not my father!"

Todd seemed like a decent guy and I hoped Phyllis wasn't sorry to bring him into the family, like I had been at times with John. I didn't want to relive my stories, but told Todd it would all work out. I had come to realize that somehow things always do.

In class, I found the technology of this company way beyond me. When Kathleen, our spunky little teacher with big blue eyes tried to teach us about our Outlook email program, I sat in wonderment. It was a good thing they had a cheerleader type for this role. She was probably too young to have heard the saying about old dogs and new tricks.

In the class I was fascinated to learn that ninety percent of a real estate salesman's clients came from people they knew, their "sphere of influence." These could've been parents from a kid's soccer team, a dry cleaner, or Aunt Millie and Cousin Larry.

I had lots of clients from my design business, so that is where I began. I called one of my favorites.

"Say Robin," I began. "I wanted to let you know I'm in real estate now." I waited on the phone for a response.

"That's great," said Robin. "Say, I've been meaning to ask: Remember that picture over the couch that my mother in law gave me? Well, I always hated it. Now that she's gone do you think it would be all right to replace it?"

"Um, sure," I said. "Like I told you before, Robin, never have anything around that makes you feel bad."

"Good," she answered.

"Great! Now, about my real estate business. Do you think you might know . . ."

"Can you go shopping with me for a new picture?" Robin interrupted.

I cleared my throat. "Sorry," I said. "I'm in real estate now. Do you know anyone buying or selling a home?"

Things didn't go much differently when I called Colette. "Come over for a drink," she said. "I have some more romance novels for you and we can talk about your new career."

Another client, Cynthia, said, "I loved those alabaster jars. Can we still get them with your decorator discount?"

Call after call I recounted the gory details of my toxic poisoning and why I couldn't continue in the design business. Nothing seemed to make them see me as a real estate agent. I was strangely out of my element. But selling was selling. I told myself I could master this.

Every day I'd show up next to Todd in the "bullpen," the herd of cubicles in the middle of the office, for "newbies" who hadn't earned office space. He was having less luck than me, since he hadn't lived here long enough to have a "sphere." So Todd began calling expired listings, with his phone banging down every few minutes to the mutterings of "You asshole," or "Son of a bitch."

One day during one of Todd's tirades, I was talking to my design client, Colette. She was in her usual alcohol-altered state when she heard Todd's language. "Say, who's that, Mary?" she asked. "Are you calling from a bar?"

Here I was trying my best to be taken seriously in my new profession. I had to talk to my manager. Toni was always happy and had the longest fingernails I'd ever seen. They even curled downward. She painted them in bright pinks with little flowers or two toned with the colors split by little gold bands. At Christmas that year she had little Christmas trees on a red background.

As I entered her office she was clicking her talons together. "I could be much more productive at home," I explained.

"No," she said. Today her nails were fuchsia with daisies. "You have to stay in the office and make your sphere calls."

"Believe me, Toni, you can trust me to work at home," I pleaded. "I'm a workaholic, for God's sake!"

"Sorry, you knew the program when you signed on here."

I sulked to my cubicle in the hermetically sealed office. I remembered to pray. "Please, God, don't let 'em suck the life out of me!"

Suddenly I straightened, wondering, where was John? Why could he sleep in late and wander in and out of the office at leisure when I worked from dawn to dusk?

I'd seen him earlier that morning. "Hey Hon," he had said. "I'm going to visit my friend, Ellen. She just got home from the hospital."

"Sure, honey," I said.

*What a nice guy,* I thought to myself now, opening my "sphere" book to a crumpled dryer sheet. *He's so sweet.*

And it seemed truer than ever: John *was* good to people. One night we were eating dinner at Anna Lou's Restaurant. We had just ordered when an older woman across from us started choking. Her husband sat looking at her while this sweet little lady in gingham and lace grasped the table with both hands trying to breathe. Her husband casually turned to the room and asked, "Can someone help us?"

John jumped up, hauled the lady out of the booth and tried to do a light Heimlich maneuver. I rushed to the kitchen. "Call 911," I yelled. "A lady is choking."

When I went back out, John was standing with his arms around the tiny lady's midsection. "I don't want to hurt her," he said looking at me.

"Go up UNDER her ribs!" someone yelled.

With one fast jerk, the lady's meat dislodged, flying across the room. Just then the paramedics arrived and tended to her.

We went back to our booth and one of the firemen came over. "Thanks," he said. "You saved that lady's life."

Then our waitress stopped at our table. "Thanks, you guys. Can I get you anything?" She looked toward our plates at the same time John and I glanced down, and all three of us caught the same sight. That little lady's slimy piece of meat sat directly in the center of our table. There was silence.

"How about some doggy bags?" John asked.

"Of course," she said, grabbing the meat up in a napkin. A soft, "ewww," came from her.

John and I looked at each other, grinning. When the paramedics left and the little old lady was reinstalled in her booth, we heard her say, "I'm so embarrassed. What will people think?"

"For Gods sakes, Ethel, who cares?" her husband grumbled. "Eat your meat, there's plenty of good pieces left."

With that, John and I couldn't contain our laughter. We had to get out of there. John pointed to the doggy bags and we muffled our shrieks of laughter, shaking our heads in unison as we left them behind.

Back at the office, I thought about John.

That night in my journal I wrote: *"Isn't John great? He always does kind things for the needy, and visits the sick."*

# CHAPTER 41

## *It's Not So Easy*

The real estate business is hard. Since I wasn't getting immediate clients from calling my sphere, I took as much floor time as I could get. One day in walked Tim and Angie. I thought they were brother and sister because of their identical wide-set blue eyes. Each had skin so pale it made us Northwesterners look tan. Tim's job had brought them here from Wisconsin, and they were excited about everything: their new life together, buying their first house and expecting their first child. "Ah, youth," my stepdad would've said to their pre-jaded outlook on life.

Since Tim had grown up on a farm, he wanted a house with land. I went to work looking for a country setting to make him feel at home. It so happened that Angie's dad was a contractor and would be coming to town to check out their house before they purchased it. He had a meticulous eye for construction so I carefully searched for a house that wouldn't need much repair.

I found a three bedroom ranch on three quarters of an acre not far from the cable company where Tim worked. Angie liked the fact that it wasn't too far out of town, since Tim traveled with his job. It was everything they wanted. It even had a nursery decorated in shades of blue. We wrote the sale contingent on her father's approval. MY FIRST SALE! It was hard to tell who was more excited, Tim and Angie, or me.

That weekend, Angie's folks came to town and we all piled into my Aerostar to drive to the property. As we neared the house, her father shook his head. "It's too close to the road."

I soon learned the front door hadn't been installed properly, the kitchen cabinets needed to be replaced and the cheap hardwood floors would take forever to refinish.

In spite of her father's remarks, Angie drew back her shoulders and carried her pregnant frame onward, leading her mom to the sunlit nursery. I could hear them squealing about the blue-painted room being fate: they'd learned they were having a boy. But their joy was short lived when they heard the bellowing of her father outside, condemning everything from the composite roof to the concrete foundation.

One by one, we trudged out of the house and got back into the van. The ride was quiet all the way back to my office. Tim and Angie were as deflated as I was. None of my massive amounts of sales training could have saved that sale.

But I knew how sales worked, so I dusted off my failure and answered a call for my first listing appointment where I met Jeff and Marianne. They had been married for twelve years, and were now on the brink of separating.

Their kids Brent and Cybil were in the hallway as I came in, leaning against the wall with their arms crossed. They rolled their eyes in unison as the parents quarreled in the kitchen.

"We are putting this house on the market and getting divorced!" Marianne yelled.

"Well hurry up! I don't want to live with you a minute longer!" Jeff roared back.

Brent turned to me and said, "They do this all the time."

"Don't worry," Cybil said, shrugging. "We aren't going anywhere."

"You aren't the first realtor they've talked to," Brent said, crossing his arms the other direction.

"Yeah," Cybil sighed, "We get a new one every other month."

Great, I thought, but undaunted I went ahead and listed the house. Over the next few months I brought Jeff and Marianne several contracts, but they always found a way to reject the sale. Then one day, Marianne called. "Mary," she said resolutely. "We've decided not to sell. We have decided to stay together . . . for the kids."

I have often wondered how those kids turned out, and whether they're still leaning against a wall somewhere rolling their eyes as their parents quarrel.

Another client, Andrea, called in a panic to see a house on her way home from work. I was in the middle of dinner at the time. "Would 7:30 work?"

"No," she answered. "I really need to see it now."

This was just one of the many interruptions of daily life that were normal in real estate. On another day Andrea called to see a house she had found in the newspaper. "I'm with another client right now," I said. "Can we set a time for tomorrow?"

"I'll get back to you," she said. And that was the last I heard from her. Andrea went to another real estate office in town, found an agent to show her the house and bought it that day. Andrea never mentioned she had been working with me for *four months.*

And on and on I learned the challenges and nuances of my new career. How different from my other sales jobs! For the first time I was working alongside more women salespeople than men, and their backgrounds were varied: homemakers, teachers, retired military and downsized employees. My past sales training had included a lot of strong-armed maneuvers I was never comfortable with. But this new batch of salespeople didn't have much training at all. They didn't even understand the basics of business. It was a refreshing change, at first.

John offered me some perspective, having worked in real estate for so many years. He told a story that pointed out an interesting difference between male and female salespeople.

One day when John was sitting at an open house, Don, a real estate agent, came in to show the house to a very interested married couple. When they entered the basement the husband pointed to the wall. "Say, I'm concerned about that huge crack over there."

"Oh, that's no big deal," said Don. "You can just spackle it in. Now let's go see that greenhouse you like so much."

The husband scratched his head, still examining the crack while being led up the stairs. He shifted uneasily and approached the subject again. "Don't you think there might be a problem with the foundation?"

"Don't think so, buddy," Don said. "I wouldn't worry about it."

"But won't it leak with all our rain?" the husband asked.

"Not if you spackle it."

On the same day, another agent, Pam, brought a different couple through the house. The husband pointed out the same huge crack in the basement wall. Pam batted her eyelashes, and raised a hand to her mouth. "Oh no!" she said. "Can it be fixed?"

The man puffed up his chest. "Oh sure little lady. You just fill it in with a little spackle and it'll be fine. Say, my wife wants to see that greenhouse you've been talking about."

That quick the matter was no longer a concern.

I was getting a chance to observe human behavior in a fascinating new light through my experiences and those of the other agents.

One agent, Susan, was overly dramatic about everything. She gathered quite a crowd, throwing her briefcase down on the desk when she arrived in the office. She would begin her latest tale of woe with, "You won't believe what happened this time!"

Agents gathered to hear how she had been done wrong and how all her deals were falling apart. The agents then joined in with their own sagas of despair. Eventually it would be the market's fault for them not being able to close a deal. And of course, the mortgage rates were much too high and rising.

Soon some agents would go home, defeated before they even began their work for the day. The agents that stayed would try to get on with it, but were so affected by the hopeless tragedies of their profession that nothing would go right. And so, more stories were created for the morning pity party.

On another day, a brand new agent, Liz, burst into the office with the news she just closed on a million dollar property at full commission. "I can't believe this sale has gone so smooth," she said. "Not one hitch in the whole process."

I was excited to hear more but the agents scattered.

"That's great," Susan said, shutting the door to her office.

"That's really cool," Bob muttered on his way out the front door.

"Good for you," said Don, ducking under the newspaper listings.

I wondered, why did more people gather to talk about the miseries of life than about the successes? Were we jealous of another's good fortune? I began to think that's why people don't like to shine. It's lonely.

When I thought about it, most of America went to sleep with the 11:00 news and woke up to news in the morning. I could understand why we were all so scared. If the salmonella in the chicken didn't get you, the spinach would. There was never enough money for this program or that. Our roads were deteriorating, gas and grocery prices were climbing and another politician was being outed for his sexual indiscretions.

At some point I pulled a book off my bookshelf from the 1970's. I was amazed when I read about the gas problem and rising prices. The divorce rate was climbing and our children's school budgets were being cut. There were dirty politics going on. So things hadn't really changed. We still had the same challenges we had decades ago. Who wouldn't be depressed?

Despite the negativity I knew there were so many advantages in staying positive. Each morning on the way to my real estate office, I passed a road crew widening one of the streets. The same flagman was there every day, directing traffic to the one useable lane. He was an older black man with salt and pepper curls escaping from his hardhat. Day after day this man would grin flashing a gold tooth at each driver as they passed. He would wave with a gloved hand on freezing mornings and always smile through the pouring rain.

Worrying about this real estate deal or that, I would see this man greeting each car and think to myself, *If this guy can be so joyous in his job, what am I complaining about? At least I have a nice warm office to work in.*

Many things could've gone wrong in my real estate deals and many did. I felt I had no control over any of it. But then I was realizing how little control I had over anything: John's drinking, Heath growing up and moving on. In my journal I wrote: *"The only thing I have control over is how I react to everything that comes my way."*

# CHAPTER 42

## Saved by a Lady

Even with all the setbacks, I focused on doing my best for each client in my new real estate career, and gradually sales did show up. Another good thing that showed up was Maggie, a black and white miniature schnauzer. Julie, a client, worked in a pet store and felt sorry for Maggie. She was the runt of the litter and shook whenever you tried to pet her, so Julie took her home. One afternoon I was helping Julie tear down wallpaper in the house I just sold her. Maggie crept into a nearby corner and began to shake. Julie put down her scraper. "Oh, *why* did I bring that dog home?" she sighed. "I already have three dogs. Hey Mary, do you think you could take her?"

I glanced over at the sweet, little cowering puppy. How could I say no? Poochers was getting old and John and I had considered that a new pup might be good for her. That evening, I rode home with a companion. The instant I opened the door, Maggie came out of her shell, wagging her tail and smiling up at us. John and I sat on the couch to watch as Maggie sneaked up on Poochers and tried to play. Poochers wouldn't budge. We laughed as Poochers looked the other way, her nose in the air, flat-out refusing to be impressed with this new pup. She didn't want to share her position as "Queen of the House." I was sure it was just the way Linda acted when they brought me home from the hospital.

As time passed, my dogs were always there giving me love when I dragged in at the end of the day. As I pet them they would pull the

Reiki energy out of my hands. They cuddled at my feet when I wrote in my journal, helping to fill the void in my life with unconditional love. They even made me forget our money worries since money wasn't exactly rolling in.

And I had to admit, though I loved looking at houses and always enjoyed a challenge, real estate was the hardest job I had ever had. All my sales training and even my well-organized black leather briefcase couldn't save me from the many pitfalls. I had always enjoyed building relationships, selling to the same people over and over, whether with business accounts when I was a rep on the road or individuals like Collette when I had my design business. But in real estate you were lucky if you saw your client again in five to seven years, buying another house.

Yet some of my fellow agents vowed that it was the best job they had ever had. How could I account for this difference?

Camping. I remembered camping: some people love it, some don't.

One summer when I was a kid, just before Labor Day, Dad came home from work and said, "Let's go camping this weekend."

We were really excited. "Can we fish, too?" Joe asked wide-eyed.

"You bet," Dad said. "Round up your poles."

"Mary Pat!" Mom shouted. "Come help me make the food list!"

"I'm on it," I said. "Are two boxes of cereal enough for eight people for three days?"

"Should be," said Mom. "One morning we'll have sausage and eggs. Now go down to the basement and get the camping stuff. Make sure we have all the pots and pans."

A few minutes later I came up the steps, dragging a cardboard box. "Is this the one you wanted?" I asked, panting.

"Let's see," Mom said. "Yes, but there's another one with the plates and silverware. Can you get it, please?"

I returned, lugging the second box. "Mom, these are heavy," I gasped.

"I know dear. Now go pack clothes for your brothers and Annie. Don't forget sweatshirts and jackets. It might be cold at night."

By the end of the weekend I had helped Mom fix 48 meals out of a cooler and on a camp stove while Linda sat under a tree with her nose in a book. On the last day Mom and I were still washing dishes when everyone came back from fishing.

"Look," Dad said, "John caught a bluegill; I'll clean it and we can have it for dinner."

"Yuck, I'm not eating that thing," I said. I couldn't wait to get home.

When we finally walked in the door from the long weekend, Mom handed me a laundry basket. "Mary Pat, can you take these dirty clothes to the basement?"

"Sure, Mom," I droned.

"And then can you make sure all your brothers get into the bathtub?" Mom asked. "And lay out their uniforms? The first day of school is tomorrow."

"Great, Mom," I said sitting down on the bottom step. "But I don't get it. Why do we do this?"

"Because," Mom sighed in a bored voice, "your father and the kids enjoy it."

"Well, I don't like it," I said, picking up the basket.

"I know, dear." Mom gave a tired smile. "Me either."

And so I learned. One person's vacation is another person's dirty laundry.

For me, selling real estate was not much more fun than dirty laundry.

Luckily, in nine months Beth saved me. She was head of the Relocation Department of the real estate firm and needed help with a special program serving our clients.

I joined her team, working with vendors instead of prospective home buyers. I jumped out of bed each morning, excited to be building partnerships again. In my journal I wrote: *"I am so glad to be back in a job I like AND with a paycheck!"*

# CHAPTER 43

## *Give Peace a Hand*

In a few months our company expanded Beth's program, focusing on home owner's needs with a wealth of products and services.

I began to see how each of my jobs had built on the next. From decorating to real estate, my work experience had provided the understanding that I needed to get the deal closed. When there were conflicts between contractors and homeowners, I had my peacemaking skills learned from Mom.

My new boss was Kathleen, the perky little blue-eyed technology teacher. I hadn't had a woman boss since college. And now, through real estate, I had Beth as a boss and now Kathleen. Times had changed for sure. Kathleen herself had risen in the company because she was very articulate and good at dealing with the agents. Although she said she could never be a salesman, she could sell the agents on any new program like no one I'd ever seen.

As I met with Kathleen in her office one afternoon, I was distracted every few minutes by a co-worker, mail deliverer, or someone's client passing by. Kathleen's office walls were windowed on three sides, and I felt like I was in a fish bowl. How could she work like this? Meanwhile, Kathleen swiveled in her chair to respond as we talked, or to field a telephone call, or take a sip of her tea. She never even seemed to notice the commotion surrounding her glass walls.

"Okay, Kathleen," I said, as the UPS delivery guy wheeled a dolly down the hall. "I need to tell you. I really need to work from home."

"Seriously?" Kathleen paused and looked up from her computer screen. "I don't see that as a problem. As long as you get vendors signed up."

I sighed with relief and we went on to discuss the program. As we talked, I realized how much we had in common. We each had the ability to come up with new ideas and also to implement them. We could see the big picture while not losing sight of the details. We were both direct, to the point, and moved fast. We knew where we wanted to go and the steps needed to get there.

From the start, we had an easy relationship and worked well together.

This new job was great, but there was one problem. I was used to being the "Golden Girl" at all the companies where I worked, and I had the Dolly Parton in a miniskirt trophy to prove it. But in this job, there were no trophies. My achievements were never publicly acknowledged. I thought my ego had died after failing in my design business, but after several key accomplishments went unpraised I questioned whether I was doing a good job. But then I realized I didn't need trophies. I knew I was doing a great job.

One day in Kathleen's office I was relaying a story about the handyman that walked all over the customer's new white carpet with muddy boots.

Kathleen shook her head. "I can't believe these guys. Don't you wish every contractor would show up on time in an Armani suit?" she said wistfully as she propped her chin on her hands, "AND would drive a spotlessly clean truck?"

"How boring would that be?" I laughed as I answered a phone call. On the line was an agent screaming about a door latch needing repair by closing tomorrow.

Some days all I heard from were angry customers and agents. It was hard to take in all that negative energy. But since I worked at home, it was easier to deal with. Sometimes I'd punch pillows to expel my anger. Sometimes I'd dance it out to *Roll with It* by Stevie

Winwood. Sometimes the only satisfying outlet would be to belt out Aretha's *Ch-Ch-Chain, Chain of Fools*. And sometimes, quietly meditating on a problem helped me solve it.

More often than not, these times of meditation would center me, working wonders. Once, when I had a roof problem, I half joked with Kathleen that I would light a candle and pray to the roofing gods. But in a corner of my mind, I was completely serious.

"Nice," she said rolling her eyes. "But really, I don't care *how* you take care of it, just take care of it."

Every problem was a chance to make our program shine. Nothing went perfectly, but what customers remembered was how we came to their rescue.

One day I heard from Rosie, the supervisor in our call center. "Mary, I don't know what to do with Rhonda Logan," she sighed. "She has complained about every contractor I've sent her. Jim, from Bushman Landscaping showed up ten minutes late with his shirt tail hanging out. His crew talked constantly on their cell phones and took smoke breaks. Since she was paying by the hour, she was livid."

"Great," I sighed.

"The floor refinishers had to come back three times," Rosie went on. "They were lucky. The painters had to come back five times for missed spots and the handyman will probably *never* be done."

I held the phone a little further from my ear while Rosie's frantic voice continued. "I've talked to all the contractors. But I don't think there is any way we can make this lady happy."

"Okay," I said. "Give me her number."

Dialing the phone I took a deep breath and wondered how this one would turn out. I introduced myself and said, "Rhonda, I understand you are fixing your home up to sell."

"Yes," she said. "My husband took a job in the Midwest."

"That sounds great," I said. "When are you moving?"

"As soon as I can get this house sold," she said in a tired voice. "But with work and the kids, I'm going crazy. My husband has already relocated and, to be honest, I don't really want to go." Her voice broke, and I could hear her pushing down a sob. "The kids don't want to go either," she added. "All my family and friends are here—and I *love* my job."

"That's a tough one," I said. "Have you talked to your husband about this?"

"I've tried. But he's on to his new life, *our* new life while I'm stuck here at least until the end of the school year."

"Oh, are you waiting for the kids to get out of school?"

"Well that," she said, "and also, I'm a teacher."

"No kidding? What grade?"

"Third."

"That sounds like a fun age," I responded, trying to be enthusiastic.

"I like it," she said with a half-hearted laugh. "But honestly, I'm getting burned out." she sighed resigning herself to the move.

"Will you teach after you move?"

"No, my husband is earning three times what he made here and I will be able to stay home with the kids. You should see the mansion we have been able to buy! Home prices are much lower in our new place. I can't wait to start decorating!"

Soon she was filling my ears with facts about the kids' great new school, the beautiful architecture, the wonderful culture of their new town. One by one, Rhonda was listing all the good things about her move. Her voice grew peaceful, her sighs contented. Finally she wound down. "Don't bother having the handyman come back out," she said at last. "He did a good enough job."

I chuckled silently to myself as we said good-bye. All she had needed was a listening ear.

In other situations, problems needed to be worked out between homeowners and contractors. They were often able to solve them between themselves—except when agents got in the way. Kevin was one of those agents.

Kevin called about his client, Betty, a widow with all her retirement locked up in the home she was selling. Her house needed a lot of work in order to sell, and Kevin was seeking a contractor to drywall her basement ceiling.

We had a contractor named Josh give Betty a call, giving her a bid of $1100 over the phone, sight unseen. When he got to her house, the room was much larger than the dimensions she had given him, so he raised his bid to $1700. He wasn't sure he could finish before the open house scheduled for the weekend.

Now Kevin was practically yelling into the phone as he called Cheryl in our call center. "I think this guy is pulling a fast one on old Betty. He's just trying to get more money out of her!"

"Josh is one of our best contractors," said Cheryl. We've used him many times. I don't think he would do that."

Finally, I called Kevin and listened to him gripe. It was an outrage, he explained, that the contractor wouldn't be done in time for his open house. Now I better understood Kevin's problem.

Quickly, I talked Josh into putting more guys on the job to meet the deadline. Then I checked in with Betty. "Wonderful," she said. "I need to get this house sold."

Later that afternoon, Kevin went to Betty's house, looked at the job and called me. "This job is horrible" he shouted, "absolutely horrible! "The guy has no idea what he's doing."

I was determined to smooth things out between these two. "Look," I said. "You're looking at a drywall job that's only half done. Why don't you call Josh and talk to him about your concerns?"

Wrong move.

Within seconds, Kevin had called Josh and was berating him for a lousy job.

Naturally, Josh became defensive. "My contract is with Betty, not you," he said. "And she's happy." Josh hung up.

Now these two egos were in a full-blown war.

Things were only getting worse. I jumped in with more calming calls, finally getting Josh and Kevin to agree on meeting at the house the next morning. How could I be assured there would be no bloodshed at this meeting? I did the only thing I could: meditated in silent surrender. Or, as I jokingly put it to myself, I prayed to the drywall gods once again.

Luckily the two had a civilized conversation and decided to part ways. Kevin then needed to find a new contractor to finish the job scheduled for completion in just a couple of days. I thought to myself: *funny how some people would rather be right than happy.*

In each problem, there was a puzzle, a gift, or some lesson to be learned. I loved the challenge. In my journal I wrote: *"Give me a business problem any day. Personal problems—forget it. I still don't have an answer for John and his drinking."*

# CHAPTER 44

## *Stuck in the Center*

One afternoon on the way home from the office, I was sitting in the parking lot otherwise known as Interstate 5. I looked at my watch, *6:15. Hmmm . . . John will be passed out by the time I get home,* I thought.

But I was surprised. "Your Mom called," John announced as I walked in. "She says they're trying to find you for your thirty year reunion in Ohio."

"No kidding?" I threw my briefcase on the chair, trying to be casual about the fact that John was alert, without a drink in his hand. "It was nice of them to invite me, since I actually graduated in Phoenix," I said as I unbuttoned my jacket and thought about it some more.

In the back of my mind for years I had been trying to make sense of my Catholic roots. Now it occurred to me that maybe some of my classmates could help. They, too, had been raised Catholic. Some, like me, had even been divorced. I wanted to see how they were handling the guilt, and were *they* still going to church?

"I think I'll go," I said.

Walking into the reunion the first thing I saw was the bright poster with day-glow red letters: "Booze, Broads, LSD, We're the Class of '70!" Our anti-establishment class cheer made me laugh. Yet, as I thought about it, it wasn't all that funny.

That chant had found an eerie way of coming true in my life. I'd been surrounded by alcoholics, called much worse than a broad and had my own trials with my drug of choice, food. No doubt, I'd chanted it just one too many times.

Now as I looked around the room it hardly seemed that thirty years had gone by. I turned to an old friend with a haircut like Katie Couric. "Martha," I said. "How is your Mom doing these days? I can still hear her yelling at us to come in for dinner."

"She's good," Martha said, giggling. "And she still has that deep, raspy voice that puts the fear of God in all of us."

"I was sorry to hear about your Dad," I continued. "He was always so sweet to drive me home in the middle of the night when I woke up crying."

"He was a good Dad," Martha said, staring into the drink in her hand. Then Mary, my high school cheerleading buddy joined us to tell about her kids. It was great catching up. Mike came over and gave me a bear hug in his strong arms that were sprinkled with gray hairs. "How have you been?"

"Good," I said. "And I hear you've been having fun."

"Oh," he said. "You mean the divorce?"

"Yeah," I sighed. "I've had one, too. Sit down. Talk to me. I'm wondering . . . do you still go to church?"

"Sure," he said lifting his glass as if to give a toast. "I go."

"And do you go to communion?" I asked between sips of wine.

"Yeah, sure," he said, sitting up straighter. He held out his glass and looked thoughtful, as if he might recite a line of Shakespeare. Then he looked at me. "Why not, don't you?"

"Nope." I shook my head and slumped back. "I don't."

If only I could find a way to be at peace with my divorce, after all this time.

When I got divorced from Dan, I didn't dare go to communion because I had been excommunicated. I knew the rules of the Catholic Church, and to me the rules mattered. Why would I continue to belong to an organization and not follow the rules? How could I possibly consider another divorce now when I hadn't resolved the first one?

I got up and mingled some more, and almost bumped into Jeff. He was the first boy I ever kissed in grade school. He got together with Marcy in high school and they had a dramatic on-again, off-again relationship. I thought they would marry and battle it out for eternity. But, I came to learn that they married other people. Each came to the reunion without their spouses. I could see them exchanging glances all night. Later in the evening Marcy marched up to Jeff and shoved his class ring in his face. "Here, this is yours," she said.

I had to laugh. Their drama continued, even after thirty years. People really didn't change that much.

On my way to the bar I met Margaret, her hair shorter and thinner than I remembered. She grabbed my arm, "Mary Pat," she said, "I am so sorry about that incident with the shoe."

"The shoe?"

"Freshman year."

"Huh?"

"You've *got* to remember," Margaret said, "how you were sent to detention for tying Janice's shoes together."

"Sorry," I shrugged. "I don't remember." Then I smiled. "But it does sound like something I'd do."

"Well," she said, "you didn't do it this time. It was me. And I've felt bad ever since."

I put my arm around her shoulders. "Margaret," I said. "I can't believe you've been carrying this around for over thirty years!"

"I guess I have," she said, looking down. "Anyway, I'm really sorry."

"Please, forget it," I said, hugging her. "How can it matter, when I can't even remember it?"

With that, I had to sit down. Why do we carry so many forgotten things around—regrets that keep us awake all night, that haunt and harass us? Here I was, carrying the guilt of my divorce. Whether or not the church approved wasn't the point. I had to recognize the baggage I was carrying. What good did it do?

Later that night, as the crowd was thinning out, Martha and I sat down at a table. "Where's Christina?" I asked, realizing I'd never caught sight of my sweet pal from grade school.

"Oh," Martha said. "She doesn't come to these things. Something about growing up on the poor side of town."

"Great," I said. "That's the side of town *I* grew up on. Another thing to feel bad about. I'm just glad I didn't let it keep me away."

Martha laughed. "Well good for you," she said. "Here's to the poor side of town!" Our glasses clinked in a toast.

"You know," I said, after my sip. "Someone who never changes is Joan. She's always been such a free spirit. I admired her in high school because she never conformed to fit this group or that."

"I know," Martha said. "She is a character."

"As for me, I was so shy growing up," I said taking another drink, "that I spent most of my time trying to hide because of Dad's drinking."

"Funny," Martha said. "I never knew that about your Dad."

"I know," I smiled. "We were pretty good at hiding it. But didn't you think it was strange that I spent the night at your house more than you did at mine?"

"Not really," Martha said. "Our families melded because of our moms."

"True," I said. "They helped each other through some chaotic times."

"For sure," Martha said. "All those kids—ten at our house and six at yours. What a mob!"

As I headed to my room after the reunion I wondered when was the last time I'd had a heart-to-heart talk about my past, my family, and what really mattered. The next morning I woke up early. I pulled my journal out of my suitcase, sat down and wrote:

*"It's time to let it all go. No more guilt about:*

1) *my divorce*
2) *going bankrupt*
3) *not being perfect (hadn't I let that one go a long time ago? I guess not.)*

# CHAPTER 45

## *Gravity Keeps Dragging me Down*

I couldn't believe I'd lived this long: I was turning fifty. Finally, I felt like a grownup. I took the day off work to celebrate by myself. I woke up early and scooted several boxes filled with thirty-five years worth of journals up the hall to the couch.

I pulled out my first diary from high school. Burgundy leather etched in gold filigree with a sturdy lock, scratched up by the pick marks Linda had made with a hairpin when she broke into it to read about my latest adventures.

Next I dragged out the psychedelic autograph book my classmates gave me when I moved to Phoenix in 1969. There was a black journal with pink Georgia O'Keefe flowers from my artsy phase, and a cloth Indian print journal in peach and turquoise from when I was really missing Phoenix.

The paisley green and blue book reminded me of a man's tie. Obviously, I was focusing on my career with that one. Various angels in red, blue and gold decorated a journal from a spiritual stage. There was a fuzzy gray snakeskin and a shiny, pink book with black boots and high heels from a silly, high fashion craze.

The green notebook embellished with sad, tired peach flowers reminded me of all the characters in a rehab class for spouses. Crowding another box, there were stacks of various spiral notebooks in hunter, lime, Irish green, teal and aqua. Navy, lapis and sky blue.

Black and gray. Sunshine, daffodil and mellow yellow. Scarlet, maroon and ruby red. Peach, sherbet and sunset orange.

Some pages were yellow from age or spilled coffee. On others, the writing from my angry pen pierced right through the paper. Asterisks marked profound discoveries. A dog-eared corner showed a great revelation I might need to refer to later. All together they were the story of me.

With my afghan wrapped around me and my dogs at my feet, I began to read. I laughed, but mostly I cried. By the end of the day I no longer cared to keep my dinner plans. John picked up my favorite Vietnamese dish and a slice of chocolate cake from Safeway and we dined in silence. I was exhausted from the highs and lows of my life story, but I came away with more understanding about me. I learned:

1) The very first words in my very first diary were "lose weight". It was my New Year's resolution for 1967 and the first goal on every list since.
2) I had been through rehab with my husbands six times.
3) Through everything, I remained positive no matter how difficult it was. During one particularly trying episode I wrote, *Life is good—when I'm asleep."*
4) When I surrendered saying, "Okay, God, take over," things always got better.

As I reviewed my journals, the theme of friendship came forward. Memories of my college roommates came to life. They were turning fifty as well, and I wondered how their lives had turned out. I'd seen Kathy several times since she visited me when her daughter lived in Portland. I kept in touch with Candy when visiting family in Phoenix. I knew Ali had moved to Albuquerque for George's job, and we talked occasionally. The night Clinton won the presidency, Ali and I reminisced about going door to door for McGovern. "I remember what you said when Nixon was elected," Ali remarked. "Give the American people what they want. They'll be sorry."

Now that all our kids were grown, wouldn't it be fun to meet for a weekend and catch up with all my old buddies?

I called Candy with my plan. "Great idea," she said, "as long as it's after tax season." She was a big mucky muck for H&R Block now.

Kathy was a nurse and had traveled a lot on her time off. Her job was fairly flexible. "Count me in," she said.

Ali was a teacher. "Sounds like fun," she responded. "As long as school is done how about June?"

At the Seattle Airport I saw Candy floating off the plane in her earth mother style from college. Ali could be spotted immediately with her head above the crowd. Was she still wearing those high heels? Next came Kathy—tan and fit as usual. Nothing much had changed in their appearances and I soon found out we all gelled like we did 30 years ago at the *Republic and Gazette.*

At the hotel we settled in and shared stories about our kids. Hearing about the mood swings and personality changes of their daughters, I felt lucky to have had a boy.

We talked about our jobs. I told about a "Come to Jesus" meeting I had with one of the contractors. Ali held up her beer. "Oh, you were always like that, Mary Pat, direct and to the point."

Her words warmed and surprised me. It meant so much to be back with friends who knew me when I was "coming of age," and saw strengths in me that I'd forgotten or overlooked . . . back before life beat the crap out of me.

As the night wore on we ended up lying on the floor drinking and sharing pictures of ourselves back in the day. Candy grabbed a photo. "Look at that," she said. "I thought I looked fat in those jeans. Oh, what I'd give to look like that again!"

"No kidding," Ali said. "Why didn't we appreciate it then?"

"I'm not sure," I said. "Just make sure you tell your daughters to enjoy it!"

"What about the aches and pains?" Kathy said. "I'm have to have both my feet operated on."

"I know," Candy said. "I'm having my gall bladder out soon."

"Ugh," I said, getting up for more wine. "My friend Alice says she's saving money for the face lift, but she keeps having to spend it to keep the carcass going."

We all laughed and agreed.

On my drive back to Portland I thought about how they had all turned out much like their mothers. Kathy and her mom both had beautiful olive skin and straight elegant frames. Both were quiet, easy people to be around. Kathy smiled just like her mom with an inner knowing.

Candy was a carbon copy of Rosemarie, the calming force in the tribe of three boys and Candy. We never entered her kitchen without hearing, "You girls look beautiful." Candy had been my cheerleader for years, just like her Mom had been for us. And Candy, too, was the maternal peacemaker.

Ali was as formidable as her mother, Eloise. They both had a stately air of superiority, perhaps because of their height, but probably because of their intelligence. Eloise was the only working mother I had known growing up. As a teacher, she wasn't afraid to vocalize her opinions, which were as well regarded around the kitchen table as the men's. As a young college student, I was really impressed. It seemed to me there was a secret rule: working women were allowed to speak up.

Ali followed in her Mom's footsteps and became a teacher.

Back in Portland, I wrote: *"My Mom, Madonna, is soft spoken and has a saintly sweetness about her. She's tiny and petite. None of that sounds like me. But then:*

*I married addicts who were just like Dad.*
*I worked to keep the family together, just like Mom.*
*I was a pacifist, just like Mom.*
*Yikes!*
*I've turned out just like my Mom, too!"*

# CHAPTER 46

## *The Time Has Come For Me*

When I got home from Seattle, I had to face facts. John and I were losing our house. We were so far behind in payments we couldn't afford to live there anymore. This was the home Heath had grown up in, and held so many memories. On the couch with Poochers and Maggie at my feet, I whimpered, "Where's my afghan?" They cocked their little heads, trying to help. I settled in, wrapping my arms around my knees, rocking back and forth watching the Oregon lights flickering across the Columbia River. I had seen this view from morning to night through many seasons, and it saddened me to know I would soon be missing it. I opened the newspaper to look for apartments. There was one that took dogs. When John came home I showed it to him.

He wrinkled his nose. "I don't think so, but what about the rental in Washougal? The one my Mom and I own. We could get the tenants out."

The place was dark and depressing. It had dingy, smoke-marred walls and stained, raggedy office carpeting. I agreed to take a look anyhow, and when we visited I felt the same dreary horror that Heath had expressed during our move to "the dump" after my divorce from Dan. Thank God Heath was away at Washington State now and didn't have to go through this again.

I packed the last box of dishes and scraped the spaghetti from the kitchen ceiling. I thought of all the fun times we had in this home. Goodbye to another big house with a view. Was there no end to my degradation? There wasn't enough ice cream in the world to hide my shame.

On top of everything, John had been having trouble with his eyes. He looked like a frog, the way they were bulging out. The doctors couldn't figure out what was wrong and I didn't know what to do, so I tried not to think about it. Instead, I jumped into fixing up the rental.

Heath came home from college one weekend to paint the walls. I chose a light creamy yellow to offset the depressing gray of the northwest. We hung black shutters and installed window boxes outside. I filled them with red geraniums and ivy trailing down the sides. I stacked bricks on both sides of the porch to make flower beds.

My stepsister, Chrissy, and Kay and Claudia from my book club scrubbed out the cupboards and shined up the windows.

Soon it became a cozy cottage with new carpet in a pebbled sand color and faux travertine countertops in the kitchen. The yard was perfect for the dogs and I could walk to Hathaway Park, sit under a mystical arrangement of sequoias and imagine all my troubles being carried away by the Washougal River.

John had an operation to remove the tumor from behind his eye, but instead of getting better he seemed sicker. He hadn't wanted me to go to the doctor with him, but I insisted on knowing why he wasn't recovering. When the nurse went over all the drugs he was taking, I was in shock. There were eleven prescriptions: blood pressure pills, blood thinners, prednisone, pain pills and many more that didn't seem to have anything to do with his tumor. Did anyone know the ramifications of mixing all these pills together? If he was adding alcohol, no wonder he wasn't getting well.

At the dry cleaner's one day I ran into one of John's friends, "It was so nice that John came to visit me when I got home from the hospital," he smiled, "even if it was just to get some of my pain pills."

Slowly it came to me: there was a reason for all of John's visits to ailing friends home from the hospital. With disgust, I realized he had been seeking free drugs. I had no clue what to do now. I dragged John back to Karen, the counselor we had gone to many times over the years. In the first session we had barely sat down when Karen looked John in the eyes. "John, as long as you are drinking, I won't treat you."

"Fine." John looked up and smiled more relieved than anything. Since he had no intention of quitting drinking, he was off the hook.

I sat there, clenching and unclenching my hands.

"But Mary," said Karen, turning to me. "I can see you clearly need help. Why don't we make an appointment?"

"Okay," I said, and took a deep breath. "The sooner the better, I guess." The next day I settled into the light blue barrel chair across from Karen. "Mary, John is conning you," she said as she took the pen away from her lips. "He CAN work. But instead he's drinking and drugging himself to death, because he doesn't need to. You're doing everything. You are not helping him." She went on tapping her pen on her note pad.

I sat there stunned. I didn't know what I was expecting, but it wasn't this.

"You pay all his bills and take care of all the household chores," she went on. "Why won't you let him do these things for himself? You are creating a monster."

Karen was right. And all my rescuing was making me exhausted. Physically, my blood sugar was on another roller coaster. In *You Can Heal Your Life,* Louise Hay explains that blood sugar issues happen metaphysically when you don't have enough sweetness in your life. That was for sure. I was so busy taking care of John and keeping the money coming in, I wasn't paying attention to myself . . . again.

At our next session, Karen informed me, "I'm gathering participants for an *Artist's Way* class. It's a weekly meeting based on the book by Julia Cameron. It promotes taking care of you for a change."

"Taking care of me?" The concept seemed so foreign. I was so used to taking care of everyone else.

It had always felt like a badge of honor to power through my problems alone. As with that strep infection, which I ignored completely until it showed up on my face appalling the doctor for my lack of concern about myself.

"Won't you join us?" Karen continued.

Maybe this was a way to get back that sweetness I was missing, I thought.

I accepted her invitation to this weekly class, which consisted of five women. We had to complete three assignments each week. One was to write three pages in our journal every morning. *Only three pages?* I thought since I was used to writing reams of paper each day.

Another assignment was to take ourselves on an "Artist Date." We had to go somewhere that fed our soul for an hour each week. It didn't have to cost money, just make us feel good. I could easily spend my hour feeling the latest, rich hues in silk, chiffon, velvet, suede and tapestry at The Fabric Depot in Portland. I would imagine the clothes I would sew or the chairs I would recover or the drapes I would make.

Another of my pleasures was to spend an afternoon at Powell's Bookstore, browsing the aisles then stopping for a latte at their coffee shop. Sometimes when John was passed out, I would take myself out for a nice dinner alone and read or write. Sometimes I would just walk down to the river and watch it flow.

The third task for the class was to walk every day. It amazed me what I could figure out while walking and letting go of all thought. It became my favorite way of meditating.

In one class we danced, focusing on really feeling the music. The movement was freeing. I learned that letting my body move got rid of all the kinks. And, I never felt the same after a dance. My body was more relaxed and my emotional state always changed for the better.

Another week our class connected with sound. We were told to scream, grunt, cry whatever. I had never given myself permission to do that. It became another way to get out negative emotion. How many times have you just wanted to scream? Or sing a song full blast without worrying about being on key?

As I practiced these techniques, I was able to let go of so much that didn't matter. I'd always journaled to purge my mind of negative thoughts. Now dancing and singing relieved my body of things I never realized I was carrying.

One week in class we created collages from magazine cutouts. On poster board, we glued pictures and words of what we wanted in our lives. This exercise was full of surprises, such as with Lynn the quiet mouse of a lady who worked for social services. When I looked at her board, I couldn't believe it. Bright reds, purples and yellows with phallic symbols galore. Everything on her board screamed SEX!

My board surprised me too. It was covered with blue skies, green trees, waterfalls and rainbows. "Live your dream" and "You can do it" were cut out sayings. But what was my dream? I had been so busy keeping things afloat for John and Heath I had forgotten me and what I really wanted.

Unless I took care of myself, I couldn't be of help to anyone. And, I had to take a hard look at my actions. I wasn't helping John by paying for his gas and real estate dues so he could keep pretending to work. Even worse, along with John's insurance, I was paying for all his pills and even cigarettes. I had to admit, I was buying his booze and street pills, too.

At tax time that year, I sat in our accountant's office armed with our sad financial story. Rob reclined in his office chair, crossed his arms and looked over his glasses at me, "Mary, what are you thinking?" he said. "John hasn't made money for three years! I see him around town. He's not that sick that he can't make some money. The real estate market is really good right now. Why are you letting him drag you down? You need to look out for yourself and your future."

"I know, Rob," I said as I sat back in my chair. "But how do you leave a sick man?"

In my journal I questioned, *"Is John really so ill that I should be taking care of him like this?"*

# CHAPTER 47

## *One Drink Over the Line*

One Thanksgiving Heath, John and I went to Phoenix. One day Mom and I were making lunch when John walked into the kitchen. "I'm going to check out that Harley dealership I heard about," he said.

"What about lunch?"

"I'll pick up something."

The door slammed behind him. "He's drinking again, Mary Pat," Mom said, turning to me.

"No, Mom," I sighed, "he says he's not." I kept my head down, slicing tomatoes for the salad.

That night Linda and her husband Robert invited us to a Mexican restaurant. John and Heath were playing pool in the bar, while all the women chatted over chips and salsa. I thought I saw a drink in John's hand, but turned my head quickly and became absorbed in Molly, Linda's daughter, telling her latest escapade with the cheerleaders she was coaching.

When dinner arrived, I heard John drop his fork at the end of the table. "My God," he blurted out. "This is awful."

He staggered up the long table, turning to each of the guests. "Is yours salty?" he slurred. Lurching forward, he rested on Robert's shoulder then Linda's. "Is yours as bad as mine?" he asked leaning in.

The restaurant owners were friends of my sister and her husband. I wanted to run and hide. After dinner Heath and Molly said goodbye before going bar hopping. I stood up. "Let's go, Mom," I said grabbing my purse. "Heath, tell John we're leaving."

The next morning Mom was folding the guest sheets. "Mary Pat," she said, "can you help me fold up this bed?"

I sat down on the sofa bed and began sobbing into my hands. "Oh, Mary Pat," Mom sighed, "I'm so sorry. But you can tell he's drinking again by that outburst last night."

"I know, Mom. I'm so embarrassed."

"I can't tell you how many times your father embarrassed ME like that," Mom added, sitting down beside me. "It's uncalled for. What are you going to do?"

"I don't know, Mom."

"Well, he's never going to get well if he doesn't stop drinking." Her voice stiffened.

"I know."

"He's going to be just like your father and drink himself to death," she whispered, staring ahead. A deep sadness filled her eyes.

"But Mom," I spoke up. "I don't think I can stay and watch like you did."

"I know. But Mary Pat, I never would have stayed with your father if I'd had a way to support all of you kids." She got up, straightening the covers. "And you can support yourself," she said, throwing a pillow on the bed. "You've been supporting Heath, yourself *and* him for how many years?"

I shook my head, "I don't know. I was just trying to keep the family going like you did, Mom."

Mom reached over and patted my arm.

When Heath got out of the shower we all decided we would confront John about his drinking after we got home from Phoenix.

---

Heath set down the last suitcase as we arrived home from the airport. "John, we need to talk," he said, placing a hand on his stepfather's shoulder. "You have GOT to quit drinking. You're killing yourself."

"I know," John said, walking to the bedroom. "I'll take care of it."

"You'll take care of it?" I repeated, watching him in disbelief. "What do you mean, YOU'LL TAKE CARE OF IT?" I yelled after him.

"Don't worry," he said, turning toward Heath and me with gritted teeth. I could see the red flush of rage creeping into his face. "I said I'll take care of it."

"Okay, then," Heath said, shrugging his shoulders, "I guess that's the end of that."

I dropped down on the couch, deflated. I didn't know what I had expected. I'd told myself that things would somehow get better, that we could make a difference with our mini intervention.

What happened next was one more visit to rehab. John made arrangements and I dropped him off in Portland as the rain poured down. I drove home, barely able to focus. I wasn't sleeping, and with my exhaustion and blood sugar issues, I was a mess. By the time I got home the rain had stopped. I walked down to the river, shivering in Heath's Camas High School basketball sweatshirt. I sat on my favorite bench and thought how great it would be to have a week off from worrying about John.

But the third day of rehab, John called and said he was coming home. How could he detox that fast? I told him he needed to stay longer and I wouldn't pick him up. I needed the rest.

Yet, a few hours later, John was home. He had called a friend to give him a ride. I couldn't believe they let him out so fast. Then I recalled how skilled he'd become at reciting a new plan for his life: *get up at 7:30, eat eggs and toast, don't socialize with old drinking buddies, attend a meeting a day.* He had the lingo down, so they set him free.

I wasn't convinced by another of John's show of resolve. Then, when Heath came home at Christmas after graduating from WSU, he commented on how good John looked. He'd lost all his bloatedness and his complexion was pink instead of gray. He acted like the old Johnny we knew and loved.

I began to think the change would stick.

Then John's eye swelled up again and he was back to sleeping in late. Before long, his doctor placed him back on several medications, as well as a sleep apnea machine. I tried to imagine the swooshing of that machine was simply the sound of the ocean, but when I couldn't sleep through the tsunami, I had to move to the other bedroom.

With some of my design clients, I had seen that once they moved to separate bedrooms they lost their closeness. Sadness overwhelmed me when I thought about the passion and fun we'd had in the beginning of our relationship. Alcohol had taken its toll on my life . . . again.

I still worked from home, only now my office was in the corner of the living room. Every morning John would get up at 10:00 or 11:00 and scream as he tried to walk. His hip bones were deteriorating from all the prednisone. This created complications for my professional persona. How do you explain the sound of your husband screaming like a little girl when you're on the phone talking business?

Our daily life limped on, some way or another.

Mom came to visit that summer. "Mary Pat," she began, shaking her head.

I knew what she was going to say. I simply sighed and looked down. "I know, Mom. I know."

Despite what everyone was telling me, I just couldn't give up on my marriage. In my journal I wrote: *"I know love can conquer all."*

# CHAPTER 48

## *To the Hustle*

With Heath's graduation, I was the proudest "Coug Mom" on the planet. He moved home, but wasn't exactly happy in our little house, with only two bedrooms and my office in the living room. Sure, it was crowded, but I hoped he could make the best of it since Heath was a happy diversion for me.

One of his friends, William, had known Heath since second grade. He helped him get a job offer as account executive for a mortgage company.

Heath never wanted a commission job since he'd seen the ups and downs of John's and my businesses, but he decided to make an exception since the mortgage business was hot. Every night after dinner, John and Heath sat on the porch and talked interest rates, cold calls and business maneuvers. Heath immediately started making money.

Seeing him in this job made me prouder than I'd ever imagined. Once, I'd heard the first President Bush say the proudest day of his life was the day his son was inaugurated president. I had thought to myself, *why wouldn't it be the day* you *were elected President?* But now I understood. I was more proud of Heath and his accomplishments than anything I had ever done.

Within six months, Heath bought a house. It had a beautiful view of Mt. Hood from the deck. I could see his pride as we began furnishing the new bachelor pad. We found an overstuffed chocolate brown couch with matching chair and ottoman, perfect for watching all the Cougar games on his new big screen TV.

Heath and I always had fun together, but spending time with him after he'd been gone so long was especially great. We shopped for the massive faux marble bedroom set, the dark cherry dining room table and the beige upholstered deck furniture. He bought a six-foot long carved wooden alligator to put on the high shelf in the great room. I decorated around it with lots of greenery, old trunks and pottery for an "Indiana Jones" look.

We spent days together shopping for his Nautica dishes, new silverware and pots and pans more for looks than for cooking. We chose a tablecloth and placemats in gold and rust autumn colors. We added plush towels in the same tones to jazz up the earth tone look.

Early one Sunday morning, after our two eggs over easy with hash browns and a side of country gravy, we stopped at Wal-Mart. We needed some nails to hang pictures. As we made our way to the hardware section, suddenly over the loud speaker we heard, "DO THE HUSTLE!" followed by "Do do do do, dododo, do do." Heath looked at me, grinned, and broke out dancing in the aisle. The music stopped; Heath shrugged his shoulders and continued pushing our cart down the aisle. A few minutes later, again we heard, "DO THE HUSTLE!" Heath dropped the nails he was holding and burst into dance steps again; this time I joined him. The music stopped as abruptly as it had begun. Heath picked up the nails, threw them in the basket and we moved on. We received a few blank stares as we intermittently boogalood to "DO THE HUSTLE" a few more times before checking out. "Hey," I asked the gal at the register. I was still out of breath from all that dancing. "What was all that 'hustle' stuff about?"

"Oh, that. We play "The Hustle" to remind the sales associates to check their aisles," she explained.

"Cool," Heath said, and struck the Saturday Night Fever pose with one hand on his hip and one pointed to the ceiling. I shook my head, smiling. Life had been anything but easy lately, with John's challenges, my sense of paralysis and having no idea what to do about it, or whether I even should or could fix things. I was glad for this break with Heath who reflected back to me my own sense of humor. He, too, always looked for the positive in everything.

When he was a freshman in high school he had been thrilled over the start of basketball season. All four grades were practicing for tryouts. When I stopped at practice to pick him up on Friday, he signaled a thumb's up from across the court. After practice he ran up to me. "Guess what, Mom!" he shouted. "I made Varsity!"

"Are you kidding? That's wonderful!" I threw my arms around him.

"Yeah," he said, hugging back. "And, I'm the starting point guard." I was as excited as he was.

At the first game I thought how small he looked next to those big, hairy, muscular boys, but he made 10 points and had 12 assists. The next Monday when I picked him up from practice, he ran to the car, got in and slumped down in the seat. "What's wrong?" I asked worriedly.

"Can you believe it, Mom?" He pounded his fist on the dashboard. "The league came up with a new rule . . . freshman can only play on freshman teams."

"Why?"

"Because some of the high schools in this stupid league only have sophomores, juniors and seniors," he said with a big sigh.

I felt so bad for him. Later I heard the basketball bouncing outside with Heath's nightly thousand practice shots. I hoped this new rule wouldn't get him down.

The next morning he came into the kitchen. "Well, Mom," he said confidently. "I'm just going to have to dominate all the freshman teams and rack up as many stats as I can."

And he did. I was SO proud of him turning another bad situation around.

Maybe I could recapture that kind of spunk. Maybe I could find a new approach at home, and create a positive outcome. In my journal I wrote: *"I am so glad to have Heath. I am the luckiest Mom alive."*

# CHAPTER 49

## *Freedom is Just Another Word for Nothing Left to Give*

Over the years Heath had several long term girlfriends but I had never seen him gush the way he did with Melinda. He was enthralled with her and I could see why. She was petite with honey colored hair and beautiful with no makeup. She was a great mother to two little girls, ages five and eighteen months. Heath fell in love with them, too, and soon they all moved in together. Melinda didn't even seem to mind the obvious bachelor style décor.

As for Heath, he had dreamed of being a dad since middle school. One day he'd said, "Mom, we have such a puny, little family. When I grow up I'm going to have at least four kids—two girls and two boys." He held up two fingers. "I'll have twins, Heath and Heather and two more." I had to laugh, thinking he had plenty of time to change his mind.

Now, with Melinda, he was halfway there. "Sometimes, though," he told me over coffee, "I feel like a babysitter with the girls. It's not easy blending a family, is it? I remember when John moved in with us."

I sighed and stirred my latte. "It's true," I said. "There were so many issues to work though."

Heath smiled. "Next time I see John, I'm going to apologize for the hard time I gave him. He deserves that. I understand now." And at the next opportunity, he did exactly that.

Heath soon bought a bigger house for Melinda and the girls. I couldn't have been happier when they asked for my help with the decorating. I tried to contain myself and act nonchalant, but I practically danced onto the showroom floor when Melinda and I went shopping for furniture.

"Say," she said, as we roamed the store, "Wouldn't that table look cool in the kitchen?" She pointed to a tall café table with bar stools.

I swallowed. I had always hated trying to get up on those things. I had visions of taking a running jump and twisting an ankle. "Don't you think a larger . . . ?" I began, but then bit my lip.

Melinda was standing there with a small hand on her hip, waiting.

I smiled. "Sure," I said. "Whatever you like is what counts." This was no longer my decision.

I was used to being the decorator in Heath's life. Now Melinda was taking my place, in more ways than one and so soon after I had him back. I knew it was all part of the deal. But why was it so hard to do?

Heath and I had always been close. In high school he told his girlfriends, "You better get along with my mom because I'm a momma's boy."

Now I was losing that boy to the woman he loved. Each morning, the ink on my journal pages became blurred with tears as I wrestled with my loss of Heath, again. In *The Prophet* it says, "Your children are not your children . . . They come through you but not from you. And though they are with you yet they belong not to you." I knew this was how it was supposed to be but I wasn't ready for the deep grieving of this loss.

Eventually I got to where I could write, "*Thank you,*" to Melinda in my journal. *You can take over for me now. I love you.*"

Without Heath to focus on, I had no choice but to take a hard look at my own home life. At Christmas, Kay from my book club threw a party for relatives and friends. Fred was one of the guests. He stood in the corner, leaning against the wall, drink in hand. His red rimmed eyes looked out from a weathered face. Kay introduced him as a drug and alcohol counselor. My ears perked up. I wondered if I could gain some wisdom that might help me with John. I walked over to him casually, "So," I said with one hand on my hip. "Have they found a cure for that disease called alcoholism yet?"

"Not that I know of," Fred said, hugging the wall. "I am so burned out on all of it." He rubbed his forehead and looked as if he might collapse.

"How long have you been doing it?"

He dropped his head like a tired, old dog. "Fifteen long, hard years," he rasped. "Wow," I said feeling his frustration.

"Yeah, and if I get one more fifty year old guy in who's going to CHANGE his life," Fred shook his head in disgust, "I'm going to quit."

A wave of nausea came over me and I put my hand on my stomach. At fifty-four, John was *that* guy. He could never stop drinking. He had his own life to live, his own deal with God. Who was I to change it?

It took this stranger to get through to me what my Mom, my counselor, my accountant and many friends had tried to get me to see for years.

---

Sometime later, I flew into Phoenix to visit Mom. As she placed my favorite dinner of baked chicken on the table, she said, "Mary Pat, you look exhausted. I'm so glad Candy is doing the driving to Albuquerque."

"Me too," I said. My college roommates and I were having a gathering at Ali's house. I could hardly wait. I was so glad to be out of the house and away from my John dilemma.

The next morning, for old time's sake, Candy and I began our trip at Coco's, our former second home in college where we'd down mega doses of coffee discussing religion and politics under the guise of studying.

"Remember *Silva Mind Control*?" I asked, sipping my coffee. "I still make my mental grocery list on the hood of my car."

"I know, me too," she laughed, pouring cream in her coffee. "I still can't think about orange blossoms without my eyes watering up." We both chuckled.

"Those were the days," I sighed, head in hands.

"What's up with you?" Candy asked, peering at me closely. "You look worn out."

"I am," I sighed. "I think I have to leave John."

"Leave him? Why?" Candy looked up from the plastic menu.

"He drinks so much on top of all his medications. He's out of it most of the time." I sighed again. "I've gone through I can't remember how many rehabs with him and he continues to drink and do pain pills." I played with my coffee cup. "He's going down the same path as my Dad and I can't stay to watch."

"Wow," Candy said. "Why haven't you said anything?"

I shrugged. "I didn't want to dwell on it. I kept focusing on the positive. I was detaching like they taught me in Al-Anon, but really I think I was in denial. I can never get those two straight."

"You were always so positive," Candy smiled.

"I try. But that's not the worst of it," I giggled, "I haven't had sex for many years."

"What?" Candy looked at me like I was lying. "You? You've got to be kidding."

"Nope," I shook my head, "I wish I was."

We were both quiet, no doubt drifting into the sex-crazed memories of our youth. Then we got in the car and cranked up Kenny Loggins to full blast as he sang, *"Even though we ain't got money, I'm still in love with ya honey,"* and we headed east across the desert.

For lunch we stopped at a tiny Mexican restaurant on an Indian reservation and ordered chile rellenos. They were all puffy in their egg batter, made with real chilies, not the canned, mushy ones in the Northwest. We decided to spend the rest of our lives looking for the perfect chile rellenos. It suddenly seemed like the most worthwhile quest we could embark on.

After lunch, when we climbed in the car, Candy said, "You *do* have to leave John. You can't keep doing what you're doing."

"I know," I said closing my eyes and resting my head against the seat.

When we got to Albuquerque, I admired Ali's house, a Santa Fe style with Saltillo tile floors she laid herself. Her walls of paprika and plum showed off her mastery of color from her art background. I was glad to be surrounded by friends at last. As we sat down to our first bottle of Two Buck Chuck, I told Ali and Kathy my sad news.

"I am so sorry for you," Ali said.

"Thanks," I said, slamming back my wine. Maybe I thought a little alcohol would help me process the situation with the alcoholic.

Kathy patted my shoulder. "I remember some of John's—adventures, shall we say," she told me. "I knew he had a problem."

"It's sad," she continued. "But probably what you need to do, MP."

"Thanks, Kath."

The comforting words were interspersed with laughter and memories.

When the weekend was over, it was hard to leave. With the chorus of encouraging voices still in my ears, I arrived home from Phoenix, tossed my suitcase on the bed, and told John, "We need to talk."

John sat down on the loveseat, staring ahead. I stood up and began pacing. "I can't do this anymore," I said, wringing my hands, "I have to leave. I am exhausted from worrying about you. I can't stay and watch you kill yourself like my Dad did."

"I understand," John sighed sadly, looking at the floor.

That was it? No outburst? No argument? I was surprised he didn't have more to say. Maybe this was a relief to him. He wouldn't have to hide his drinking anymore.

A few days later, I put a deposit on a condo in downtown Vancouver. Across from the park, three floors up, visitors had to be buzzed in. It felt like a fortress—and more than anything I just wanted to hide out.

On the morning of my move, Heath walked in to our little kitchen and almost crashed into Leslie Ann, a friend from my *Artist Way* group, as she wheezed in the corner from her COPD. Three other dear friends, as old or older than me were loading boxes of books, clothes, and pictures onto one of their husband's trucks.

"Um, is anyone *else* coming to help?" Heath said, scratching his head as he looked around at each helper.

"No," I said. "This is it. Sorry!"

"Great!" he said, throwing up his hands in exasperation, but smiling anyway.

I didn't think I had that much to move, but under the circumstances, it took a while. As I carried the last box out of the bedroom, John came home and stood in the kitchen, empty eyes following me. My heart lurched. Behind him I noticed a few spaghetti strands dangling from the ceiling. I felt a smile breaking at the same time that sobs forced their way up from my chest. John and I hugged and cried as everyone stood uncomfortably, watching with tears in their eyes.

Though feeling sad and guilty, I had to go. I left John, my sweet little dogs, the spaghetti on the ceiling and took the bills. *Another divorce filed in Clark County, Washington*, I thought. *This place has not been so lucky for me. Maybe I should move back to Phoenix.*

Yet through my heartbreak, I focused on getting well and decorating my new condo. It had purple carpet. How was I to decorate around that? I thought about my recent trip through Sedona with Candy and envisioned the red rocks against a sky so blue, it was purple. So I bought a sofa so red it was orange. Orange, the color of joy against the purple carpet transported me back to Sedona. From my windows all I could see were blue skies. Things were looking up.

It was summertime. Bands played across the street in the park. It didn't get much better than sipping Duck Pond Chardonnay, listening to K.C. and the Sunshine Band's, "That's the way, uhuh, uhuh, I like it," on a warm August night under the evergreens by the Columbia River. On Saturdays and Sundays, I pulled a little cart to the Farmer's Market and filled it with fresh strawberries, raspberries, tomatoes, eggplant and zucchini. I began to heal.

It was like I had been hitting myself over the head with a hammer for years and when I finally stopped it was a strange sensation. I had thought it wouldn't be much different than living with John—who passed out most nights by 6:30. Yet the reality of this freedom was strange.

In my journal I wrote: *"I am really alone now."*

# CHAPTER 50

## *You've Gotta Have Fate*

The same week I left for Albuquerque, I received an email from Greg, my fiancé from college days. He was living in the Northwest and we had met several times over the years when he traveled through Portland. He sold his business and was retiring. He wanted to make sure I had his new email address. *"I'm coming through Portland on my way to Seattle,"* he wrote. *"Can we meet for coffee?"*

*"Perfect."* I sent back, *"I live on top of a Starbucks."*

I had just ordered my double tall latte when Greg came up behind me leaning in and smiling. "I'd know you anywhere. How long has it been?"

I looked into the bright brown, shiny eyes of the guy I fell in love with thirty-five years before. As he walked to the table I saw he still had the short trimmed boxy hairline as Mr. Stevens! How could I have forgotten about Mr. Stevens?

Greg and I talked for over an hour catching up on our careers and our friends from college, Stan and Candy and George and Ali.

As we strolled past the park, Greg told me he and his wife had grown apart over the years while he traveled for business and she raised the kids.

In turn, I spilled out the sad stories of my marriages. I didn't know which story was worse—his or mine. My marriages had ended, but they were never devoid of passion. Or was that really anger? We kept walking and reached the Columbia River. The water sparkled

250

like diamonds as we began talking about our kids. We laughed and shook our heads in amazement at all the changes in our lives.

Then Greg took a deep breath. "Mary Pat, you should know I still see you as that same little 19 year old girl, fresh out of Catholic School, full of spunk and energy." I had been the girl he loved, so long ago. I looked into his eyes and knew he loved me still.

Some things weren't meant to change.

I still saw him as my strong protector who had the world figured out—just like Mr. Stevens.

Over the next few months we developed a long distance relationship filled with intellectual banter. Greg was an engineer and all logic. I was more touchy-feely. In our twice daily phone calls, he challenged my spiritual beliefs and I poked holes in his scientific ideas.

To keep busy, I spent a lot of nights in downtown Portland helping feed the homeless kids through our charity at work. The kids reminded me of Heath and his friends as teenagers. But unlike Heath and his friends, these kids were caught in the cruel world of drug addiction and trying to live on the streets.

One of the kids, Emily, came to work in our call center. She had a young son and I watched her get slammed with the same "left hook from heaven" I got hit with many times as a single mom. But Emily kept on through custody battles, getting her police record cleared and eventually going to college. She reminded me of me.

After a while I realized I became too attached to these kids. It was a good thing I had such a small place or I would have taken them all home to live with me. It became clear I needed more healing from my issues before I could help anyone else.

My downtown condo was fun, but a bit like living in a hotel. As time went on I decided that a grandma needed something better suited for the role, so I bought a condo in another part of Vancouver. On moving day, I climbed a stepstool and checked the ceiling of my empty kitchen, but there was no spaghetti. It was time to move on, alone.

I loved my new place: a two-bedroom, two bath condo with bamboo floors throughout. The only drawback was the colors. The bedroom which would be my office was lime green, easy enough to ignore. But the master was deep burgundy. To me it was the color of death.

That burgundy bedroom reminded me of my friend's father's funeral home in grade school. We had big slumber parties in that house with its burgundy theme. Sometimes Patsy would call at the last minute. "We got a body in," she'd say. "So we have to call off the party this weekend."

When we did have the parties, we'd play around in the coffin room trying some on for size. We'd rat each other's hair into beehives and tell ghost stories. And God forbid, should you be the first one to fall asleep. We'd freeze that girl's bra in orange juice.

When we settled down to sleep we'd spread our pillows and blankets across the burgundy floor in the viewing room. As I looked up at the matching heavy drapes I felt suffocated.

One night Patsy's brothers sneaked down from their bedrooms and rubbed those burgundy velvet curtains together to mimic the sound of someone moving around. Then came the wailing: "Woe is me, woe is me-e-e-e-!"

We all jumped up screaming, running to the coffin room. One brother was inside a coffin, banging and shouting, "Let me out! Let me out!" I never got back to sleep that night.

Now every morning in my condo I woke up believing I was back at Beckman's Funeral Home. To my relief, Greg offered to paint the bedroom for me. It took many coats of my favorite yellow to squelch the horror of that blood-red color, but I finally could connect my new place to the color of sunshine and the feeling of new life. Greg never complained. It was nice to have a guy around.

Greg and I fell into an easy relationship as comfortable as if no years had passed. We saw each other on his way through Portland for his scuba diving trips or ballroom dancing contests. On his way back through town he brought me presents. There was a silver bracelet from Taiwan, a pearl bracelet from Shanghai and a jade Buddha from Hong Kong. Greg made me feel cherished just like I had imagined Suzanne felt with Richard.

But the best thing Greg brought me was information about a new technique called Neuro-Emotional Technique (NET). He had sat next to a chiropractor on the plane and explained it was a way to let go of physical ills by healing emotional issues held in the body. I researched the method on line and found a chiropractor in Portland that performed it. It was so different than anything I had tried before. Soon I felt freer and healthier than I ever had.

Greg encouraged me to get my health back. From all my classes with Karen, I realized my dream was to write a book, and Greg encouraged me to do it.

As I carried in the mail one day, the Clark College catalog slipped to the floor, and opened to a page of writing classes. One called *Wildfire Writing,* jumped out at me. *Unleash the writer within,* it read. This was it.

I signed up. The first class was cancelled because of a rare snowstorm. When I arrived at the next class I was greeted by a pretty, angel-like teacher who asked, "So what did you do during the snow days?"

"The same as I always do," I said shrugging. "Work."

One by one, each student told their stories of being snowed in at the airport, home with hot chocolate, relaxing with a lover by the fire, or digging out old board games with the kids, not to mention combating lots of cabin fever. I looked at my life and realized I was becoming a hermit. All I did was work and read. Every spring my garage was stacked high with boxes from Amazon, but what I was missing was a real relationship.

Greg and I had all the pieces, but he was married. It hadn't bothered me in the beginning because I had rationalized it by thinking, *he was with me first.* But soon I realized that was like rationalizing Hawaiian style pizza was good for me because it had fruit on it.

Greg said he and his wife lived separate lives. Yet they shared a home. I wondered if she knew he considered them "separate?"

Painfully, I examined this pattern of choosing guys who really weren't there. Dan was gone all the time, but came in to make big decisions. John was emotionally unavailable because of his addictions. And now, Greg was married, whether he and his wife had separate lives or not.

But then, Dad wasn't there for me either. I remembered back to the time when it happened. I had been the one Dad took on all his handyman jobs until one day everything changed. My overalls couldn't hide my developing breasts. Dad backed off from me when I hugged him after our Saturday workday together. I was no longer Daddy's cute little helper. After that, my brother John took my place helping Dad on his jobs.

As I looked at my life in this new light, I copied down a quote from Carl Jung into my journal and dog-eared the page: *That which you do not bring to the light of consciousness continues in your life as fate."*

# CHAPTER 51

## *Sweet Boy of Mine*

I continued to reminisce about my life choices. I recalled a name from the past: Abe Steinberg. I met Abe when I was 21 and worked at the front counter of the *Republic and Gazette*. Abe came in each week to deliver the ads for his family's jewelry store. Everyone in Phoenix knew the place. Steinberg's was the chi chi place to go. He'd say hi to me looking over horn rimmed glasses on his way to Display Advertising, bent over with his briefcase under one arm and his hands in his pockets.

One day my boss, Lorene, came out of her office and handed me a telegram. "For you, Mary Pat."

I read out loud:

*I would love the pleasure of your company. Please meet me for a drink at Oscar Taylor's Thursday night at 6:00.*

*Abe Steinberg*

I looked at Lorene, "What should I do?"

"I would go," Lorene said shrugging, "Why not? I've known his family for years. It could be fun."

"I must say, I'm intrigued," I said, fanning myself with the telegram like a well-to-do southern belle.

Oscar Taylor's was the new ritzy, cool place to go in the Biltmore area. On Thursday night, dressed in jeans and a white silky halter top, I strode into the lounge, dazzled to be in a place frequented by hotshots. *Is that John Stewart at the end of the bar?* I knew he was in town for a concert that weekend at Grady Gammage.

I looked around as a smiling Abe walked up, took my hand, then kissed it while dropping to one knee. "Come, M'Lady, I have a table over here."

Was this for real?

Still holding my hand, Abe ushered me to the corner. I blinked in disbelief at his white shoes and white belt. And did he have to wear green plaid pants, too? I'd hated plaid since Catholic School.

There was an uncomfortable silence as we sat for several moments. "So, Abe," I finally said, leaning across our table in the candlelight, "How long have you been in the family business?"

"Since college," Abe said, leaning back, twiddling his thumbs on his white belt, "for about 10 years."

*Wow. That means he is . . . 31 or 32?* His white shoes were blinding me.

*Never trust anyone over 30*, came to mind as Abe rattled on about the jewelry business. It was good I didn't have to think of anything to say for a while. When I did talk I made a reference to a Beatles song.

"Who?" said Abe.

"The Beatles. You know, the Beatles?"

He shook his head.

After a couple of drinks I'd had enough of this strange evening. I told him I had to get home to study. One quick peck on the cheek—ewww! And he was gone. It was awkward, as if I were being kissed by my father. I ran home and washed my face.

When I walked into work the next day there were two dozen red roses at the front counter. The card attached thanked me for the great time. It was shaped like a check written out for one million dollars. In whatever he did, there was always the message of money. Soon, he was asking me out again.

"Sorry," I told him. "I have too much schoolwork right now." As his invitations kept coming, I tried other excuses until the invitations stopped.

As a middle-aged, twice-divorced woman thinking about her security, I now wondered: *Why couldn't I have gotten over the plaid pants and white shoes?* But it was more than Abe's money that would have made my life different. Abe had cherished me. At the time, it had made me uncomfortable, but now I understood what a gift it was.

As it turned out I'd chosen men who didn't exactly cherish me, nor did they provide a sense of security. I had always hoped to feel protected by my husband from life's trials. Instead, with each marriage, there were three times the problems: his, mine and ours.

Marriage hadn't been the thing to provide security.

My next hope was that I would experience a sense of security once I had a baby to love unconditionally. Such was not the case. I didn't know the meaning of the word "scared" until I had Heath to worry about, too.

My search for security continued. I thought once I was a manager in my job, I would be in control. But after my promotion, I discovered I still had a boss to answer to, and the added responsibility of my employees.

Finally, I was sure that having my own business would be the key. But when this materialized, I soon found out that EVERYONE was my boss, from customers to suppliers. Not to mention, the IRS and the state revenue department were the biggest bosses of all.

At other times in my life, I'd sought security in being perfect. If I could just be the perfect wife, perfect mother and perfect employee, with dinner on the table every night, the house clean, the laundry caught up and Heath finishing his homework. I would make it to all his games and keep my sales at the top of the pack, then I could be assured of peace. As unrealistic as this was, there were times when I did seem to manage it. Yet, I found out, I could never relax or capture the feeling of peace I longed for.

Looking back I realized I was a salmon swimming upstream, overcoming odds but never attaining real happiness. When I was exhausted and could do no more, I turned everything over to a source bigger than I was. The elusive ideals of security never brought me peace, but surrendering did.

Surrender brought peace from the first moment I said, "Okay, God, take over," when Heath visited his drug abusing dad. It brought peace when I didn't know where our next meal was coming from and Angela, the soccer mom, fed Heath and me. It brought peace when John's drinking became too much, and I received the wonderful gift of detachment.

Now I was learning to say it much sooner with any problem whether business or personal. When I took a breath and said, "Okay, God, take over," I could let go enough for an answer to flow through the cracks of my crowded mind.

Heath stopped by one day on his way home from work. "Mom," he said. "I want to marry Melinda."

They'd been living together for a year, so this was no surprise. "Great, Heath!" Finally I'd get to call her my daughter-in-law. As our relationship unfolded, it was better than having a daughter—we could shop together, and meet for lunch, but without the mother-daughter baggage.

The day was warm and I snatched two water bottles from the fridge.

"I want to surprise her," he said, biting the lid of his water. "I thought I'd propose when we meet Dad in Minnesota."

"That's cool," I said evenly. But inside I wondered why his jerk of a dad got to be around for this, when he hadn't been around for anything important in Heath's entire life.

"I want to ask Melinda's parents first, though," he said, gnawing on the cap again.

"They'll love that," I said.

Later that month, Heath called from Minnesota, ecstatic about all the details of the proposal. He had taken Melinda out on a boat to an island in the lake. I was surprised my son was so romantic.

The Saturday after they came home he called to meet him for lunch at our favorite Mexican Restaurant. As we were chomping chips he said, "Um, there's something I have to ask you."

"Sure," I said, smiling back at him.

"Melinda and I have been talking about our wedding," he began.

"Yes. Did you set a date?"

"June fourth," he nodded. And we've been talking about the wedding party," he hesitated as the waiter set our quesadilla in the middle of the table.

"Go on," I told him, while panic rose within me. Were Heath and Melinda eloping, leave me out of wedding plans altogether? Were they planning a tiny wedding on a tropical island with just the two of them? I had no idea what to expect. Once again, I was getting the chance to let go. I took a deep breath. *Okay, God, take over.*

"I've been thinking about who should be my best man," Heath said. "I've been lucky to have a lot of friends."

I nodded. So many great kids had come into my life because of Heath. Who would he choose for his best man? Tyler? Will? Kit?

Heath went on, his voice getting stronger. "As I looked at all of them I thought, who's my *best* friend? Who's always been there for me?" He paused. "Then I realized, that's you, Mom." He looked up, tears in his eyes. I felt my own eyes flooding as he smiled at me. "Mom. Will you be my best man?"

All the years I had spent trying to seize security, trying to be as good as the guys in business, and here I was winning the best prize of all—the chance to be my son's best man. Overwhelmed with the happy thought, I choked the words out, "Yes, of course, Heath."

I realized that even though I felt alone, I would always have my son and his family.

That night in my journal I wrote: *"Maybe true peace of mind comes from making it through all the trials of life. Because now no matter what life throws at me, I am sure I will make it through."*

# CHAPTER 52

## *My Body is a Wonderland*

Now that I was at peace with most of my life, it was time to make peace with my body. Forty years of journals showed "lose weight" as the number one goal on any list. No matter what I weighed I hadn't been happy with my body since fifth grade. I looked back at pictures of myself at different ages. There was the middle-sized me in a purple blazer with linebacker shoulder pads meant to make my waist look smaller. There was the slightly pudgy me with short permed hair in a coral pantsuit. Then there was me in college in a floor length green leaf print halter dress. I had to agree with Candy's sentiment: *I remember that day. I thought I looked fat in that outfit. What I would give to look like that now.*

And then there was the snapshot showing my white legs under the red and black pleated skirt with pom poms held high—me the cheerleader.

In one of my group therapy classes Lynn said to me, "Oh, you were a cheerleader! Like I couldn't tell."

"What do you mean?" I asked. "And when did it become *bad* to be a cheerleader?"

"Oh, you just have that cuteness about you that all cheerleaders have," Lynn smiled.

"Listen," I said. "We cheerleaders have our own set of problems. How would you like trying to meet everyone's expectation of being perfect? Or listen to people talking behind your back at reunions about how much weight you've gained? Trust me, it's not fun."

I thought about whether a few extra pounds should make so much difference in my self esteem. When Candy gained or lost weight, did it make a difference to me? No. She was still my friend. Nothing changed, except for my bit of jealousy when she lost weight, immediately wanting to know how she did it.

But, why did I have to wear my addiction? An alcoholic didn't show his addiction for years. Maybe then the red nose and cheeks showed up on their bloated faces like W.C. Fields. Even cocaine addicts could pass off their sniffing and red noses to a cold or allergies.

But when your addiction is food, the whole world knows. I was just glad I didn't have my gains and losses recorded on film like Oprah did.

Food served me well, comforting me in fifth grade when I was betrayed by the nun and priest. It insulated me from the world. Later in life it was a way to make myself unattractive, so I wouldn't be tempted to stray from my marriage. And, I can never forget the deadening comfort of going comatose from a carbohydrate high.

Food, like cigarettes, had been my friend. But food is not like cigarettes. You can give up smoking, but you always have to eat.

Many times, with countless diets, I tried to starve my body into behaving—but it was useless.

For example, there was the "whatever you want" diet, which Heath had found particularly amusing. I would eat nothing all day, and then for one hour each night I could eat whatever I wanted. Maple frosted doughnuts, sausage pizza, peanut butter and chocolate ice cream. It didn't matter, as long as it was within one hour.

Another of Heath's favorite diet moments was when I went to the doctor with stomach problems. "I'm trying to lose weight," I told the doctor, "but the only thing that makes my stomach stop hurting is ice cream."

"Then eat ice cream," the doctor shrugged.

Every day when Heath came home from basketball practice, I'd be sitting on the couch eating ice cream straight out of the carton.

He'd shake his head, laughing, "I thought you went to the doctor to lose weight, Mom."

"I did," I said defiantly. "He said eat ice cream."

I could hear Heath laughing all the way down the hall to his room.

Of course, neither of those diets worked but I continued to starve myself with every diet known to woman. I would also beat my body into submission with exercise.

When Heath was in grade school, I was into the aerobics craze. In the morning he sat on the couch eating his Cheerios (with sugar) while I worked out to a Jane Fonda tape. After about twenty minutes he said, "Well Mom, you sort of look like the girl on TV, except your legs are fluffier."

"Thanks, Heath."

Try as I might, my legs will always be fluffier than Jane Fonda's. God built me for comfort not speed, as my friend Ali would say.

But then I tried gyms, jogging and judo.

I hired a personal trainer, built like Arnold Schwarzenegger, who shouted orders like my Dad, "Hut, two, three, four," until I popped a rib while bench pressing. In another gym stint, I was running around the track, tripped, and tore a ligament in my knee. As I limped back to the locker room, one of the gym rats turned to me, "You know, not everyone is made for running."

"Thanks for that," I said looking down at my well rounded body, built way too close to the ground.

When I sprained my ankle falling off a treadmill I finally realized some people are just not gym material.

So I decided to appreciate myself. I thought of everything I had done to my body over the years—overeating, starving, binging, insane exercises, fad diets.

I looked down at my little feet. "I'm sorry I've given you so much to carry," I said. I took a good look at my legs, thighs, stomach, chest, arms. "I'm sorry," I repeated. Through all the torture my body had served me amazingly well.

"Thank You, Body," I said out loud.

With that I made a promise to be nicer to me. I got rid of my scales and no longer judged my day by how much I weighed. I thanked God for giving me a pear shaped body early in life and then changing it into an apple. Two different body types in one lifetime!

I realized that I had treated myself poorly for a long time. Not only was I more considerate of other people than my own self, but I even treated my car better than I did myself! The golden rule says, "Treat others as you would like to be treated." The question was, how was I treating myself?

I reasoned further: Why would anyone treat me well, if I wasn't good to myself? I had kept my college promise to always buy good booze and good toilet paper. Now I could add more things to the list: good shoes, good face cream and especially good food. I realized that I deserved the best food that money could buy: no more burnt toast or questionable leftovers in the fridge. These were all ways to start treating myself well.

I began learning to treat my body like it was a part of me, instead of something outside of me I had to have control over. I started giving my body massages and pedicures. Also, I learned to ask my body what it wanted to eat, rather than thrust upon it what the latest health studies said was good for me. This way I could truly enjoy every bite and I didn't need as much. When I was full, I stopped. I no longer ate like a wood chipper, mindlessly downing food, like Dr. Phil said. My blood sugar came in line because I had more sweetness in my life. I began asking my body what it wanted for exercise that day. A walk? Yoga? Or to rock out to old seventies music? (My body loves seventies music.) I began to really love my body fluffy as it was. And if there was to be another guy in my life, he would be sure to love my fluffy body too.

In so many journals I had struggled with the truth of the statement: *"Love can conquer all, right?"* Yes, it was true. But, with one change: *"Love of MYSELF can conquer all."*

# CHAPTER 53

## *Joy in my World*

June 1, 2007 was like no other day in my life. At 5:30 a.m. I was driving to the new Legacy Hospital in Salmon Creek for the birth of my granddaughter. Melinda had invited me to be in the room with her before her Caesarian, and I felt honored beyond belief. I was further honored that Delaynie DeYon's middle name would be John's and my last name. Heath was as happy as the day of his wedding. Dressed in his surgical garb with his arms opened wide, he said, "Hey Mom, do I look like a marshmallow, or what?"

I shook my head and hugged Melinda as she was wheeled off for the final surgical preparations. The nurse led Heath and me to a little room. Seeing my son pacing in anticipation of his daughter's birth made my heart so proud I thought it would burst. When Heath was called into surgery, I went to wait with Melinda's family for my newest granddaughter.

Melinda's mom, Dixie, was playing a game with Kyrstin while Craig, Melinda's dad was getting his camera ready. Delaynie would be their fifth grandchild, so they were old pros at this. I was a wreck. I paced up and down the hall counting my steps, then the tiles in the ceiling. There were one hundred fourteen.

Then she was born. When I finally held Delaynie I was filled with that same awe I felt the first time I held Heath. Only this was better. Maybe because I hadn't been through fourteen hours of labor. Or maybe because I would be there for all the fun but not the worry.

I made a vow to myself that I would be like my Aunt Rose. She was the best influence a girl could ask for. Twenty years older than my mother, when Aunt Rose blew into town she'd turn our house upside down with her flamboyant hats, colorful jokes and sense of adventure. Aunt Rose had been a flapper in her day and there was nothing subdued about her.

On one trip, she was wearing a rose colored pill box with netting that dropped over one eye. She barely got in the door when she motioned for Linda, Annie and me to go upstairs. She closed the door to our room and slowly opened her suitcase as she sat down on Linda's bed. "These are all the rage now, girls," she said, pulling a tiny ruffled thing out of a bag.

"Here, Mary Pat." She handed me a peach silk fabric with black lace that vaguely looked like underwear.

I held it up in wonder. Was it something for a doll? Tiny, not like the utilitarian, white cotton we were used to.

Mom came in and gasped with her hand to her mouth. "My goodness, Rose, what *are* those?"

"They're called bikinis," Aunt Rose said, standing defiantly. "These girls need to feel like girls, Madonna." She grabbed her suitcase. "And while we're at it, where are the boys? I have some things for them."

Mom ignored her and turned to us. "Girls, you will not wear those things to school or church, ever, do you hear me?"

"Yes, Mom," we said in unison. Then we shared some secret smiles, knowing she'd be too busy to check.

The next Sunday, I felt incredibly naughty, sitting in the pew wearing my new lace bikinis.

Then, a couple of years later when I was fourteen, Aunt Rose took me shopping. "It's time you had a grown up outfit," she said. "Something that isn't a hand-me-down from Linda, or home-made, or part of that God-forsaken uniform you wear every day."

We drove to a dress shop on the north side of town. I'd never been here before. As Aunt Rose sauntered along the racks, she acted like she owned the place. She gestured to the salesgirl. "We need something," she began. "I don't know . . . mmm . . . maybe a suit. Something that will look stunning on my niece here." She moved me forward with her arm around me.

The clerk brought out a beautiful blue linen suit. It had a straight skirt with an open pleat up the back. The jacket was long with beige linen lapels topstitched in the same blue. It even had a matching beige linen blouse that zipped up the back.

I tried it on and walked shyly out to Aunt Rose who stood waiting by a three-way mirror. "It's exquisite on you!" she said, and hugged me. I agreed, though I didn't know what that word meant. I just knew that whenever I wore that suit or those panties under my uniform skirt I felt "special." Aunt Rose knew all about what a girl needed.

That's what I want for my step-granddaughters: Kyrstin and Addy, and my new granddaughter Delaynie. I want them to feel loved and special by someone besides their parents.

Later that year after Delaynie was born Mom and I took a trip back to Ohio to visit friends and relatives. We stayed with my Aunt Dodie and were treated like royalty. Her husband Paul, took us anywhere we wanted to go, served us drinks and anticipated our every desire.

"Hey, Big Daddy," I said after my second glass of wine, "you're going to spoil me for other men."

We all laughed. It was nice to enjoy drinking again. For so long I thought alcohol was the devil incarnate. But it wasn't the alcohol that had taken the toll on my life. It was how it was used. It was the same with pain pills. If someone breaks a leg, the pills are good. But if someone needs them to get through the day, not so good.

At Dodie's, Mom and I were sleeping in the same guest room. I couldn't remember ever sleeping with my Mom before. The next morning we woke up laughing about the joke of the night before: Big Daddy ruining me for other men.

"I don't know why you've had such a hard time, Mary Pat," Mom sighed. "And I'm so sorry. I've been lucky to have two wonderful husbands."

I sat straight up. "Are you kidding me? Where do you think I learned about men, Mom?" Laughing I said, "From my Dad, your *first* husband, remember him?"

Mom started giggling, too. We both realized how good we were at living in denial. Or was that detachment? I still hadn't gotten those two straight.

We laughed so hard, we woke up Paul and Dodie.

That day my family gathered for a reunion. I found myself in the middle of the most gracious women I had ever seen. They were my aunts and cousins, ranging from my age up to my Mom's—beautiful women, inside and out. I'd heard about them over the years: their terrible losses and plights with cancer, alcoholic husbands and the loss of children. Yet they exuded a kind of peace that overwhelmed me.

Just like Mom. Now in her eighties, she was still beautiful and strong, with the peaceful aura of a holy person. I was humbled to be part of this clan. In my journal I wrote: *"I have no reason to worry about my granddaughters. They are blessed with the strength to endure whatever life brings them—just like Heath was. Just like I was. The hard times only make us stronger."*

# CHAPTER 54

## *Life is a Tapestry*

One day the following summer, the sun was shining bright through the white wood blinds in Heath and Melinda's dining room. It was the morning of Delaynie's first birthday party. Dan had traveled from Tucson with his wife and eight year old daughter, Kelly, to meet his granddaughter for the first time.

Heath, Melinda, John, my ex and three beautiful granddaughters were all seated around the table with Dan and his family. We were sharing old pictures while eating breakfast burritos.

"Wow, Dan, your hair was really long back then," John said.

"I know," Dan chuckled. "I sure don't have that much now, and for some reason it's much lighter than it used to be."

We all laughed.

"Boy, look how much Heath looks like his sister," I said, holding up a picture of him when he was eight.

After the plates were cleared, John asked, "Say, Heath can you and Dan come to my house and help move that antique carved chest?"

"Sure," Heath said, then looked hesitantly at Dan. "That is, if it's okay with you, Dad."

"Fine," Dan shrugged smiling.

As my two ex husbands and my son walked out to share an otherwise mundane chore, I was reminded of all the years of struggle the four of us had been through, in various scenes and stages. And now, look at us. We were all together and Heath had become a great dad because of—or in spite of—Dan and John. After all those years of worry.

Later that summer my brother Chris, and his wife, Pat, came through town. Sharing drinks one night I said, "Mom says she had two wonderful husbands and wonders why couldn't I have done the same."

Chris burst out laughing. "Did she mean our Dad?" he said, rolling his eyes.

"Yes." I laughed with him. "Our Dad—the wonderful husband."

"Yeah, right," Chris said.

"All I know is, I feel bad about my choices in husbands," I sighed.

"But Dan and John weren't deadbeat, alcoholic drug addicts when you married them," Chris said. "How could you have known?"

"That's true," Pat echoed.

"Thanks, guys," I said, getting up to follow Chris into the kitchen. "It's just that I feel like such a failure."

"You were always too sensitive about everything," Chris said, nudging me with his elbow while pouring another whiskey and coke. "I remember you always crying."

"Great," I said. I rolled my eyes, took a breath, and toasted with my wine glass.

"Yeah. Remember when you and Linda would babysit us?" Chris laughed. "If Mom and Dad weren't home exactly when they said, you'd sit by the front door and cry."

"Thanks for that memory." I popped the cork on another bottle of Duck Pond.

"When we moved to Phoenix, the floodgates really opened." Chris sat down. "Was all that crying about that skateboard champion, or Abe Steinberg?"

"No," I said defiantly. "*You* try moving in your senior year of high school."

"I guess it wasn't much fun for any of us," Chris sighed.

After their visit I sat down with my journals, as well as all my guilt and regret. I had processed and overly processed my marriages until they were like baloney or Cheese Whiz. It was time to let it all go.

I could have married that geeky, geezer jeweler in the plaid pants, but I picked someone just like Dad—twice. Dan was a controller and in the end Dan and I had religious differences. (He thought he was God. I didn't).

I had to get rid of Dan and get someone even more like Dad. I thought I was getting a 50-50 relationship with John but I went overboard and started doing it all.

Going through the pain of my bankruptcy, my second Dad sat me down. "Mary Pat," my stepfather sighed. "Life is like a tapestry. We all go through suffering. We encounter certain trials, meant just for us. Every problem adds to the back of the tapestry, with all its whips and turns and knots." I nodded, thinking about all my struggles and through them how I became stronger and more spiritual.

"And then," Dad continued, "When you turn the tapestry to the front, you see a beautiful work of art." So it was with my life.

I had to admit that even the worst problems had brought beautiful things into my life. I'd married "two wonderful husbands" just like my Mom. Because of Dan I didn't need a "Mr. Stevens" to show me how the world worked; I could learn it on my own. And finally I had learned to cherish myself.

From John I learned to lighten up. Life didn't have to be so serious.

From my bosses, Fritz and Tom, I learned I could do anything.

Linda prepared me for the mean women in my life. Their attitudes toward me were balanced by the love from Mom and great friends.

The salesmen who branded me an outcast at work helped me develop my own kind of selling: a kinder, gentler approach that helped fulfill my customer's dreams.

Because of Catholic School, I learned to find a spirituality that was truly my own.

My struggles with weight taught me to enjoy food and exercise and appreciate my body.

All these people and issues taught me to love myself. They were the perfect whips and turns and knots for my tapestry, my life.

*August 4, 2009*

*Today as I write from my living room I am surrounded by all my favorite books. I am reminded of the house on Camelback Mountain where Candy and I visualized what we wanted in life.*

*Candy and Kathy just left one of our get-togethers. I have great friends to laugh and cry with. I have another new granddaughter, McKynlee Beth, and no worries about any of them because Melinda is a great mother and Heath is a wonderful dad.*

*The fantastic new guy in my life treats me like Mr. Stevens would have; probably better.*

*Mom is turning eighty-five in October and doing great. Even Linda and I are friends now.*

*I have a job I love and am writing like I always dreamed I would.*

*I have many people in my life to throw spaghetti on the ceiling with.*

*Life just flows for me now. I know I am divinely guided.*

*I am truly blessed. It was all worth it.*

# BIBLIOGRAPHY

Brontë, Emily, Fritz Eichenberg, and Bruce Rogers. *Wuthering Heights.* New York: Random House, 1943. Print.

Cameron, Julia, and Mark A. Bryan. *The Artist's Way: a Spiritual Path to Higher Creativity.* New York, NY: G.P. Putnam's Sons, 1992. Print.

Carnegie, Dale. *How To Win Friends.* New York: Simon & Schuster, 1981. Print.

Emmanuel, Pat Rodegast, and Judith Stanton. *Emmanuel's Book: a Manual for Living Comfortably in the Cosmos.* Toronto: Bantam, 1987. Print.

Gerber, Michael E., and Patrick O'Heffernan. *The E-myth: Why Most Businesses Don't Work and What to Do about It.* Cambridge, Ma.: Ballinger Pub., 1986. Print.

Gibran, Kahlil. *The Prophet.* New York: Knopf, 1951. Print.

Hay, Louise L. *You Can Heal Your Life.* Santa Monica, CA: Hay House, 1987. Print.

Hill, Napoleon. *Think and Grow Rich.* Hollywood, FL: F. Fell, 2002. Print.

Mitchell, Margaret. *Gone with the Wind.* New York: Scribner, 1964. Print.

Peale, Norman Vincent. *The Power of Positive Thinking.* New York: Prentice-Hall, 1952. Print.

Peck, M. Scott. *The Road Less Traveled: a New Psychology of Love, Traditional Values, and Spiritual Growth.* New York: Simon and Schuster, 1978. Print.

Twain, Mark. *Letters from the Earth*. New York: Harper & Row, 1962. Print.

Wolfe, Tom. *The Bonfire of the Vanities*. New York: Farrar, Straus Giroux, 1987. Print.

Yogananda. *Autobiography of a Yogi*. Los Angeles: Self-Realization Fellowship, 1971. Print.

# Acknowledgements

I especially thank Christi Krug for without her this book wouldn't be. Christi opened me to writing from the first Wildfire Class and I haven't been able to stop since. Her undying enthusiasm for my message and her week after week encouragement to "unpack" each of my painful stories has kept me going. "Your writing is meant to be shared," she kept saying. And then she became my editor.

Thanks to my Guinsler family of teachers. From my Mom, Madonna, I witnessed the quintessential female in action. My Dad gave me my work ethic. Linda made me toughen up. Annie made me appreciate the little things in life. John is my reminder of Dad. Chris taught me I could stand up for myself, even to Dad. Joe taught me how to be a mom.

Thanks to the Murphy's: Chris and Mary Ann for taking care of Mom; Chrissy and Mike Maerz—it was good to know you were just across the river if I needed you; Michael Murphy for sharing your music and Janet for sharing your sweetness as a friend.

I thank Heath, who taught me more about myself than anyone. From you I learned a kind of love I had never known before. Your positive attitude showed me we really can change things.

Thanks to my two wonderful husbands: the first taught me to be independent and the second taught me to have fun.

Thanks to my friends: Kathy Jones for saving me in high school; Candy Haley, my best cheerleader in good times and especially bad; Ali Hicks who taught me that women can have opinions and be heard; Alice Jorgensen who supported me through two divorces and single momhood; John Hess for pushing me to my dream; Jim Loeb for his friendship all these years.

Thanks to all my writing buddies: Theresa Bond, for reading my story and dressing me well; Tricia Christensen for her devilish "Lutheresqueness;" Greg Bell who let me know my stories are nothing to hide; Lisa Feather for her creative insights and Val, a kindred spirit.

Thanks to my bosses: Fritz Munsinger and John Caldwell for valuing their women employees as much as their men. Kathleen McRae for your friendship and letting me run my show without a choke chain (most of the time).

I thank: Cheryl Winter for reading my story and keeping me laughing through writing it; Rosie Kaufmann for your constant support and friendship; Emily Scroggins for showing what can be overcome.

Thanks to Dr. Allen Knecht for writing the Forward for this book and working your NET magic on me. Without you I never could have let this book out.

Thanks to Rhetah and David Kwan for believing in my book; Herman Johnson for getting the lumps out of my psyche; Sharon Lee for being brutally honest; Rebecca Singer for helping me birth this baby; Erin Donelly for helping me market my truth; Ben Edtl for your bright marketing ideas and trying to teach me social media; Ross Hall for your political and writing inspiration; Melody Patterson for her friendship, support and organizing my closets.

I thank Joe Vitale for sharing his personal journey to make mine easier. I thank Louise Hay for her work and her inspirational authors at Hay House.

Thanks to Krista Hill and John Potts of iuniverse for all your support.

I thank Dennis for the joy and happiness I have found in someone who supports my dreams.

I also thank all of you that have been in my life, but have not been in this book. Don't worry there is probably a sequel.